John R. Leifchild

The great problem

The higher ministry of nature viewed in the light of modern science, and as an aid to advanced Christian philosophy

John R. Leifchild

The great problem

The higher ministry of nature viewed in the light of modern science, and as an aid to advanced Christian philosophy

ISBN/EAN: 9783742844231

Manufactured in Europe, USA, Canada, Australia, Japa

Cover: Foto ©Andreas Hilbeck / pixelio.de

Manufactured and distributed by brebook publishing software (www.brebook.com)

John R. Leifchild

The great problem

𝔈𝔥𝔢 𝔊𝔯𝔢𝔞𝔱 𝔓𝔯𝔬𝔟𝔩𝔢𝔪.

THE HIGHER
MINISTRY OF NATURE

VIEWED IN THE

LIGHT OF MODERN SCIENCE,

AND AS AN AID TO

ADVANCED CHRISTIAN PHILOSOPHY.

BY

JOHN R. LEIFCHILD, A.M.,

Author of "Our Coal Fields and our Coal Pits," "Cornwall; Its Mines and Miners," &c., &c.

WITH AN INTRODUCTION BY
HOWARD CROSBY, D.D., LL.D.,
Chancellor of the University of New York.

NEW YORK:
G. P. PUTNAM & SONS,
23D STREET AND 4TH AVENUE.
1872.

INTRODUCTION TO THE AMERICAN EDITION.

The royal Psalmist said, "The heavens declare the glory of God, and the firmament showeth his handy work." The modern Huxleys respond: "The heavens declare nothing at all, and the firmament is ultimately but eternal protoplasm." In this happy and hopeful response the materialists are as much traitors to science as enemies to religion. They *ignore all the facts of mind.* This whole department of cognitions is neglected in arranging their premises. The very first canon of science is thus violated, which demands that *all* facts be collated as data. Then, a second fallacy of which they are guilty, is *leaving scientific proof and leaping, by the imagination, to the conclusion that life is merely matter.* They find an ultimate matter (only ultimate, however, owing to the limited power of the microscope), and straightway say, "this is *life*," although it is known to exist without life, and has not a single characteristic of life in it. By such unscientific methods these scientific men, whose names are now so famous, have imposed upon the unlearned and credulous, and made men lose their faith in the eternal truths of God. Darwinism is another form of the same infidelity, working its evil by the same unscientific methods. Darwin leaps to his conclusions against every axiom of science, and Darwinism is, instead of science, mere theory. Science and Religion are at one. They both come from God and lead to God. "The heavens declare the glory of God," and "the statutes of the Lord are right, rejoicing the heart," are accordant strings of the same harp.

We need sensible and learned men to come forward and show the world what fools these pseudo-scientists are, and thus break the spell, which is as groundless as the Cock-lane Ghost, but which holds so many all-agape at their fantastic tricks.

Mr. Leifchild's book is popular, and yet sound and thoughtful. Its style is terse and clear. He represents the materialists and pantheists (the extremes are one) with fairness, and exposes the core of their absurdities, showing the higher ministry of Nature in declaring the glory of God, vindicating the equal authority of our intuitions and our senses, and the separateness, yet intimate connection, of mind and matter. It is a book that should find its way to every parlor, where the materialistic poison has been scattered, to straighten and strengthen the weak knees, and give color to the pallid cheek, letting the light upon the frightful spectre, and showing it to be but a man of straw. It is high time that this buffoonery in the name of science were played out. Scientific and religious men must join to put out the intruder with a brand upon his back. To hold serious talk with him is only to set him up in his assumption. Mr. Leifchild's book exposes him to the world, pulls off the lion's skin and turns the public fear into laughter. Let the voice of truth be heard through a thousand such books, and the cant of materialism shrink into silence.

HOWARD CROSBY.

PREFACE.

THE work now laid before the reader requires an explanatory preface, although it sufficiently unfolds its purpose and plan upon perusal. It needs some apology for shortcomings in the fulfilment of the great design which the author had proposed to himself; but it may be allowably pleaded that the field of research is too extended, and the whole subject too vast for satisfactory treatment by any one writer in a volume of moderate compass. This book deals moreover, in many portions, with inevitable, and probably insuperable difficulties. It occasionally touches upon the extreme limits of human intelligence, where no thinker can hope for clear solution, in the present state of our knowledge. In such themes no author can accomplish so much as he ardently wishes, nor indeed do more than give, as he thinks, a right direction to the minds of those who follow his course of meditation. Hence, too, it is certain that the treatment must to the inconsiderate appear fragmentary and incomplete; and, to employ a geological figure, the volume may seem a conglomerate of angular pieces rather than a slowly deposited and regularly formed sedimentary deposit, in which layer lies formally upon layer, and every layer denotes orderly succession and gradual subsidence.

A special difficulty has been felt in adapting the book to general perusal, while it so often treats of matters which are remote from common consideration. Had it been exclusively philosophical in its form and language, it would have repelled the mass of ordinary readers, and thus have missed its mark. As much, therefore, of popular treatment and interest has been imparted to it as lay within the author's powers and the volume's scope; and it is believed that no one of ordinary culture and habitual thoughtfulness will find any obstacle to his comprehension of the whole.

Many of the thoughts here recorded have dwelt in the writer's mind during long and solitary walks, through the valleys and over the passes of the high Alps of Switzerland and the neighbouring countries. This is mentioned to account for the frequent occurrence of Alpine metaphors and illustrations.

The author is fully aware that his mode of controverting some current hypotheses, and of treating certain systems, will fail to satisfy those of his readers who regard them from other stand-points than his own. This is inevitable, since he often stands upon contested ground. He is in the condition of one who wishes to make peace between ardent combatants—between nations at war with each other. If he cannot find terms and conditions mutually acceptable—if he be charged by the one side with demanding too much, and by the other with yielding too much—if he be assured that the foes are practically irreconcileable, and that war must continue even to the extermination of the one party or the other—then he must retire discomfited for the present, although he fondly cherishes the conviction that ultimately peace will be secured on some such terms as he has proposed.

It is unhappily almost a settled conviction amongst a large portion of the various existing religious communities that modern Science, and especially Natural and Physical Science, is pursued in a spirit hostile to Biblical belief and Christian faith ; and that discoveries in Science are available rather as weapons against Christian Faith, than as aids to it. Hence, there has arisen an indifference, and even a dread of, and an aversion to scientific studies which no Christian, who has himself gained a true conception of Science, can view without deep regret. Hence, too, that prevailing ignorance of Natural Science amongst even many educated persons, which eminent philosophers have so plainly exposed and so loudly lamented, has been too patiently tolerated.

Those, indeed, of the present generation who are advanced in life, and are likewise engaged in active and absorbing occupations, must be excepted from the charge of voluntary ignorance of Science, simply because during their educational period many important discoveries had not been made, and the books on Science, then commonly accessible, were few, and incomparably inferior to the numerous excellent volumes which now so frequently appear. Manuals, Handbooks, Elementary Treatises, and condensed and convenient Cyclopœdias of Physical and Natural Science, and

Natural History, form one of the leading literary characteristics of our time; and it is to those who are at present in their earlier years, that the charge of culpable ignorance is more especially applicable, while by them, probably, it is the less felt to be culpable, because Science itself largely bears the reproach of opposition to religion—a reproach which, as the author hopes to show, has arisen from misconception, and from the perversion of the scientific knowledge of things from its true tendency, were men's minds unprejudiced against religion.

If it can be shown that from this very domain of Natural Science the interests of Religion will be aided rather than hindered; if it can be established that the contemplation of Nature, and the study of it in its various parts and properties, and modes and changes, when pursued in a reverential spirit, is a direct help to Faith, and a powerful promoter of religious thought and speculation; if it can be made manifest that such reverential contemplation and research is the principal, and, apart from Revelation, the only means of which we can avail ourselves in the present stage of our existence, in order to acquire some definite and adequate conceptions of the greatness, the power, the wisdom, and the goodness of the Almighty Father; and finally—if it can be rendered apparent that in this present period, far more than in any preceding one, these attributes of the Deity may be exemplified and illustrated, so as most impressively to strike the mind of any one disposed to receive impressions and illustrations of this kind,—then surely the ignorance of, or indifference, or aversion to Natural Science to which I have adverted, will give place to zeal in its pursuit, and will ensure a welcome for its evidence and its suggestive intimations.

These ends the author humbly hopes to attain, in part at least, by the publication of this volume. It is not a systematic treatise on Natural Theology, or on any one branch of it; neither is any one subject treated exhaustively; but a number of subjects are selected for consideration which seem best fitted to secure the proposed ends, and to interest the reader by their attractiveness or importance. Although the author has discussed and weighed several metaphysical and metaphysiological theories of Natural Phenomena, and has selected some results of very high research, he trusts that every page of this publication will be intelligible to educated readers, who will bear in mind that a book of the nature of the one now before them, cannot be perused without much exercise of thought, or become beneficial without a considerable amount of reflection.

It appears desirable to explain in what sense the word *Nature* is here employed, since it is so differently and sometimes so vaguely used. From the manner in which most purely scientific men of our time use it, we infer that by Nature they mean the entire, vast scheme of things visible and sensible, subordinated to law and system. The various laws which govern it are called *Natural Laws*, or the *Laws of Nature*, which are regarded as universal and inviolable; and being so, never have been, and never will be broken. With men entertaining this view of Nature, the idea of anything Supernatural is excluded from the realm of the Natural.

Theologians, Natural or Doctrinal, have employed the word Nature in a more limited sense. They also mean by it the entire vast scheme of things visible and sensible to man, and they likewise regard this as subordinated to law and system, but as nevertheless a great unreasoning mechanism, when viewed apart from that Divine and Personal Will which has created all and keeps all in motion and in order. It is in this more limited sense that most religious men still employ the term Nature. It is impossible to use the word definitely, and with uniform precision, in a volume which has partly a scientific and partly a religious bearing, especially when the opinions of persons are cited, who themselves employ the term in an indefinite manner.

The present author, as may indeed be anticipated, always regards Nature as a manifestation of the Creator's power, and wisdom, and goodness, existing apart from Himself, and as a scheme of things to which He is external, but to which He perpetually sustains many direct relations. It is an assemblage of things which could not exist without Him, although He could exist without it. Generally the conception of Nature adopted in these pages includes man and all that is in man; but oftentimes, in conformity with common language, Nature is spoken of as distinct and separate from man—and as teaching him certain truths which it is the purpose of this volume to disclose and enforce. In such a view the spiritual part of man stands at one time aside from, and at another in connection with his material part, and he is regarded as a reasoning being in relation to the external universe. This, indeed, is the manner in which Man and Nature have been generally regarded by Natural Theologians, although not distinctly defined by them.

Those who have been educated in Theological Schools, and hold Theological Truths with a firm grasp, ignorant of the internecine war waged between them and Modern Science by many of the sceptical writers and popular speakers of our day, may think that I have given too much prominence to difficulties and theories which do not affect *their* faith. Let such persons but slightly acquaint themselves with the pretensions of Positivism and absolute Naturalism, and they will alter their opinion. Able men are labouring sedulously to overturn certain beliefs which we hold to be fundamental. Plausible advocates assure us that the alarm we feel as to the inroads of Science upon Religion are groundless and foolish. This is true of of Science itself, as this volume aims to establish; but it is untrue of certain philosophers and men of Science, as a few quotations would establish.

Before me at this moment lie the two large

volumes which Mr. G. H. Lewes, the advocate of Positivism, has very recently (1871) issued as the latest and largest edition of his clear and comprehensive History of Philosophy. In several pages of these volumes, and particularly in the additions now just published, Mr. Lewes' anti-theological spirit is manifested. He speaks of "The Radically Incompatible Conclusions of Theology and Science;" and his favourites are the determined opponents of what is generally accepted as Theology. Of Mr. Herbert Spencer, so well known as a clever Evolutionist upon the strictest principles of Naturalism, Mr. Lewes affirms, "It is questionable whether any thinker of finer calibre has appeared in our country; although the future alone can determine the position he is to assume in History. He, alone, of British thinkers has organized a System of Philosophy. His object is that of the Positive Philosophy, namely, the organization into a harmonious doctrine of all the highest generalizations of Science by the application of the Positive method, and the complete displacement of Theology and Metaphysics."*

* It is very amusing to contrast with Mr. Lewes's encomium, Dr. Porter's severe condemnation of Mr. Spencer and his phi-

Now, if such be the aim of the thinker of finest calibre in our country, a thinker of a different calibre may, however timidly, offer his thoughts and conclusions. Over displaced Metaphysics I do not lament, but over doomed Theology I may be allowed to mourn. Mr. Spencer's vaunted system is nearly completed, and Theology, therefore, is speedily about to be displaced! Before that removal is thoroughly effected, I claim to say something on Theology in connection with Nature. In so doing, I aim to establish it more firmly, and to widen its foundation, and to enlarge its

losophy, in an essay entitled "Science and Humanity," which has been re-published in England since this book was written. Dr. Porter, the President of Yale College, America, is as merciless to Mr. Spencer, as the latter is to others; and thus concludes:—"No well-read student of philosophy can hesitate to believe that, notwithstanding the zeal of his admirers, he will cease to be the wonder of the hour; that so soon as the secret of his plausibility is exposed, he will suffer a more complete neglect than he will fairly deserve." It is plain that the President of Yale College has a very low opinion of "Our Great Philosopher," as Mr. Darwin styles Mr. Spencer. The President delights in pointing to the "incoherencies of Spencer," for whom it appears his American adherents claim that, like Kant, he is the all-crushing philosopher of these times. Dr. Porter, however, is the Spencer-crusher, and charges him with "his stealthy subreptions, his cool word-plays, his confounding of inductions with axioms, and his sacrifice of common sense to the requirements of an unproved theory."

scope. Though Natural Theology be pronounced moribund, I am not yet too late; at all events, it is more animating to pronounce a defence of the living than a eulogy of the dead. Possibly I may reinvigorate my departing friend; certainly I shall vindicate him from unmerited calumnies

LONDON.
February, 1872.

THE HIGHER MINISTRY OF NATURE.

I.

THE FLEETING AND THE ENDURING.

THE whole animate creation as placed upon, and encircled by, the inanimate masses of inorganic matter, is a collection of things fleeting in the midst of things enduring. Man in his present state of existence, by sacred and secular writers, by poets and proverbialists, is likened to many common things which are of briefest endurance. He is compared in this respect to a flower, a leaf, a blade of grass, a wreath of vapour, a drop of dew, a cloud, or a bubble. So frequent and so familiar are these comparisons, that they cease to affect us. Who amongst us is led to reflect deeply on the brevity of his human life by the ordinary or even the Scriptural metaphors illustrating it? Nay more, the multiplied cemeteries, the long rows of tombstones, monumental piles and inscriptions, effigies and funeral pomp, and mortuary emblems of all kinds, lose their utterance to our ears, and their significance and impressiveness to our hearts. We require something new, or sudden, or strange, to enforce their lessons. Perhaps even that slave who by royal command daily repeated in his royal master's ear the warning, "Remember that thou art mortal," at length became monotonous in tone, and saw that his admonition was unheeded.

An unexpected or extraordinary event, however, may bring us into the desired condition of thoughtfulness, and such an event which took place in 1867 at Paris, during the time of the Great Exhibition, will perhaps have this effect upon us at present.

An Egyptian mummy was unrolled at Paris in the presence of several savants—at the period named. There was indeed nothing particularly novel in the uncovering of one of those long and curiously preserved Egyptians. Mummies have been often unrolled before, and perhaps nothing worthy of special record would have been noted of this embalmed body, but for the singular accompaniment of a few leaves in its armpits, and the complete preservation of their forms, although they had lost their colour. Here there certainly was a very suggestive fact and a striking contrast. The leaves themselves required no embalming, no curious case, no balsamic preservatives. Simple things as they were, they had once quivered in the cool breezes of evening, they had not withered under the burning meridian beams of an Egyptian sun, they had been refreshed through every tiny pore, and along every thin vein by the drenching dews of heavy night. They had been plucked, before they naturally faded and fell, by some human hand, on the banks of the Nile; and now here they were in the city of Paris, after having been torn from a living tree some three thousand or more years ago, by a living human hand, and placed under a dead human arm. Here they were as well preserved as the human body itself, though as dry and as sapless!

Who was it that placed these leaves under the dead arm? Did he do so thoughtfully or carelessly? Did he thereby mean to teach a symbolic lesson, or did he regard these leaves as themselves conservative in their effluence?

Did he thereby purpose to speak to a remote posterity on earth, or thus to influence the spirit of the deceased? We cannot determine, but this we see—here lie together two kinds of once living organisms—the vegetable and the human, and these two are both symbolic of a short life; both distinct in outline, yet both unrecognized in their minute features; both alike in their end, yet each very different in its previous existence.

Although nothing precise could be pronounced relating to the kind of plant to which these leaves belonged, and although nothing definite could be deciphered of the rank and character of the individual who once animated this human body, yet they both came from that land of marvels and mysteries, where even language lies entombed in strange pictures, and where care for the dead often exceeded care for the living. They came from a land where the Fleeting and the Enduring stand in more conspicuous contrast than in any other country.

While men died and leaves decayed, while animate forms lived out their little span, and passed away as though they ne'er had been, there slowly rose up by their side those gigantic monoliths, those tall, slender obelisks, and those massive pyramids; those mysterious sphinxes and vast temples, of which many to this day remain, and long will remain, to testify to the bold conceptions and the patient toil of dynasties otherwise unrecorded, and of races of men utterly unknown. Men of to-day can remove obelisks from Egypt to Paris and to Rome, and in those great cities can exhibit to the moderns the scarcely injured works of the ancients; but the men and the women, the natural growths of those remote periods, are gone from this earth for ever. Sometimes a mass of dried flesh and a few dried leaves are exhumed and displayed as singular relics rescued from general decay and departure. By stones in temples, by pyramids, by monoliths, Egypt still in part endures; in her Pharoahs, in her priests, and in her many generations of common people; while in the human race, and in nearly all that appertained to the daily life of the race of oldest days, Egypt has been as fleeting as the leaves that once rustled on the shores of her great river.

Nearly the same tenor of comment is applicable to the great world of Nature in which men live and die year after year and century after century. Mountains and rocks—those huge pyramids of Nature—remain to us through all time, and we must learn from them what we best can. Natural hieroglyphics are recorded in the strata composing rocks and mountains, and we may interpret them when, after long study, we have discovered the key to their meaning. But the once living things themselves—those forms which once had voices that might have sounded forth to us—those forms which once performed actions, and displayed motions which would have instructed us —which were born and grew and died upon a soil or in a sea adapted to their existence—all those living things have vanished away, as though they had never lived at all. The scanty remains of them which are now found embedded in various deposits have been safely sepulchred like the mummies of Egypt, and they alone are our natural hieroglyphs. They alone are the enduring relics of innumerable fleeting existences. We ourselves are also passing away with like resultless lives. We are the fleeting things in the midst of an apparently enduring world of matter.

Should not we, then, who are so rapidly passing away, investigate and interrogate the outward world which has appeared in immeasurable time before us—which is marked by an eventful history of change and life—which has ever been under the sway of wonderful, irresistible, and divinely-originated laws—and which may yet remain under those laws for unknown ages to come? If by assiduity and thought we can learn and record and leave behind us some certain knowledge of this vast external world, of its hidden secrets, of its general constitution, of its majestic order, and of its impressive grandeur; above all, if we can show how these its characteristics illustrate the Omnipotence, Providence, and Bounty of the Creator of the entire universe of things, and how He designs that we should discern them in His works, and be drawn nearer to Him in spirit by the close examination of what He has set in glorious order before our eyes; then we shall have served one principal object of our earthly existence. The purpose of our present life is not to live in mental blindness, but to learn as we live, and to become full of knowledge and wisdom in proportion to our years. He who has passed through our great School of Nature without learning its important lessons—without regarding it, and listening to it as a teacher of great truths, and a symbol of things higher and nobler than itself—might as well have been placed in a chaotic and barren planet. He has neglected to gather and store the sweetest fruits of Time—fruits which bear in them seeds that may germinate and mature in Eternity. That man who goes from this world with no other acquisition than gold, or the memory of bodily satisfactions and enjoyments, is most fitly symbolized by the already-described Egyptian mummy, which bore no other final token of its earthly grandeur or industry than a few dead leaves under its arm.

II.

THE TWO MINISTRIES OF NATURE.

FOR the purpose of this book, I distinguish between what may be termed the Lower and the Higher Ministry of Nature. The former is that by which she subserves our present individual and collective interests, makes highly civilized man what he now is, and promises to make him even more than he now is, and to place him on the highest eminence of physical attainments. This is the result of what is commonly styled the March of Science, and is without doubt a wonderful result. It might be dwelt upon with great effect and at great length; but to do this would be superfluous in these pages, and quite unnecessary, since nearly every lecturer and popular writer on Science takes up this theme, and decorates and illustrates it with visible complacency and general acceptance.

Within little more than the period of the present century, the achievements of Science have been marvellously fruitful in practical benefits. "She has made," to employ the words of the Rev. T. W. Farrar, "the shattering force of the electric spark obediently speed her messages through the heart of iron mountains, and under the waves of raging seas; she has kindled her silver beacons on the wave-tormented crags, as though to light up an avenue to her palace front; she has enabled the sailor to steer in security amidst the breakers' wintry surge; and the miner to work in safety amidst the blasting fire-damp of the mine; she has drawn the forked lightning in harmless splendour out of the purple cloud; she has discovered the precious anodyne which lulls the senses into a calm and dreamless sleep, while the work of agony, agonizing no longer, is wrought upon the human frame. With a scratch of her lancet she has stayed the loathsome ravages of disease; she has forced upon reluctant selfishness, and branded into the brain of invincible ignorance, those beneficent laws which paralyze the fury of the pestilence, and restore health and buoyancy to the factory and the hut."

In every direction to which we may specially turn, we shall find more and more to excite our interest in this March of Science, while the astonishing displays, made of late years at National and International Exhibitions, have engrossed the thoughts of men in the multiplicity, and realized value of mechanical improvements. Periodically, too, other similar, but superior Exhibitions may be opened to immense assemblies of mankind. If not, the world will never cease to be instructed in the attainments of practical Science, in the need and extension of Technical Education, and in the prospects of an ultimate mechanical millennium.

No right-thinking man will deny this progress or under-estimate these benefits. He will own and anticipate the most promising issues; and although this is comparatively the Lower Ministry, it has near relations to the Higher Ministry of Nature. In truth, the two are intimately associated and mutually helpful, if neither the one nor the other be displaced or disproportionately magnified. Let an illustration be selected from what is at this time, the most conspicuous and promising of all our practical applications of scientific discovery—Telegraphic Communication. Without entering into many details, I will simply give the results of the energies manifested in this department of enterprize. In the year 1867, there were upwards of 10,000 miles of insulated wire submerged in the form of submarine cables, in daily use for transmitting intelligence under different seas; while at least an equal length was lost in the same form, chiefly by the development of faults after a lapse of time. This was a surprising result, but how much more surprising is the recent statement of a careful investigator of this subject, who leads us to conclude that the submarine telegraph cables laid and worked up to the month of June 1870, or in course of manufacture, and about to be laid that same year, amount to no less than 32,076 nautical miles in length. We are further informed by Mr. J. C. Parkinson, that he assumes that by the end of the year 1874, England will be supplied with news not twelve hours old, from every part of the civilized globe.*

Does not such a statement suggest something more and something higher than the mere fact of an enormous development of practical tele-

* *Edinburgh Review*, No. 269, and J. C. Parkinson's " Ocean Telegraph to India."

graphy?—than the mere speed of national intercommunication, and the facilities of commercial operations? Does it not demonstrate to us that mind will advance as well as commerce, that goodness may communicate with goodness between the ends of the world, that the souls of men are now put into nearer relationship, that all over the civilized earth whatever is noble, lofty in aim, benevolent, sympathetic, and Christian, can be sent forth from soul to soul; that the slender submarine electric wire can communicate a message of love which no intervening waters can cool, and that if any man has a God-like purpose of promise in one country, it may find even in a few hours, a welcome home in every receptive heart within the entire circle of nations.

There can be no question that one of the deepest desires of every high-minded student of Nature is to know its end, its relation to man in time and in eternity. The soul that strives to free itself from the baseness and paltriness of present human pursuits, earnestly seeks for every observable token of the presence—the all-pervading presence of God in Nature—such a soul is not content with physical or utilitarian ends. These may be good, but they terminate with the present life, and if there be nothing higher within human reach, then all this unfolding magnificence and endless complexity of Nature seem superfluous. Much less would have sufficed for man's ordinary wants; if he needed only food and raiment, light and heat, a little cradle, and an obscure grave, the world is too good and too grand for him. Nature is in such case, a richly-embroidered garment, wrought by royal hands for a beggar and an outcast. It does not suit him, it does not fit him; and it renders his very wretchedness the more conspicuous by its richness and its ornaments.

True that no one can positively say what the entire relations of Nature to man actually are. Still many of these may be conjectured, discovered, and to a great extent gathered from a careful and reverent consideration of the antecedent history of our earth and our race, and from an examination of the emotions and courses of thought which Nature excites in the most cultivated and contemplative minds. If Nature should awaken similar emotions in many similar minds, if the wider the cultivation the greater the appreciation of her manifold characteristics, if souls seeking after communion with God should frequently find in an enlightened communion with Nature that she lifts them up heavenwards as though on eagle's wings; if the successive discoveries of Science shall, when rightly regarded, be capable of arrangement into a series of altar steps stretching through space upwards towards the throne of the Invisible Almighty One, then Nature has a higher ministry than is known to the unreflecting, or cared for by the mere utilitarianism of this life.

It is the object of the present work to accomplish somewhat, however limited, in this direction, and it may suggest much more than it accomplishes. Thoughts of this kind, regulated by adequate knowledge, and chastened by due reflection, appear to be the least frequent of all associated with Nature. The poetical imagination, the pictorial, the æsthetic in general, discerns continually more and more in her, and appropriately depicts it, but unhappily our religious instincts and emotions do not seem to have been brought into an intimate relation with Nature. We do not habitually resort to her as a great teacher sent to us from God; we seldom think of her as a rarely and richly-stored revealer of divine truths; we treat her as dumb because we do not listen to her voice; we pass our lives in her midst and think she says nothing to us. We are like travellers who traverse a wood by night and are impressed by its awful silence, not knowing that in the morning every tree will be instinct with visible life, and every glade vocal with the sweetest song. A thousand singing birds are now roosting on a thousand branches. Darkness hides and hushes them, but he who in a few subsequent hours follows the present nocturnal traveller on the same path, will descry far-spreading green and brightly coloured foliage, and rapidly beating wings, and will find light in every woody interstice, and listen to love in every changeful lay.

The physicist or naturalist, simply as such, does not regard it as within his province to refer to this Ministry of Nature; he is engaged in questioning her about her physical properties, and when he has elicited what these are, he has performed his part. The anatomist is concerned only about structure, the naturalist about order and organization, the biologist about life, the geologist about stratification and origin and change of material, the paleontologist about the life that has been as the antecedent to that which now is on the earth and in the seas. All these inquirers usually restrict themselves within their respective circles, and find more than enough to occupy them therein. Such men may treat the suggestion of a higher ministry of Nature in accordance with the structure of their several minds. Newton and Faraday derived from their scientific researches sublime conceptions of God, to which, however, they rarely gave public utterance. The number of religious students of nature is probably greater than anticipated, and probably greater than can be known, because many such are reluctant to give prominence to their opinions, or do not court opportunities to make them public. Thus not a few pious men pass away from the ranks of science, and none but their intimate friends know their religiousness. Turner the chemist, Dawes the astronomer, and several others almost unknown to survivors, might be named as examples of this class.

Others who have an incredulous cast of mind will either resent or disregard the idea of any higher ministry of Nature than that which she presents to them phenomenally. Some will deny it, and some ridicule it. Many will remove it into the region of the "unknowable," or the "unthinkable," or the "unprofitable." Such has been and will long continue to be the state of some philosophic minds in relation to Nature. So few persons investigate Nature and Science on their own account, that the multitude are apt to take the teaching of certain scientific men in respect of morals or religion, as the teaching of Nature, or rather as the legitimate issue of scientific pursuits. Nothing can be more erroneous, though perhaps nothing is more habitual in unreflecting minds. Nature is around us, just as the Bible is before us; much the same kind of treatment is given to both. They who find little or nothing Divine in the Bible are not likely to find much that is Divine in Nature. They who do not derive life, hope, and consolation from the one, are very unlikely to derive any such things from the other. If the Bible have no higher ministry than its letter, neither has Nature. But as tens of thousands have derived, and will yet derive, their noblest thoughts and most animating hopes from the Bible, so tens of thousands may derive the same, in a different measure from Nature.

Throughout these pages it will be apparent

that a due respect is paid to both of these great teachers, and that while the author is not indeed forgetful of the great advances of modern criticism in the explanation of the Sacred Book, so he is on the other hand by no means unmindful of the very much higher ground on which any true religion of Nature must be based than heretofore. And it is on this very account that he thinks his book may be useful to many even moderately cultivated and intelligent persons. So far as the impressions, and emotions, and aspirations to which he presumes to give utterance are his own, and are the results of his personal experience and reflection, so far they may or may not be chargeable with individualism, or fancifulness, or speculativeness, accordingly as they may strike the minds of various classes of readers. Indeed, the same views may be taken of them as have been taken aforetime of the spiritual treatment of natural things. They are open to all kinds of fair criticism, and subject to all kinds of literary animadversion. Nay, to a considerable number of naturalists, and philosophers of material schools of thought, they will be positively objectionable and distasteful. For without doubt they are at the opposite pole to much current teaching. They strive to show its feebleness and its fallacy, and though the author's aim has always been to accomplish this courteously and considerately in respect of persons, he cannot avoid speaking as strongly as he feels of erroneous systems and speculations.

That there should exist such an exalted Ministry of Nature as the author describes, he is himself convinced. That it may be made a most powerful and persuasive ministry, he is likewise persuaded. That it *will* be made such in years to come he is much inclined to hope and believe. That it is at present the most neglected of all higher ministries, he is painfully aware. Its greatest force will be exercised in conjunction with a Biblical ministry, and not apart from it. Separately it may do something, but it will do most in combination. All true ministries must grow in influence by combined forces which shall touch our manifold nature on all sides. Any theological creed which reaches to and rests in one part of our nature only, and which is in contradiction to others, may have its day and its disciples, but is doomed inevitably to perish. In like manner, a scheme of natural science or philosophy, which exclusively touches another side of our nature, is equally doomed to perish. Only when a physical hypothesis satisfies all the requisite conditions, does it pass into a law of nature, and only when a higher scheme comprehends the whole man, his religious instincts, his noblest emotions, as well as his reason and intelligence, can it be credited as universally applicable.

The present is pre-eminently an age of investigation, and of searching inquiry into fundamental beliefs; consequently there prevail much doubt and much fear. Even in any one community of philosophical observers, there are wide variances of opinion, and as a president of one of the boldest and least reverent of our scientific societies recently remarked to the author respecting the tendency of certain researches, " In all such matters no two of us think alike." There is, as there should be, unrestrained freedom of thought and expression. Every man says what he thinks and what he pleases about religions and sciences, and therefore, as previously observed, the utterance of individual opinion corresponds to the structure of the speaker's or thinker's mind. Ill-informed and narrowly circumscribed men, who stand without, are appalled, and believe their lot to be cast in evil times. The remedy for this state is not to retire into narrow and still narrower limits, but to examine what is alleged, to see what really scientific basis it has, or has not. The march of science is in many respects a march of destruction, in order that it may subsequently become a march of restoration. If any man feel that he holds his religious opinions at the mercy of Science, if he believes only at the point of its sword, he lives an unworthy and valueless life. Baseless superstition *is* at the mercy of the sword of Science, and must be slain by it. Where in the present day it exists at all, it exists only by virtue of an armistice, its death is deferred only by the grant of a reprieve.

Doubt even, on great and vital truths, while it is painful to a believer in them, is not necessarily a total evil to the community, for it leads to deeper inquiries, to a winnowing of the chaff from the wheat, and to the re-edification of truth on a broader and surer foundation. The revival of old infidelities and the republication of old anti-theistic schemes in a new dress and with modern ornaments may be in one aspect discouraging, but in another hopeful, since intelligence is thus kept alive and vigorous, and no man is permitted to sleep at his post. He who comes out of the conflict victorious has confidence in his weapons, and for the future fears no human assailant. His conquest may cost him severely in hardship, in toil, possibly in hardly-healed wounds; but he cherishes the just pride of a conqueror, and is incomparably the superior of the credulous sluggard or the self-congratulatory coward. All may be equally safe, but who would compare the sluggard or coward with the conqueror?

Yet a continued state of doubt about fundamental questions of religion and philosophy, is fatal to the Ministry of Nature. We must arrive at certain fixed points to which such ministry may attach itself; at certain centres of truth around which it may circle, and a certain veneration for the Supreme Being, which it may fortify and illustrate. If the mind remains undecided about the existence and character of God; if a man thinks it to be best to hold such tenets, with all that flows from them, ever floating about in a haze of doubt and mystery; if he banishes them from his daily meditation to a remote region rarely visited by a stray and feeble thought, then Nature is to him simply a system of law and order, never reflecting the glory of the Creator, unlit by any but natural suns, and eloquent about Hipparchus, Newton, and Kepler, and a number of great observers; in fact, Nature to such a mind is the mere glorification of the highest human intellects.

The Higher Ministry of Nature is that by which she serves us as a handmaid to Religion, and becomes our servant in showing herself to be the servant of God. This, while it is her higher, so confessedly it is her more delicate and difficult service. The mind requires to be trained to perceive it, and the spirit alert to receive it, before it will be available or interpreted. There is indeed a close analogy between the effort, the patience, and the perseverance of the physical discoverer, or the mechanical inventor, and the research, the contemplation, and reflection required on the part of him who would spiritually profit by Nature's teachings. Intimate acquaintance with the lives and labours of scientific observers shows how devotedly they have served Nature before she usefully served them. In like manner, in respect of Nature's higher ministry, every man must become her devoted attendant before she becomes his instructive teacher. If there be no royal road to geometry, there is none to natural knowledge, and assuredly none to the higher knowledge of Nature. In the study of this latter, pre-eminently we must exercise all our powers, and patiently and perseveringly pursue every clue and every path that appears to lead us to a favourable issue. Definite results in this direction are not easily attainable, while the inquirer is repeatedly baffled and thrown back upon the insufficiency of his faculties. In this region we are as children searching in the twilight, with an impenetrable darkness ever threatening us, and ever drawing closer upon us. Some one has suggested that as seekers of truth we are like wanderers in a large park, who delight ourselves in pacing numerous paths, beautifully bordered by shrubs and plants and stately trees, all of which, though alluring, nevertheless delude us; for whenever we pursue any promising avenue to its end, we find ourselves stopped by a lofty wall, over which we cannot look. Everywhere stands the wall. It may be concealed by vegetation; it may be ingeniously hidden by woods and herbage; circuitous paths may be planned to keep it long out of view, to wile us into sideways, and to beguile us with the imagination of unlimited space. Nevertheless on all sides rises the wall; and we turn away defeated in one direction, only to find ourselves alike defeated in another. The domain is on all sides bounded; our faculties in all directions are limited; we have only at best to explore what we can pace over; and if we do that, we shall obtain the utmost results that our present liberty will permit. The time, however, will come when we shall pass beyond the baffling wall into the unbounded expanse beyond; and in all probability our acquired knowledge of the little paths of this world will qualify us for future explorations without limitation and without defeat.

These observations naturally lead us to consider briefly the character and conditions of our present ignorance, how far it is removable, and how far voluntary, and therefore culpable.

III.

IGNORANCE:
DEFINITIONS, DISTINCTIONS, RESPONSIBILITY.

THAT the scope of the following chapters may be understood, it is necessary to define what is really meant by *Ignorance*, a term which is continually employed, with indistinct apprehensions of its true and relative significance.

Ignorance, simply stated, is a deprivation of knowledge, and therefore an intellectual deficiency, but it may be very differently viewed in relation to its opposite, Knowledge. There is, for example, a *necessary* ignorance, viz., of that which cannot possibly be known, or the unknowable; and there may, again, be the absolutely unknowable and the temporally unknowable. The essential nature of the Deity may be considered as absolutely unknowable by man, while many of His actions and motives may be considered as temporally unknowable, that is, by our present faculties, though possibly apprehensible by us when endowed with higher faculties in a superior state of being. The ignorance of a human being may be merely his as human, while equal ignorance does not becloud higher orders of intelligence; and therefore our present ignorance of many things as yet unrevealed is merely a temporal bar, and may be removed in the future.

There may be likewise a *conditional* ignorance in relation to certain states and conditions of the knower. The ignorance of childhood is conditional to that early stage of existence, and is in gradual process of abatement as we grow up, in exact proportion to our efforts to remove it. Man at his birth is a being of conditional ignorance; at his maturity he is less ignorant; after his death, if he has carefully cultivated his faculties, he may be the possessor of comparatively enlarged knowledge.

The term *ignorance*, if strictly used, can only be applied with reference to that which may be known; for the term nescience, properly expresses that which is beyond the possibility of knowledge. In truth there can really be an ignorance only of that of which there can be a knowledge. "The ignorance," says Ferrier, "which is a defect, must not be confounded with a nescience of the opposites, of the necessary truths of reason; in other words, with a nescience of that which it would contradict the nature of all intelligence to know. Such nescience is no defect or imperfection—it is only on the contrary, the very strength or perfection of reason."

Ignorance which is remediable—is morally culpable—and more or less culpable in proportion to the importance of the object of knowledge. There are many things of which we may continue ignorant, which it would be of some advantage to know; there are other things of which we may be ignorant, but which are of the highest moment, and of which, if we remain voluntarily ignorant to the end, such ignorance is culpable in proportion to the importance of the objects.

Now, in this light, ignorance of what may be learned of the Divine Being, and His designs in the world around us, appears to be voluntary and culpable; voluntary in proportion to the amount of light and knowledge capable of being discovered in the natural world; and culpable in proportion to the value and elevating influence of such knowledge on the mind in relation to God. Moreover this culpableness increases in proportion to the bearing which all such knowledge has on our condition in a future state; and if we extend our ignorance voluntarily to what belongs to the state of the soul in the next life, then we become responsible for all that we may there have to endure. We are morally responsible for all the neglect of natural enlightenment which is voluntary, and morally culpable for the loss of all to which it would lead us and all which it would illustrate and corroborate.

This remediable, and therefore morally culpable ignorance has two aspects in the present consideration — one towards those who are voluntarily ignorant of attainable knowledge of Nature, but who may yet possess more or less acquaintance with spiritual truths—the other towards those who are pursuing researches in natural things, while they at the same time voluntarily ignore things spiritual. True knowledge of God, and of Nature in relation to God, constitute, in the author's opinion, the two halves of that grand whole which ought to be the ardently desired good of every human soul. Therefore, as much blame rests upon ignorance in one direction as in the other. That soul is not in a healthy condition which separates God from Nature or Nature from God,— and moral disease must be the consequence of such mental severance. There may be the conceit of Science as well as the conceit of ignorance, and in either case conceit is the forerunner of barrenness in the highest truths. Hence it comes that religious men of culture are so frequently pained at the opinions expressed by men of Science in public lectures, and in books, or popular papers, designed to explain certain results of their scientific researches. An example may be taken from a periodical in which a distinguished physiologist publishes one of his Sunday Evening Lectures to the People :—

"If a man," says Professor Huxley, "asks me what the politics of the inhabitants of the moon are, and I reply that I do not know; that neither I nor any one else, have any means of knowing; and that under these circumstances, I decline to trouble myself about the subject at all, I do not think he has any right to call me a sceptic. On the contrary, in replying thus, I conceive that I am simply honest and truthful, and show a proper regard for the economy of time. So Hume's strong and subtle intellect takes up a great many problems about which we are naturally curious, and shows us that they are essentially questions of lunar politics, in their essence incapable of being answered, and therefore not worth the attention of men who have work to do in the world. And he thus ends one of his essays :—

"If we take in hand any volume of Divinity, or school metaphysics, for instance, let us ask, *Does it contain any abstract reasoning concerning quantity or number?* No. *Does it contain any experimental reasoning concerning matter of fact and existence?* No. Commit it then to the flames; for it can contain nothing but sophistry and illusion."

"Permit me to enforce this most wise advice. Why trouble ourselves about matters of which, however important they may be, we do know nothing and can know nothing? We live in a world which is full of misery and ignorance, and the plain duty of each and all of us is to try to make the little corner he can influence somewhat less miserable and somewhat less ignorant than it was before he entered it. To do this effectually, it is necessary to be fully possessed of only two beliefs. The first that the order of Nature is ascertainable by our faculties to an extent which is practically unlimited; the second, that our volition counts for something as the condition of the order of events."*

On one passage in the above extract, let us here make remarks:—" Why trouble ourselves about matters of which, however important they may be, we do know nothing and can know nothing? We live in a world which is full of misery and ignorance, and the plain duty of each and all of us is to try to make the little corner he can influence somewhat less miserable, and somewhat less ignorant than it was before he entered it." In these sentences lie more than one fallacy. First, there are certain matters which it is confessed may be highly important to us. If so, the Deity (and Professor Huxley does not deny His existence), would not leave us in *total* ignorance of them. But whatever their importance, we *do* know *nothing* of them, according to the Professor. If this be true, how do we know their importance? It is added that we *can* know *nothing* of them; but if they are important, we can know this fact, and it is presumable that in proportion to their im-

* *Fortnightly Review*, Feb. 1869.

portance we *ought* to learn more of them. Is not this a plain instance of voluntary and culpable ignorance? Is it not culpable to reject all inquiry about important subjects, although by their very nature they are incapable of the same treatment as physiology?

About our actual position in relation to the present life and our eternal destiny, somewhat at least has been revealed, and that somewhat is of the highest importance to us; while it is true that we are largely ignorant of such things as may be hereafter revealed to us. But our present ignorance is partial and temporal, and, however deeply it may humble us, it should never have the effect of terminating inquiry, and benumbing our spiritual instincts. Let us listen to the meditations on this subject, of one who well knew his ignorance as man, and, perhaps, dwelt too despondingly upon it; but who at the time was acquainted with the source of true knowledge, and rightly estimated the culpableness of voluntary ignorance.

In referring to the subject of the duty of reflecting on the end and purpose of human life, Pascal reasons that it is assuredly a great evil to be in doubt of this; but it is nevertheless our indispensable duty to examine things while in this doubt. He who doubts, but does not seek a solution, is altogether very unhappy and very unjust. If he be tranquil and satisfied and makes a profession of this, and finally even make his ignorance a subject of sport or vanity, then "I know," says Pascal, " no terms suitable for so extravagant a being. What source of pleasure can one find in expecting miseries without relief? What theme for vanity is there in finding oneself in impenetrable obscurity? And how can such reasoning as this pass for that of a rational man?"

" I know not who has placed me in the world nor what the world is, nor what I myself am. My ignorance on all subjects is terrible. I do not know what my body is, or my senses, or my soul, and that part of myself which thinks what I utter, which reflects on everything, and on itself; and has no better knowledge of itself than of all the rest. I behold these appalling depths of the universe which shut me in, and I feel myself fixed to a corner of that vast space, without knowing why I am placed in this spot rather than in another, nor why the little moment which is given me to live, has been assigned to me at this particular point, rather than any other in the whole of that eternity which has preceded me, and the whole of that eternity which is to follow me. I see nothing but infinity on all sides, which encloses me like an atom, and like a shadow which abideth but an instant and returneth not. All that I know is that I must shortly die; but the thing I am most ignorant of is that very death which I cannot escape.

"As I know not whence I came, so I know not whither I go, and I know only that when I leave this world I fall for ever either into annihilation or into the hands of an angry God, without knowing to which of these two conditions I am for ever condemned. Behold then my state, full of misery, of weakness, of obscurity. And from all this I conclude that I ought to pass my days without a moment's reflection upon that which shall befall me. Perhaps I might find some ray of light to guide me in my doubts; but I will not take the trouble; I will not take a single step to seek it; and after treating with contempt those who do engage in this task, I will go without forethought and without fear to encounter so great an event, and suffer myself to be led softly to death in utter uncertainty of what shall be my condition to all eternity." *

* "Pensées," Havet's Ed., p. 135-137.

"Who would desire," says Pascal, " to have for a friend a man who discourses in this manner? Who would choose him from others to communicate his affairs to? Who would have recourse to such a friend in one's afflictions? And, in fact, for what purpose in life could one assign him a place?"

If we estimate the value of different kinds of knowledge even by the utilitarian scale of measurement, surely that knowledge is the most useful which concerns our highest being, and the longest ages of our existence. Hence instead of such knowledge being regarded as superfluous, we may affirm that all knowledge besides is by comparison superfluous, or in the words of Milton,

"is fume
Or emptiness, or fond impertinence,
And renders us in things that most concern
Unpractised, unprepared, and still to seek."

My present argument rests in part upon the culpability of ignorance of the higher ministry of Nature in relation to God and religion; and here it becomes necessary to speak of what seems to be knowable and what unknowable in Nature. This word has been so diversely employed, and is even now so vaguely used, that it may be well to determine its proper acceptance. We hold, then, the term Nature to express the totality of all corporeal or material existences such as they have been, are, and will be, with their diverse activities, and with the invariable laws which govern those activities. It is therefore the totality of second causes distinct from and acted upon by first and free causes. God is the great and perfect First Cause, and though omnipresent is not to be confounded consubstantially with Nature, but is distinct from it, though throughout directive of it. And we believe the whole scheme of Nature when rightly interpreted, illustrates His perfections and promotes a perpetual recognition of them by human beings. This we take to be the higher ministration of the totality of things around us, while numerous secondary and temporary purposes are served by the scheme of Nature, many of which purposes man discovers by scientific research, and applies to his own benefit by practical skill.

It is maintained by the soundest thinkers that of the essences of things we must remain ignorant in this world, for phenomena are not the manifestations of hidden essence, but only the result of the relations of things between each other. Here we speak of things material and of necessary limits, as in the biological and physico-chemical sciences. Adopting the expression of Claude Bernard, in all kinds of experimental science, when we have found the nearest cause of a phenomenon, in determining the simple condition and circumstances in which it manifests itself, we obtain the scientific object or end which we cannot pass beyond.

The phenomena then which we behold are by no means the manifestation of the undiscoverable essences of things, but merely the results of their relation to each other; so that two things become known to us by their relations or their contrasts to each other. Both are objects of knowledge only by relation or by contrast. Thus the idea of empty space would not present itself without its opposite idea; viz., of full or penetrable space. Each of these ideas is a unit of knowledge which we can consider in turn, although the one originally revealed the other. Hence we must always have two units, and a relation or contrast between them to form a cognition. All our knowledge of things natural is therefore simply relative.

It would be beyond our design to enter into farther details respecting the doctrine of the alleged relativity of all human knowledge, and to distinguish the differences of opinion on this doctrine entertained by metaphysicians. Mr. Mill has clearly and sufficiently shown these differences in his Examination of Sir William Hamilton's Philosophy; but it is as well to notice that some philosophers believe that the Noumenon or thing, *per se*, is in itself a different thing from the Phenomenon, and is equally or more real; but that though we know its existence, we have no means of knowing what it is; all that we can know is relatively to ourselves, the modes in which it affects us, or the phenomena which it produces. Other and perhaps the greater number of philosophers, hold that we know things partly as they are in themselves, and partly as they are in relation to us.

For the considerations involved in these pages, it is quite sufficient to take the phenomenal as the object of scientific intelligence, and as the ground of reasoning. We need not here discuss degrees of relativity, but may deal directly with the phenomenal as that which is within universal cognition.

But beyond and above all that appertains to scientific or natural knowledge we have to erect a higher and holier superstructure—

the important superstructure of spiritual apprehension and of faith, founded upon revealed truth. In the region of spiritual apprehensions, of psychological intuitions, and of religious faith, we aim at far higher results than the phenomenal. We are not content with the nearest cause of a phenomenon; for we seek the farthest and the first cause. In Science we cannot pass beyond the scientific object; in Religion we can and do, even by taking the nearest cause into account, and as a step in our advance to the first. We proceed the more surely because we have previously taken this step in our progress, and it is the object of all worthy religious philosophy to comprehend natural phenomena, and not to suppose that they assume an attitude of perpetual contradiction to it.

An appropriate illustration may be taken in regard to the human soul. Professor Owen recognizes no advantage in speaking of "an immaterial entity, mental principle, or soul." Professor Huxley affirms that "matter and spirit are both names for imaginary substrata of groups of natural phenomena." He also signifies that thought is the effect of protoplasm, yet that protoplasm exists without thought.

Here I have no concern with the philosophical defect of this argument, though it has been noticed that it violates a first principle of induction, viz., that the cause of a fact must precede it when it does take place, and that we can only omit this precedence when it does not take place. Here my concern is this: two distinguished naturalists do not recognize as philosophical the cognizance of soul or thought in the form of a distinct spiritual principle. This may be called a statement consistent with our knowledge of the phenomenal, and of nothing beyond it. Am I on this account justified in disbelieving the existence of any soul? Either I believe in its existence as a distinct spiritual principle, or I do not. If I do, am I unphilosophical? if I do not, am I irresponsible?

If I believe it, I plainly go beyond the materially phenomenal; if I disbelieve it I deny the possibility of any psychology, not to say the dictates of revealed truth, which in many places assumes the existence of the soul, and bases human responsibility upon our care for it, and use of it. But because I adhere to psychology, and because I believe in revealed truths concerning the soul, am I therefore neglecting the limits of the phenomenal, and overpassing the boundaries of any true knowledge? Assuredly not; I am in such belief obedient to a conviction out of and beyond the range of the phenomenal, but not contradictory to it. With such a conviction I may be still strictly philosophical in all that relates to the philosophy of the phenomenal world, and strictly correct in what relates to the supra-phenomenal world, to which the higher ministry of Nature, as well as the constant teaching of Revelation conduct me. I may entertain the profoundest respect for the scientific attainments of Professors Owen and Huxley, and fully confide in their physical and biological science; but beyond that, and in relation to the soul, I may altogether disagree with them, and feel myself quite capable of judging of the existence and distinctness of my soul. Their justly-granted reputation rests not upon their psychology or anti-psychology. Recognition of the soul rests upon supra-phenomenal science.

Here, then, we see how responsibility for our knowledge of things surpassing the phenomenal, finds its due place. Ignorance cannot be pleaded to bar this responsibility, since we are as much bound by the supra-phenomenal world in our higher as by the phe nomenal in our lower nature. The soul being recognized, it has its needs, its sustentation, its proper objects, and its destiny. These form the conditions of all higher human life, and the satisfaction of these is as imperative in the spiritual kingdom as the satisfaction of bodily wants in the corporeal and material. A man ought not to remain in ignorance of the demands of any one part of his compound nature.

Outside of the province of the physical and phenomenal there lies the whole region of our primary intuitions which are not controlled by physicism. Hence come our conceptions of causation, of free-will, of morality, of responsibility, of God. With those who denounce our primary religious conceptions as unscientific, we can hold no argument, for we have no common ground of standing. In despite of such persons, we say there is a science of the supra-phenomenal as well as of the physical, and you cannot monopolize the term science and always limit it to the physical. If you deny the possibility of a true science of the supra-phenomenal, then for you at least who deny it, there is no goal but complete scepticism, within the black shadow of which all varieties must vanish—all, God, man, self, others than self, personality, individual existence—in short all distinctions and all certainties. This is nihilism, universal scepticism, in which the word *ignorance* has no proper place.

With the inherent difficulties, doubts and indefiniteness of our primary intuitions, the purely physical school often contrast what they are wont to term the "certainties" of physical science and its methods. This language is however in a great measure illusory, and quite unsuitable by way of disparagement. Nothing would be easier than to specify some of the uncertainties of physical science and its methods. What are called the "exact sciences" can only be justly so called by comparison. Absolutely there is no such thing as an exact science, for the exactness is merely relative. To quote the language of a scientific writer, Professor Jevons, borrowed from his lately published Theory of Political Economy: "Astronomy is more exact than the other sciences, because the position of a planet or a star admits of close measurement, but if we examine the methods of physical astronomy, we find that they are all approximate. Every solution involves hypotheses which are not really true: as, for instance, that the earth is a smooth, homogeneous spheroid. Even the apparently simpler problems in statics or dynamics are only hypothetical approximations to the truth. We can calculate the effect of a crow-bar, provided it be perfectly inflexible, and have a perfectly level fulcrum, which is never the case. The data are almost wholly deficient for the complete solution of any one problem in natural science."

Were a contrast to be drawn between the methods of physical science and primary intuitional knowledge, it might be drawn in favour of the greater certainty of the latter, inasmuch as primary intuitions are bound up with consciousness, and are direct exercises of it, productive of immediate effects, while mathematical conclusions require the intervention of a train of reasoning.

Although then we cannot be culpable for nescience, we are so for not seeking and satisfying all attainable cognitions,—especially if these are acknowledged as proposed objects of pursuit, and as attended with corresponding mental and moral benefits. Such we cannot but think are the Divine intimations in the scheme of Nature as manifested to our minds, and as presented to us for perpetual inquiry. And if our present position in relation to it be that of highly capacitated beings,—of beings specially qualified to comprehend progressively more and more of the seen in order that we may thereby be led ardently to desire higher capacities and larger and fuller revelations, then voluntary ignorance is not only a loss but a sin. It is the choosing of darkness rather than light.

When, moreover, we believe that the whole visible universe is a magnificent representation of the power of the Creator, and the beneficence of the Provider, then the sinfulness of remaining wilfully ignorant of what he has revealed of himself becomes more apparent; and the question of our *responsibility* for neglect of opportunities of knowing Him in His mighty and manifold works comes before us for deliberate consideration.

In proportion to our conviction of the real purport of our present life in relation to God, will be our sense of this responsibility. If we feel that the chief object of our existence is to know the Divine Being in all the relations he sustains to us, and to do all that such knowledge will prompt us to perform, and if we admit that our opportunities of knowing Him in outward nature are many and perpetual, and more than ever so in the present age of the world, with its brighter lights, and surer methods of observation, and numerous aids and instrumentalities; then, emphatically, may we pronounce upon human responsibility in relation to a sanctified knowledge of nature. We shall urge upon ourselves and all men, that this is one of the most incumbent duties of our daily life, as well as one of its highest delights. We shall not take shelter under a presumed incapability of tracing God in his works; we shall not magnify the difficulties, or rest contented under an endless night of human ignorance; while we lament that we cannot know more, we shall study to know what is really knowable. We shall be deeply sensible that we cannot here expect to see God as He is, but as He chooses in His wisdom to be seen by us; and that if we wilfully close our eyes to what He here shows of Himself and of His attributes, it will be but a just judgment upon us, if in another life we should be far removed from His glory, and consciously responsible for our distance from the Source of light and love.

Men have too long been accustomed to regard responsibility merely in a religious sense, and as limited to the sphere of what is termed Divine grace, and to overlook the fact that responsibility to God is as extensive with his entire manifestations of Himself. Let us freely admit that responsibility is broad and universal, and to discern that it is so, we have only to read St. Paul's words in Romans 1. 18-20. "The wrath of God is revealed from heaven against all ungodliness and unrighteousness of men, who hold the truth in unrighteousness. Because that which may be known of God is manifest in them, for God hath shewed it unto them. For the invisible things of Him from the creation of the world are clearly seen, being understood by the things that are made, even His eternal power and Godhead; so that they are without excuse." If gentiles and heathens were thus without excuse for not observing the Divine light shining in the "things that are made," what greater degree of inexcusableness must attach to Christians of this age for averting their eyes from the multiplied lights of centuries of observation, and the broad beams of this century in particular, which most brightly illustrate the "invisible things" of God."

This responsibility we may term *natural*, in order to distinguish it from spiritual responsibility, which latter may be held to have regard to the revelation of grace as commonly understood; although in truth all responsibility must hold in reference to the individual, and to the Personal God to whom the individual is accountable for all that he is and all that he enjoys. And of natural responsibility be it observed that it clearly rests upon voluntary and on remediable ignorance; the willingness being judged of by the opportunity of removing it, and the remediableness by the faculties, and the position of every man in relation to existing knowledge. He who is frequently engaged in studying the constitution of the world of matter —the student of science in general, and of any natural science in particular, by neglecting the light that such studies should throw upon divine truth, and on his own standing as a dependant upon, and a worshipper of God—may be incurring a solemn responsibility upon which he has seldom duly reflected, and which perhaps he has never rightly estimated. He, again, who is not professedly conversant with such studies cannot on that account cast off all responsibility, for he is accountable for what he might attain, if he would fairly and fully exercise his natural powers of observation and reflection.

It must continually and strongly be impressed on the good, though half and scarcely half-informed men of Christian Churches that a serious responsibility rests upon them on their side; and here I prefer to quote the words of a great Christian writer, rather than to appear to presume in my own. On this topic Coleridge pointedly observes: " If acquiescence without insight, if warmth without light; if an immunity from doubt, given and guaranteed by a resolute ignorance; if a mere sensation of positiveness substituted—I will not say for the sense of certainty—but for that calm assurance, the very means and conditions of which it supersedes; if a belief that seeks the darkness and yet strikes no root, immoveable as the limpet from the rock, and like the limpet, fixed there by mere force of adhesion ; if these suffice to make men Christians, in what sense could the apostle affirm that believers receive—not, indeed, worldly wisdom that comes to nought, but the wisdom of God *that we might know and comprehend* the things that are freely given to us of God? On what grounds would He denounce the sincerest fervour of spirit as defective where it does not likewise bring forth fruits in the UNDERSTANDING ?"

IV.

THEOLOGIES AND NATURAL SCIENCE.

THE course of human studies has separated between ecclesiastical and natural theology more for reasons of convenience than from any really necessary distinction. There is only one God in Nature and in Grace, the same author of Natural and Biblical Revelation. He manifests Himself to us in divers manners, but always in divine characters. In the universe and in the Bible He is the same, only two revelations display themselves to us from one source.

Natural and Spiritual religion are therefore two branches from the same root. An old tree will sometimes (and one in particular, a singular thorn-tree, suggests this analogy to the writer), send up divided trunks and branches, which soon fork out in opposite directions, and seem to be distinct growths. In winter, a spectator, may think so; for he sees nothing but bare and knotted ramifications. Let him, however, tarry till the summer time, and then he will behold the leafage, and the flowering, and the fruitage, as alike the products of one hidden and buried root. So is it with Natural and other Theologies.

The religious student of Nature will ultimately escape from the heated atmosphere of the halls and the schools, and discern that true and broad religion is not the product of a particular place or a special priesthood. Ecclesiastical Theologies are at best but the vestments of real religion. They may change with the creed, the church, and the era. Some adopt one and others another vestment; some are dazzled with the showy embroidery of one garb, others are delighted with the simple purity of another. On one there is an array of fine needlework, of systematic network, of nice distinctions; in another there is a prevalent simplicity and a colourless uniformity. So it ever has been, and so probably it will long continue to be through the various ecclesiastical vicissitudes of Christendom. He who looks dispassionately upon the systems of his own day, as they pass before him, will perceive that they are all at best but varied vestments, while he feels that there is a living and enduring personality beneath them all. If, indeed, these flowing vestments often hide rather than hallow the living personality, still the thoughtful observer will reflect that the garments may be put off while the personality remains. The disrobed religion is vital still, and most adorned when unadorned. It possesses a superhuman principle of existence. It may be disguised, but it cannot be destroyed. It is vital above time, though it passes through time. It is powerful beyond place, though it exists for destined periods in numerous localities. Men may contend for long centuries to come, as they have contended for long centuries past, about its investiture—about embroideries, borders, symbols, emblems, and colours. Respecting these, men may combat with such animosity as to forget the living thing, and even to slay each other in ecclesiastical zeal. Nevertheless they cannot slay the thing itself. It is a thought, a creation of the living God. He made it, like man, in His own image, and He planted it in the heart of man as His own reflection.

This is the essential, the everlasting religion to which Nature ministers with a holy and efficient ministry. To ecclesiastical vestments she has nothing to say; they belong to Art and to Fashion, and change with them. True, she may be forced to give a momentary countenance to them, but the fair flowers plucked from her bosom soon perish, even on the gaudiest altar, where they have no root and no nutriment.

He who thinks the devout contemplation and study of Nature, and the Sciences explaining Nature, to be one of the chief ends and one of the most glorious privileges of man's present existence, finds the two classes of persons already referred to equally indisposed to agree with him, the one thinking natural religion unnecessary, and even injurious, to revealed religion, and the other regarding revealed religion as unnecessary and as injurious to scientific pursuits. From the former class we hear the narrowest conceivable applications of great religious doctrines; from the latter, the most limited and exclusive applications of great scientific truths. The Christian student of Nature sometimes finds a strong barrier raised against his endeavours to unfold science, in the one-sidedness of the views of contracted Christians, who affirm that the one great doctrine of Redemption by Jesus Christ is exclusively sufficient for all the powers of the mind, and that it exercises and fills all its capacities apart from natural religion. They do not perceive how this exclusive view would narrow the goodness of God to one, albeit the greatest, act of His unfathomable love. They do not understand that the new relation of Sons of God in Christ Jesus, while it includes and exalts the old relation of Sons of God by nature, does not abolish it. The new creature cannot destroy the significance of the old, and the Creator always stands in a paternal relation to the created. Once this was the only relationship on earth; another is now added to it, but does not extinguish it. Doubtless Redemption is the central truth of Revelation, but by no means the sole truth; and he who thinks that there is little else in this world and in all worlds worthy of investigation forgets that this and other worlds have existed for ages, with all their varied natural endowments, and all their successive forms of life, in as entire dependence upon the Creator and the Provider as they now exist; and that they have illustrated, and do still illustrate, the power, wisdom, and goodness of God, in a manner which exalts to the highest our conceptions of the Deity. To behold the sun of our system is indeed a good and a pleasant thing; but to gaze so fixedly and long upon our sun as to become dazzled, and afterwards incapable of beholding any star in the amply and broadly-illuminated sky, is not the method of gaining a knowledge of the wonderful and boundless glories of the whole heavens; while to acquire a knowledge of some of the innumerable and independent stars by no means detracts from the splendour and magnitude of the sun of our system.

I conceive the Ministry of Nature to be a corrective of-isolated and narrow views of the Divine character, and of the dealings of the Deity with man. While imprisoned within the bars of circumscribed creeds, and fettered by illiberal and sentential interpretations of Holy Writ, the character of God in relation to man too often appears utterly inconsistent and contradictory, and in such cases no alterative in psychical therapeutics is so effective as an excursion into the broad domains of natural knowledge. There Nature becomes medicinal even to the saving and strengthening of Faith. Are we habituated to regard God's action towards us individually as hard and severe? Do we see ourselves only environed by an iron necessity and impelled towards an inevitable doom? Do we discern nothing but perplexity before us, and nothing but disappointment behind us? The remedy for such a state of mind is not to be found in casuistical disquisitions—not in the mental food which has perhaps disordered us—not in keener and more torturing introspection, but in wider and bolder circumspection—in gazing openly and frequently on the scheme of Nature, in observing there that notwithstanding numerous apparent instances of harshness, of suffering, of disease, death, and waste, still the whole grand system of things marches onward by irresistible movements to its full displays of growth, increase, and all-surmounting vitality.

We are thus wholesomely impelled towards a large circle of thought and a broad outline and proportions. He only does full justice to the manifestations which God vouchsafes of Himself to his earthly children, who endeavours to view them in their various lights, and to treat them as he would a many-sided crystal, by turning it in different directions and examining all its faces, delighting himself in it at every variation of its lustre, prizing it the more for every additional hue which it may display in its different changeable positions. Every molecule of a crystal is in some sort itself a crystal; every particle of truth is in like manner in some sort divine, but in its final and definite completeness alone does the pure crystal reflect ample light. So let us reflect the union of all the divine truths in nature and in grace. They form together a perfect crystal of many sides, each and all of them reflecting the glory of one Sun.

The manner in which the natural creation leads us to, and confirms in us our idea of its relation to God has been so clearly expressed by a modern writer, that I quote his statement:

"We find in the works of God, illustrations of his revealed attributes. It is in connection with the contemplation of these that we find at once the application of our fundamental belief, and the unfolding of that primary knowledge which is involved in it. Everything which God has created or done must be a manifestation of His nature to His intelligent creatures. We are capable of observing and comparing the works of God, and by this means we are able to form certain conceptions not only concerning these works themselves, but also concerning the Being by whose agency they have been originated; and if in all our observing, forming of conceptions, and reasoning upon them, we only regulate the mind in submission to our necessary belief, our observations, conceptions, and reasonings, will all involve a discovery of truth concerning the Divine nature. It is indeed clear that the works of God are only a limited manifestation of His nature, and therefore equally clear that by means of these we can only attain a limited knowledge, but it is impossible on that account to deny that we reach a positive knowledge of the Infinite God. . . . If God has created, His works of creation have been performed in harmony with His own nature, and a finite creation is a manifestation of the Infinite God to His intelligent creatures.

"Our observation of the works of creation is not prosecuted for the purpose of rising by slow stages to the conviction of the Divine existence. Our belief, as necessary, arises by the simple contemplation of any object. We therefore start with the conviction that there is One Infinite Being, and all our observation is prosecuted for the purpose of enlarging our knowledge of His nature. In this we must be continually regulated by our fundamental belief, which involves an immediate knowledge of

God. With it to guide us, we are saved from attributing the marks of power or of wisdom which we behold in the world, to a Being possessed only of the measure of power or wisdom needful for the accomplishment of these results. Among all the works of Nature, our observation presents to view nothing more than the finite, and the only reason why we believe in an Infinite Being, or look on the objects around us as the works of such a Being, is that the recognition of the Infinite One is given in our very nature. This alone explains why it is that the finite creation is not attributed to a finite cause, or why we do not think of God only as a Being able to accomplish all we see around us. Whatever exercise of our logical faculty there may be upon the works of God, leading to the formation of certain conceptions concerning the Divine nature, it is regulated by a primary belief which is completely above the logical faculty, and not liable to be tested and criticised by its rules. This being kept in view, the way is clear for a consideration of the legitimate exercise of human thought in connection with this subject.

"In the entire works of God, the logical faculty finds a basis from which it may rise up to meet the declarations of faith. Since by the authority of an original belief within us, testimony is borne to the existence of one Infinite Originator of all finite existence, man, as an intelligent creature, must seek to form clear and satisfactory conceptions in harmony with his faith. Every form of existence is to him a field of inquiry, in which to learn somewhat of the Great Being who has created all. While our nature may involve a revelation concerning the Divine existence and attributes, we must discover, arrange, and interpret for ourselves the facts which are disclosed in the works of God. This is the province of the logical faculty; and by earnest, laborious efforts we must seek to extend our study, and gather for ourselves new conceptions of the Divine glory, which will call forth more fully the light shining from within.

"It is to be observed, however, that there are here two distinct lines of contemplation which the logical faculty may pursue—*firstly*, what the facts of Nature are; and *secondly*, what the facts of Nature teach concerning the Creator. These two are quite distinct, and may be so completely separated that the first may be considered without the least regard to the second;

but the second can be prosecuted only in the degree in which the first is pursued. The first leads to the discovery and classification of certain facts, which go to constitute a body of scientific truth; the second, making use of these classified facts, rises by their aid to the formation of certain conceptions concerning the Infinite Creator. In this way Science is the handmaid of Philosophy and Religion. The deeper we carry our research into the wonders which Nature discloses, the further do we extend our acquaintance with the works of God, and accumulate the materials that enable us to enlarge our conceptions of the Divine attributes. In this way we can re-classify for ourselves facts from all the Sciences according as they present marks of the power, or the wisdom, or the goodness of the Infinite Creator. We can thus form separate conceptions of the power, wisdom, and goodness of God, and, gathering all these together, we can form a conception, the most grand and awe-inspiring of the Infinite and Absolute Being."[*]

[*] Calderwood's "Philosophy of the Infinite," 2nd edit., 1861, pp. 148—152.

V.

THE GREAT PROBLEM, AND OUR MEANS OF SOLVING IT.

WHAT can we possibly know of the Great Creator, Himself the Uncreated and Inscrutable One, from our little corner of the Universe and with our circumscribed powers? This is the constantly-recurring question through all time—the self-proposed question of anxious and inquiring minds of men humbly and devoutly feeling after Him, if haply they may find him. In a hundred forms the question is varied and repeats itself, and we necessarily repeat ourselves in our partial answers to it. We cannot excogitate a well compacted body of Natural Divinity in reply; we cannot parcel out our knowledge into a systematic treatise, and proceed by axioms, and postulates, and numbered problems, till we arrive at mathematical certainties. The whole result is at best a groping through darkness that may be felt, if it happily be darkness that may ultimately be dispelled.

The pedestrian in the Alps sometimes meets with a number of huge ant-hills—huge as compared with those of England—which a playful fancy may presume to have been erected at the foot of truly huge mountains as if in mimic mockery of their grandeur. Both are homes of silence, yet both suggest a comparison and a contrast replete with significance to us. Disturb the still and soundless ant-hill with your staff, and in a moment it is populous with agitated insects who run in all directions, as though feebly resenting the power and rudeness of the human intruder. Conceive for a moment one of those insects as coming forth to study some enormous snow-mountain above him, a mountain which is so many million times bigger than his own disturbed earth-dome, though that has cost him and his myriads of co-operators so much labour to accumulate and complete. Conceive that the ant sagely speculates upon the way in which the Jungfrau or the Eiger or the Mönch or Monte Rosa was built up particle by particle, mass by mass, peak by peak; that it has and strenuously contends for a system of geology, for a chemistry of rock-formations, for a prevalent direction of Alpine chains, for periods of glacial prevalence and waste, for a theory of glaciers and moraines, and for all that interests and perplexes us as men in these regions of grandeur and beauty. Can any conception be more disproportionate to probabilities, more ridiculous or fanciful? And yet is not man such an insect, engaged in such a hopeless and disproportionate inquiry, when from his little mount of remotely rolling earth he speculates on the nature and attributes of the great God so incomparably above him, so incomprehensibly beyond him?

In one sense he is, in others he is not. In respect of all comparison he is, in respect of a possibility of partial comprehension he is not. The ant builds up his mimic mountain, and has then done his work; he is not capacitated to do more, and what he is capacitated to do he performs well and perseveringly. That is his world, and he will have no other. Like disproportion cannot be fairly predicated of man if he knows his capabilities and exercises his highest powers. If not, he will only build man-hills in place of ant-hills.

For the Swiss ant there is practically as

great a disproportion between ten or fifteen thousand feet of massive Alpine altitude, and his three or four feet of earth-mound, as there is between man and the Almighty Being. The difference is not one of material measurement, but of conceiving faculty. Endow the ant with man's mind, and the insect would have his own theories and speculations, his mountainologies, warm controversies with his fellow insects, his disputes respecting the possibility of knowing anything of the Jungfrau or the Mönch, his incredulities, and even his assertions that there were no such mountains; particularly when they were utterly hidden by mists and invisible for many days. He would say to some other inquiring ant—" There may or there may not be a Jungfrau. If there be, it is unknowable, and no conceptions of ours can be adequate to it. Its very existence is a needless and disturbing hypothesis, bewildering us in our serenity, distracting us in our industry. Build up ant-hills not figments. While you are abstractedly speculating abont the Jungfrau, winter is before us, storms are upon us, and the rains are washing us down. Leave the Jungfrau to itself; it is infinite, immeasurable, unknowable. Our business is structural, our science is sociology,

5 A

our burdens are heavy enough for us, and our duties are plain enough."

The application of the moral to ourselves is apparent. Let us not be deterred by disproportion; let us not say there is no God because he is not seen by us, because clouds and darkness are round about him; and because we have our little earth-homes to build, let us not say " to erect them is enough for us; though the vast mountain may really exist, we cannot ascend it; we cannot measure it; it is too high for us, we cannot attain to it. Sufficient for us is the evil and misery beneath our little terrestrial dome. All we can do is to try and diminish that. Nothing else really concerns us in our short life; while we are speculating on Alps, a ruthless tyrant may pass by and overturn our life-labour and scatter our provisions and destroy our hopes." Were we but ants, we might say all this and be justified; since we are men we dare not, unless we deny our superiority, abdicate our rights, and deny our responsibilities.

But while these ant-hills are before us, we may by an appeal to them opportunely test some current modes of reasoning. Are not these things remarkable instances of instinct, contrivance, and purpose? Are they not most evident proofs of adaptation of means to an end, of forethought and prevision elaborated into perfected results? Examine these structures, observe the labourers individually and collectively conspiring to one predestined aim, and working out particle by particle the original conception, and tell me if you know any more striking examples of what we term design? "Not at all," replies an objector, "there is no proof of design here; these are simply fortuitous concourses of atoms; they are earth mounds and nothing more. What you call *design* is an idea of your own which you bring to the ant-hills, but which never entered into the thoughts of the ants. It is your conception, not theirs; they worked out not a plan, they accomplished not a purpose, but each insect brought his particle and left it, and the whole is anything but the result of combined forethought and determination. Before you can prove that each hill is a consequence of design in the ants, you must know their minds, fathom their views, and determine their nature. You cannot affirm that here we have the effects of a cause; plainly we have nothing here but the sequences of a series, the aggregation of a number of particles, not one of which exercised any causative influence upon another. We have merely a congeries of little lumps, and what you see besides is the mere product of your fancy. If the ants wrought from design, why did they heap up so much earth, when far less would have sufficed? if they had a definite purpose, why did they add so many superfluous little chambers, and why did they erect so many shapeless protuberances which serve to no advantage, and which are actually mere abortions on the principal mound?

Perhaps you rejoin, "Well, but there are many ant-hills within our view at this spot—they all appear to be constructed upon a similar principle, and they all serve a similar purpose, so that all the builders must have been animated with similar ideas and therefore all must have worked to a preconcerted plan." "Far from it," replies again the objector, "what you call a preconcerted plan is another imagination of yours, answering to no reality in the ant mind. The multiplication is merely one of congeries, a simple aggregate of aggregates. They happen to be somewhat alike, but any intended likeness exists only in your view, for you cannot suppose that these poor insects built up worlds like a human architect. By an illusion of your own, you are anthropothorphising the ants, who only acted upon impulses selection in choosing the best atoms. Not in any one, not in the whole number of mounds can you distinctly trace a single instance of design or contrivance or preconcerted purpose. They are at best nothing more than parts of the great natural evolution of all things, including ourselves."

Such is a fanciful but faithful application of some of the current objections to one of the soundest, most available, and most generally intelligible of all arguments, by means of which we obtain aids in forming a conception of the existence and action of the Omnipotent One in that world in which He has placed us. It will be desirable to examine more directly and more strictly some of the objections by the supposed force of which it is sought to overthrow this great argument altogether, and to cast it aside as weak and worthless.

VI.

THE ARGUMENT FROM DESIGN—ITS GENERAL SCOPE.

THE object of the Argument from Design may be thus succinctly stated. It is intended to lead us to the belief that there exists a Maker and Sustainer of all that we behold in existence, of all that by the teachings of Nature we fairly suppose to have existed in former ages upon our earth, of all that may in future exist upon it, and, as an ulterior inference, of all that may at present exist or in future enter into existence in the Universe. Such is its most comprehensive bearing and aim.

Accepting and acknowledging the full force of this Argument, then He who has designed and is sustaining the entirety, is so doing for ends and purposes, a part of which we can ascertain and comprehend, but the far larger part of which we cannot now ascertain or comprehend. In accordance with a kind of reasoning which commends itself to the majority of enlightened minds, we are impelled to infer a designer from manifold evidences of design. Any one example in creation would conduct us to this conclusion, while the more numerous, the more clearly understood, and the better classified are the examples, the more distinct and the more impressive will be our confidence in the validity of the argument. Feeling that we now live in circumstances and under conditions by which our minds are defrauded by distractions of the full effect of the wonderful exhibitions of the skill and wisdom of the Designer, the multiplication of the evidences strengthens and deepens the conclusions we should otherwise draw from one or a few of them. Therefore, the original and simple argument requires and acquires corroboration by repetition and additional illustrations. Hence the value of a whole body of Natural Theology, hence the importance of frequently reconsidering the basis of our reasoning, and hence, too, the necessity of addressing ourselves to the new or rehabilitated objections which from time to time are brought against the efficacy of this argument.

Students of ancient literature are well aware that the Argument from Design has been urged as well as combated from an early period. The Stoics maintained the doctrine of final causes with zeal; and we read in Cicero (*De Natura Deorum*, ii., 150) how the Stoic Balbus defended them. Aristotle (*de part. animal.* iv., 10) offers a long and powerful statement in favour of final causes, though he thinks that the order and regularity of astronomical phenomena more decidedly imply the action of a final cause than the irregular and capricious phenomena of the organic world. In the same treatise Aristotle regards the tools made by man as proving that the tools made by Nature had the same end in view, the hand being an organ before organs, and the whole body and its parts being framed for the functions they perform, as the saw is made for the sake of sawing; the sawing is not done for the sake of the saw.

The opposite opinions are also strongly contended for by some, and especially by Lucretius, who thus exhorts his readers in the fourth book of his poem:—

> "Illud in his rebus vitium vementer avessis
> Effugere, errorem vitareque præmetuenter,
> Lumina ne facias oculorum clara creata,

> Prospicere ut possemus, et ut proferre queamus
> Proceros passus, ideo fastigia posse
> Surarum ac feminum pedibus fundata plicari,
> Brachia tum porro validis ex apta lacertis
> Esse manusque datas utraque ex parte ministras,
> Ut facere ad vitam possemus quæ foret usus.
> Cetera de genere hoc inter quæcunque pretantur
> Omnia perversa præpostera sunt ratione,
> Nil ideo quoniam natum'st in corpore ut uti
> Possemus, sed quod natum'st id procreat usum."

"And herein you should desire with all your might to shun the weakness, with a lively apprehension to avoid the mistake of supposing that the bright lights of the eyes were made in order that we might see; and that the tapering ends of the shanks and hams are attached to the feet as a base in order to enable us to step out with long strides; or, again, that the forearms were slung to the stout upper-arms, and ministering hands given us on each side, that we might be able to discharge the needful duties of life. Other explanations of like sort which men give, one and all, put effect for cause, through wrong-headed reasoning; since nothing was born in the body that we might use it, but that which is born begets for itself a use." *

It is remarkable that the Roman poet should

* Munro's Lucretius.

have anticipated in this passage the kind of philosophy now in favour with certain naturalists and others, and that the same objections against purpose should be now revived as were propounded by the heathen writer.

Many very singular correspondences between old unbelief and what is supposed to be new, might be indicated in the clever but pernicious poem of Lucretius.

VII.

THE ARGUMENT FROM DESIGN.—ITS VALIDITY AND LIMITATION.

THE illustrative supposition with which Paley commences his treatise on Natural Theology is well known to all interested in the subject, and need not be quoted at length. It is in brief this: the casual finder of a watch upon the ground would inquire how the watch happened to be in that place. It could not have been there for ever and without reason, for its several parts are framed and put together for a purpose; they are so formed and adjusted as to produce motion, and that motion so regulated as to point out the time of the day. If the different parts had been differently shaped from what they are, of a different size from what they are, or placed after any other manner, or in any other order than that which they are really placed, either no motion at all would have been discovered in the machine, or none which would have answered the use now served by it. Paley pursues the argument with perspicacity and cogency, and if he were more extensively read, it would be seen that he has many merits beyond those allowed to him by many philosophers of the present day, and that his argument is not refutable, even though it may be disparaged.

When for instance, Mr. Herbert Spencer cites this supposition of Paley's and endeavours to discredit it by imagining a reversal of the conditions, so that instead of the human finder of the watch speculating upon its maker, the watch itself should become intelligent and for itself reason about its maker, and so reason as to arrive at the false conclusion that its maker was a being like itself, and subject to the necessity of being provided with springs, escapements, and cog-wheels; he grossly misrepresents the result, for in such a case the watch would reason not wrongly but rightly according to the measure of its intelligence, that is, it would conceive of its maker only in watch-terms. To suppose, however, that man's whole reasoning about God from nature is as limited as would be that of the intelligent watch, is a palpable absurdity. Man well knows that when he has reached the conception of a great designer, he has not reached the ultimate conception of God, but only one which lies midway between himself and the Infinite Being. It is true and trustworthy enough for a mediate position, but unsuitable beyond it. Man is possessed of supramechanical faculties, and exercises them in the whole range of inductive reasoning. He reasons onward and upward, and in the case supposed, he is well aware that the conception he may derive from the watch of its maker is merely a first and imperfect conception of the perfection of the Almighty Maker. It is simply intermediate between man and God, and is by no means final, but elementary and suggestive of infinitely more than is comprised in itself.

This supposed reversal of the conditions of the watch and its human finder, is merely a fruit of David Hume's old subtle argument against reasoning from the appearances and operations of nature to the existence of an intelligent cause. By him it is adroitly and speciously argued that in reasoning about an agent or being wholly unlike all we have hitherto known, our inferences must be strictly confined to the facts whence they are drawn. Ascending from the works of nature to their cause, we are entitled to conclude that a Being exists who created them as we see them, and therefore that this Being is possessed of sufficient skill and power to contrive and execute those precise works and no other or no more, hence it follows that a finite, but not that an infinite and all powerful Being exists. This line of argument has been repeated and varied, and is sometimes at present appealed to as an insuperable bar to the foundation of Natural Theology.

It is, however, capable of a satisfactory refutation, as Lord Brougham has briefly shown,* and as might be more largely shown, if it could really deceive any sound reasoner; who would however clearly see, as Lord Brougham observes that "according to this argument, all experimental knowledge must stand still, generalizing be at an end, and philosophers be content never to take a single step, or draw one conclusion beyond the mere facts observed by them; in a word, Inductive Science must be turned from a process of general reasoning upon particular facts, into a bare dry record of those particular facts themselves."

Hence to charge Natural Theologians with

---

* "Discourse on Natural Theology," Preface to Paley, Note.

presumption because they reason in this manner, and to affirm that all such ideas of the Unknowable One must be false and misleading, is both unfair and illogical. Thus in fact the opponents of all Natural Theology as impossible and unprofitable, proceed upon assumptions which may be shown to be untenable and baseless.

Reflect upon the continually repeated charge which they urge against us of anthropomorphism—of conceiving and representing the Creator under human figures and limitations, and as impelled by human motives and adopting human forms of procedure. Our opponents allege that so long as we judge of the Divine Mind by human standards, so long as we liken His aims and ends to ours, we make a science of Natural Theology impossible or absurd; that we thus reduce God to man, and nullify the whole force of our arguments. Frequently as this charge is renewed, and specious as it seems, we think it will be found to be in a great measure unfounded and unphilosophical. For if we are not to judge by such tests as we can apply, if we are not to employ our reason in the only direction in which we can exercise it, all reasoning upon this subject is impracticable, and we must be content to confess that our faculties have been given to us in vain. Admitting that in older books and amongst contracted thinkers anthropomorphism has been carried too far, still the only way in which we can regard the Creator at all is in the manner in which our powers apprehend him naturally and readily. He has chosen to reveal Himself to us under various human representaions, as for example a King, a Ruler, a Guide, a Father, a Provider, a Director, and Friend. These and all similar terms are simply human, and embody various human relationships. But they are the only relationships we can in our present state recognize, and the only relationships which can call forth responsive affections and obedience in all. No thinker is deceived or deluded by them, because he knows that they are merely representative symbols of higher truth, and are simply tuitional indications of future and clearer revelations.

We must necessarily think of the Divine Nature as the Divine Being has qualified us to conceive of it. To attempt anything more is to lose the substance and grasp at a shadow. "That the true conception," says Dean Mansel, " of the Divine Nature, so far as we are able to receive it, is to be found in those regulative representations which exhibit God under limitations accommodated to the constitution of man, not in the unmeaning abstractions, which aiming at a higher knowledge, distort rather than exhibit, the Absolute and Infinite, is a conclusion warranted both deductively, from the recognition of the limits of human thought, and inductively, by what we can gather from experience and analogy, concerning God's general dealings with mankind."

It seems to be overlooked that our highest imaginations, our noblest poetry, our most soaring conceptions of ideal activities are necessarily anthropomorphical. The ideal *man* or the ideal *woman* is the utmost achievement of Art and Song. Neither Raphael, nor Michael Angelo, nor Dante, nor Milton nor Shakespeare, could transcend humanity. All creative genius culminates in humanity. All sanctified emotion is circumscribed by humanity. The mind cannot go beyond it, for it is the type of visible perfection. We see nothing better than the best man, we aim at nothing higher than the most cultivated humanity.

To charge Natural Theologians, therefore, with anthropomorphism when they infer purpose and design in Nature in accordance with human judgments, is simply to charge them with the limitations and imperfections of the faculties with which it has pleased the Creator to endow them. To demand of them that they shall judge by a higher standard, is simply to demand an impossibility. To affirm that inasmuch as they cannot judge by a higher standard they cannot judge rightly, is clearly a denial of the power of judging logically at all.

By an extension of this line of thought it might readily be shown that all our reasoning is anthropomorphical, in the daily emergencies and actions of civilized life, in the ultimate issues and awards of all our dealings and doings, in our estimates of the results and fruits of individual existence. Remove all anthropomorphism from our conceptions of the Divine Being, denude all creation of what wears the semblance of human aims and purposes of the purest and noblest order, and we arrive only at the intangible and inscrutable Absolute.

To those who have reflected most profoundly on the various phases which the argument of design may assume, it has probably occurred that the true solution of the difficulties which environ this subject is *a series and succession of purposes* of which we are at present only permitted to discern a part, and perhaps the first portion. Probably the vast scheme of visible things includes a progressive series of ends of which every intelligent and reverent mind conjectures a small portion, but of which no created spirit can grasp the ultimate issue. Each end or purpose may be in itself definite as far as humanly appreciable, but higher ends and purposes would transcend our faculties and elude our comprehension. On the surface of the immense expanse of nature we behold an initiative circle, and even while we gaze, this circle slowly widens and includes greater space, and gives birth to other and larger circles, and these again widen and comprehend larger space; but human life fails to endure beyond the period when one great circle is observed, and terminates long before the original impulse exhausts itself, and the broad expanse again becomes quiescent. Nevertheless every circle has been in itself complete, and has embraced a defined space, and for the time has been bounded by a distinct circumference. The entire amplitude is coeval only with Immortality and coextensive with Eternity.

To obtain clear ideas of the true meanings

and relations of the terms employed in argument respecting Cause, Design, Means, Adaptation, and End, let them be formally defined, and they cannot be defined more clearly and succinctly than in this abstract from the recent and truly philosophical work of Dr. Noah Porter, entitled "the Human Intellect."

Aristotle and the schoolmen divided all possible and conceivable causes into these four:— the *material*, the *formal*, the *efficient*, and the *final*. The *efficient* corresponds with the cause of modern philosophy, though the latter is extended to *all* those agents which, in combination, originate a given effect.

The *final cause* was and is the design or end conceived of as impelling and directing the action of a number or succession of agencies, till it was actually brought to pass. For example, the man who proposes to construct a great edifice, will realize his *end* when after a series of actions and exertions the edifice is really built. Hence by a secondary signification the *end* comes to signify a purposed result or a design, and the phrase *final cause* suggests the same idea. The purpose is a *cause* because when formed it is conceived as prompting or causing the events, which are necessary to its realization. Hence we regard a final cause as that which from its commencement as a thought or plan is at length wrought into a fact as an end or final result.

The design conceived of as directing or impelling a series of agents to an end, supposes that agencies do or may exist which are capable of bringing it to pass. The capacity of these efficient causes when combined to produce the effect, is called their *adaptation* or fitness for it. Supposing the question to arise, by what causes or agencies can it be effected in the best and readiest manner, the answer is given by showing that the agencies selected will really bring it to pass. A series or combination of causes, viewed as fitted to an end, is called the *means*, and these form the intermediate agencies between the end as thought and the end as produced. Their relation to the latter is *adaptation*.

Every one will admit that the relation of design and the means of its execution often exist and may be clearly traced in both spiritual and material phenomena. "The point which we," says Dr. Porter, "assert and defend is that this relation is believed *à priori to pervade all existence*, and must be assumed *as the ground of the scientific explanation of the facts and phenomena of the universe.* We do not inquire whether it is observed in our experience as a psychological fact, but whether it lies at the ground of all our knowledge as *a necessary relation of things*, and *a first principle or axiom of thought*—whether, in other words, *the principle of adaptation* ranks with the principle of efficient causation as *a necessary* and *à priori truth.*"

The above appears to be a concise and correct statement of terms, conditions, and relations, without which we cannot reason at all as to the world around us or any part of it. Whether the subject be an ant-hill, or a world, or the universe, we can only proceed to argue upon some such principles; for failing these, we must relinquish reasoning and research in the higher regions of thought, and subside into narrow positivism.

We find it to be inherent in the construction of our minds that we should draw conclusions respecting the existence and action of a designer whenever we behold arrangement, order, structure, and fulfilment of ascertained purposes. Whether we inspect the works of a watch or the parts and performance of a curious machine, the order of the physical or the functions of the organic world, our mental inference is the same and indeed unavoidable. The conclusion is the stronger as the work scrutinized is complex; our estimate of the skill and power of the designer is proportioned to his display of them in his work. Not more indissolubly is one part of a machine linked to another than our conclusion is linked to the visible work, and when a particular machine manifests manifold and extraordinary adaptations to its purpose, our mental conviction that it had a designer rises into admiration of his superior ability, in addition to its certain exercise. If he has achieved a triumph of mechanism beyond his predecessors, by so much do we esteem him as superior to them. Carry this esteem to its highest degree, and if the work appear to exceed man's utmost known ability, we should necessarily conclude that the designer must be superhuman. If from its vast dimensions, its extreme complexity, its unerring perfection, and its unfailing and perpetual performance of one or more premeditated purposes, it overcomes all conceivable difficulties, the mind of man could not without violence resist the inference that some power far above itself had determined and wrought out the plan. Thus our mind would make an approach to a supreme spiritual being, to a being unfettered and unconditioned by its own limitations. The mind would approach *towards* a Divine Artificer, even if it fell far short of arriving at an adequate conception of Omnipotence.

Towards a Supreme Artificer, we say, and not *to* him; that is so far towards him as the argument founded upon the evidence of his work is qualified to lead us. This is the first great and well founded act of upward progress to which Nature helps us. We may approach to the Divine Being more directly by other and more speedy modes, but these lie beyond the province of logical reasoning, which alone for the present concerns us. And if we keep steadily in view the steps here enumerated, we shall not fail to advance surely though laboriously, nor shall we be bewildered by the sophistry of those who deny the validity of the argument. Opponents have striven to weaken it by forcing on our attention the idea of sequence, and by excluding causation, forethought, prevision, and provision, and in short all that embraces the choice, adoption, and adaptation of means to an end. Undeniably, however, there do exist plainly before us the facts of co-existence, of coincidence, and of concurrence of means or forces, which accomplish a visible result. Where are we to place all these? They must be considered as terms of the physical analysis, they must be accounted for at the end if not at the beginning.

In this strain the writer of an elaborate article in one of our Reviews has also reasoned on the same topic, and I here cite an illustrative passage.

"If by the construction of our minds we are compelled to construe actual machinery which effects an end as designed to that end, that compulsion is our justification. No insoluble question outside of this act of construction can interfere with or invalidate this act itself. If Descartes then or any one else objects to us that we must know the Divine mind before we can affix design to Nature, we reply it is falsely put—we need not know God in order to put a construction upon facts; we can put a construction upon facts if we have the facts. We have nothing to do with the speculative argument at the other end of the question; we argue from this end of it, from the facts of contrivance; design is tied to those facts and cannot be divorced from them. If we cannot argue indeed *up* to a God till we can argue *down* from Him, if we cannot interpret any signs that point to Him, till we know they come from Him, then certainly the evidences of a God from Nature are impossible until they are useless, and there is no such argument as the Argument of Design. But this is not the state of the case. You mistake our argument; we assume no knowledge of the Divine designing mind; we only argue from facts towards one. Whatever be the mystery which lies on the other side of the ocean of infinity, it is consistent with those facts, and with the constitution of our own minds which obliges this construction of them."[*]

It is remarkable that some of the very naturalists who have either disregarded or openly denied design in nature, have themselves by facts confirmed it. Even Mr. Darwin is one of its most recent exponents in his book upon the "Fertilization of Orchids through Insect Agency." The numerous particular instances of contrivance and prevision or adaptation which he there displays are not only interesting in themselves but constitute manifold and wonderful evidences of the doctrine of design. This volume would form an appropriate addition to Paley's Natural Theology. Any

[*] *Quarterly Review*, No. 253.

reader of it must rise from its perusal more than ever convinced in the truth of design in Nature. Mr. Darwin indeed stops at adaptation, and at the proof he gives of purpose in the "Fertilization of Orchids." Others, however, need not do this, but may continue and connect this special evidence with the great body of general evidence all tending towards the Divine Designer.

It appears indeed impossible to escape from the presence of evidences of design in any field of natural research, and this important argument gathers strength every day, and from every department of Nature. Design is in fact Nature's index-hand, ever pointing to the Divine Designer. We have not to invent or imagine the doctrine, our only effort will be to avoid it. In Derham's and Nieuwentyt's and Paley's hand it became a mighty instrument well wielded—in our day it is still mightier, and might be wielded with far greater effect. It is one of the first lessons taught by the higher Ministry of Nature, and both microscope and telescope equally enlarge our knowledge of its meaning and application. It extends from the minutest organism visible to the microscopist's scrutiny even to the greatest. It is coextensive with all known life, and may fairly be supposed to comprehend all which is as yet to us unknown. We see it in every part of our bodily organization, and in every function of every member is an illustration of it. We see it in other bodies, and the language and reasoning of anatomy and physiology adopt its terms. Our principal inquiry respecting every organ is what is its function, and how is it formed and fitted to perform it?

Teleology, or the doctrine of final causes, has no doubt like other doctrines been subject to abuse and misapplication; but incompetence or license in its applications cannot affect its real value. The term *final* cause is not perhaps fortunate, and may occasionally mislead, for as now liberally understood, what to man appears a final cause is not assumed to be the ultimate final cause to the Omnipotent One. The word Purpose would better express the modern view. But as respects final causes in the other acceptance of the term, Bacon's reprehension of them, though often triumphantly quoted by opponents, requires to be explained. "The search after final causes," says Bacon, "is barren, for like virgins consecrated to God, they produce nothing." If, however, we refer to his writings [Advancement of Learning, book ii, p. 142] we find him adding, "not because these final causes are not true and worthy to be inquired, being kept within their own province." How greatly misconceived and misapplied the former part of the sentence of Bacon has been, even some of his own commentators have noted. In Spedding's noble edition of Bacon's works to the sentence above cited, which in the original is "Causarum Finalium inquisitio sterilis est, et tanquam virgo Deo consecrata nihil parit," we find the following judicious note of explanation appended. "No saying of Bacon's has been more often quoted and misunderstood than this. Carrying out his division of the *Doctrina de Naturâ*, which, as we have seen, depends upon Aristotle's quadripartite classification of causes, he remarks that to Physica corresponds Mechanica, and to Metaphysica Magia. But Metaphysica contains two parts, the doctrine of forms and the doctrine of final causes. Bacon remarks that Magia corresponds to Metaphysica inasmuch as the latter contains the doctrine of forms, that of final causes admitting from its nature of no practical applications. "Nihil parit" means simply "non parit opera," which though it would have been a more precise mode of expression, would have destroyed the appositeness of his illustration. No one who fairly considers the context, can, I think, have any doubts as to the limitation with which the sentence in question is to be taken. But it is often the misfortune of a pointed saying to be quoted apart from any context, and consequently to be misunderstood."

One defect in our popular Natural Theology has been its unmethodical and partial manner of treating certain phenomena, certain structures or provisions, as coming more directly from the Divine hand than others, and the directing of attention to these as so many stronger evidences of His working than those which are unmentioned. But this defect will decrease with the enlargement of our knowledge, though inherent in all partial expositions by man. Could we display all laws or provisional arrangements as parts of the grand totality of Nature which is in itself, and consequently in all its parts, the result of the Creator's action, the argument would acquire irresistible force; while we only make use of instances, and portions, and of divisions and particulars in Nature for examination, and for an exhibition of the Divine skill or goodness, we shall always fail to attain the full effect, and the impression will be that these are conspicuous and exceptionally striking, more special evidences of design or forethought, or goodness, more so than a multitude of others which we either do not know or do not enumerate, forgetting that these are selected as evidences which most frequently come before us, most distinctly appeal to us, and therefore most directly influence us. On this account all such titles as the "Wonders" or the "Marvels of Nature," or the "Footprints of the Creator," are inappropriate and misleading. The whole of nature may be called marvellous, the presence of God is universal, and His operations are coextensive with the entire Cosmos. We are apt to forget these truths when we attribute any one single force or activity of matter, any one grand natural phenomenon, or any particular organization to Him as His *specific* work. It is true we can only contemplate one object at one time, and may well aim to concentrate attention upon certain features of things, certain individual and choice instances, but this arises from the limitation of our powers of observation and comprehension, and by no means from a distinctive superiority in the objects and subjects selected. When, for example, we select the human eye for study, as affording special evidence of the exercise of creative skill and adaptation, it should not be forgotten that innumerable other objects exist which likewise display similar evidence. Since we do not know a more admirable natural optical instrument, the selection of this for study, and illustration, or the excitement of the emotion of wonder is commendable, but we are not justified in referring to it as an exceptional work of the Divine hand. In the grand palace of Nature every stone, from the foundation to the topmost superstructure, is equally a part of the design of its Omniscient Architect. A common spectator of a grand building would most admire the ornamental decorations, the sculptured capitals, the enriched cornices, and the scrolls of foliage, exhibited before him, but the more cultured student would rather observe and commend the total design, the noble plan, the combination of parts, and the impressive grandeur of the whole building. In these he would discern the master mind, and while particular details would receive his attention in due course, he would derive his chief impressions from, and pronounce his approbation of the entire structure. The subordination of the smallest details to the one all-embracing and grand conception of the skilful designer and executer of the building would elicit his admiration, and elevate his conception to a higher thinking-point than even the most perfect construction and finish of particular parts. So would it be with our contemplation of the grand Temple of Nature, could we behold it as a perfect whole. Since, however, we are limited to parts and particulars, our impressions and our emotions are proportionally fainter. Hence the multiplication of evidences of design, and prevision and adaptation serve an important purpose. At most they are but a small part of the great whole, but the more of them we observe, the more extended, the better defined is our conception of the grandeur and perfection of the entire structure. "Lo, these are parts of His ways, but how little a portion is heard of Him,—but the thunder of His power who can understand?"

Function and Purpose in Structure.—Were it compatible with our object and our limits to enlarge on the relation of structure to function in the animal kingdom, the argument from design might be enlarged and corroborated to an almost surprising extent, certainly to an extent surprising to ordinary readers. An entire volume would be insufficient for the number of examples which might be adduced. Much of this nature has already been written in well known books, and it is needless to quote from them. Such books have their distinct and undeniable value for all except the opponents and deniers of design. Some indeed are nearly forgotten, which well deserve to be read again in our day. The small tractates entitled "Animal Mechanics, or Proofs of Design in the Animal Frame," written many years ago by Sir Charles Bell, form an excellent introduction to this study. The author himself was improved and informed by the preparation of these nearly forgotten papers, for we read in his recently published letters these words, "I have written an essay on the architecture of the head, which has put Marion (his wife) and me on the study of things we little dreamt of." Here may also be introduced his remarks on the study of Anatomy and Structure. "I, for my part, have no pleasure but in anatomy. You will say that it is that I may become the captain of anatomists; but why then have I such inexhaustible delight in the whole face of Nature? No, it is the pleasure I have in investigating *structure*. Everything there so perfect, so curiously fitted, and leading you by little and little to the comprehension of a wisdom so perfect, that I am forced to believe that, in the moral world, things are not really left in all that disarray which our partial view would persuade us they are. But, sure I am, that the study of what is called Nature is infinitely agreeable, and the contemplation of the moral state is most offensive to the notions of rectitude which Nature has implanted. I wish I could persuade you to dip a little into natural history and structure. How much I regret that I did not make myself acquainted with Natural History."[*]

In another letter Sir Charles Bell wrote: "I love Nature and Nature's God, with a sense of devotion and delight inferior to no man, and I have never for a day let myself be lost in mere worldliness."

The knowledge of Animal Mechanics is now so widely extended, and the examples akin to those adduced by Sir Charles Bell are so greatly multiplied, that the want of an ade-

[*] Letters of Sir Charles Bell, 1870. In a note to this letter the editor says, "To him this (structure) was a large word; these investigations were the delight of his life."

quate and full enumeration of them in a generally intelligible form is felt by many. Here is a rich storehouse of materials for a qualified expositor. Human and comparative anatomy, zoology and physiology have so rapidly advanced, and the accumulation of observations in these sciences is so great, while the instruments of research are also much improved, that an ample harvest of illustrations is ready for the zealous reaper.

For the due success of any such work, there must be a clear statement of the relation of structure to function, and a continuous exhibition of the nearness and directness of this relation. In connection with this observation some pertinent remarks of a recent and careful writer may here be cited.

" I may be told, when I say that the relation of structure to function is the same thing with the relation of means to purpose, I am assuming as true an hypothesis which has not and cannot be verified. I reply that the relation of special structure to special function, as for instance the relation of the structure of the eye to the function of vision, is something which has no analogy whatever in the inorganic creation, although it has analogies in machinery and other apparatus of human invention. The analogy of the eye to the camera obscura is a case in point; in fact the eye is a camera. And in speaking of such organic adaptations, we naturally and almost inevitably fall into the habit of regarding special function as a proof of purpose; and of speaking of the function of an organ and of its purpose as if the words were synonymous; and this habit is not found to be misleading; on the contrary, it is a rule in physiological research (though subject to a few very remarkable exceptions), that every organ, and every structural arrangement must have its own special purpose. These are facts very much generalized no doubt, but still facts of observation, concerning which there is no room for doubt or controversy. But when it is denied that there is any discernible purpose in the organic creation, the meaning appears to be that the relation of special structure to special function, or what I have called the relation of means to purpose, is in reality only a particular case of the relation of cause and effect. It would be impossible for any man of the slightest intelligence simply to deny the existence of the most wonderful special adaptations in the organic creation. I believe that the relation of means and purpose in organization is as much a primary law of nature, and as incapable of being resolved into any other more general principle, as the relation of cause and effect. As we ascend in the scale of nature to higher and higher vital functions, and higher and higher organic forms, we find the relation of cause and effect becoming less traceable by our faculties (though no doubt it exists all through nature); while at the same time the relation of means and purpose becomes at once more traceable and definite.

No where in the universe as known to us is the relation of means and purpose more clearly traceable and more perfectly definite than in the organs of special sense in the higher animals, especially in the eye and ear, and no where is it more difficult, (I would say, utterly impossible), to assign any physical cause for the facts, as when we inquire by what cause, or by what agency, such wonderful organs have been formed, And as we ascend in nature, not only do the separate functions become more traceable, but their natural relations become more definite. The trunk, the leaves, and the flowers of a tree for instance have each their function; but it would be unmeaning to ask whether the tree exists for the leaves or the leaves for the tree. But in all the higher animals the parts manifestly exist for the whole, not the whole for the parts."*

When we begin to enquire respecting Ultimate Purpose, that is, purpose beyond the present apparent order and constitution of things, Natural Science fails to give a reply. We may show for instance how coal and metals have been stored and arranged conveniently for the use of man; but, having arrived at human advantage, we can proceed no further by any natural knowledge. Dynamical laws, modes of formation and cosmical arrangements, and present benefits can be discovered and unfolded; and this is the province of Science. In considering the entire inorganic world, Science cannot inform us in any degree as to the ultimate purpose of such a world.

Nor can Science do much more even in the organic world. At the best physiology shows to us the function of structures in their mutual relations, and the relations of parts to the complete organism. There, however, it pauses. Ultimate purpose is quite beyond its province.

* Murphy on "Habit and Intelligence," (2 vols. 1869) vol. i., p. 119, etc.

The relation of parts to one whole may be displayed with an increasing skill; but the relation of wholes to wholes, and their combination to an ultimate creative purpose, is a study in advance of Natural Science, although Science is essential at the threshold, as giving us the proper means of enquiry, and as affording us the basis of reasoning. Having, however, enabled us to lay the foundation, it has done its utmost and must leave any superstructure to other hands.

At this stage the Higher Ministry of Nature may be brought into exercise, and by its aid we may erect a superstructure upon the scientific foundation. We may safely reason in the same mode as before, but must continue in a higher direction. We may speculate from the known to the unknown, and the conditions of the former being ascertained, we may warrantably conjecture some of the conditions of the unknown. Achieved and visible purposes are all that come within universal cognizance; but far beyond the achieved and the visible, a thousand purposes may extend into unlimited space and time. All the ends which appear to us may be means in the eye of the Divine Accomplisher, and such means may conduce to other ends, and other ends to other means in a limitless concatenation. The golden chain may be stretched out into worlds beyond worlds, and the evolution of successive great purposes may mark the stages of eternity.

This is strictly consistent with our ordinary conception of one ever-living and all-wise God. What we discover of His character and objects, or of His purposes as cognoscible by us, naturally prompts us to project into futurity the same characters in relation to other and similar purposes. If we can arrive at the inference, from our knowledge of Nature, that God has hitherto been working in love for his creatures, as well as in power, the additional inference is strictly logical, that the Unchangeable One will continue to work in love as well as in power on our behalf. If he were the malignant being that many creeds and some philosophers have represented him, then his future and ulterior purposes might be malignant and terrible to apprehend. If he were inconsistent with himself, his ulterior might be inconsistent with his preceding purposes. But admitting that he is self-consistent, invariable and without the shadow of a turning, our conjectures from the present to his ulterior purposes bear something of the quality of certainties. Supposing then that we discern most, if not all, of his purposes now discoverable by us, to tend in particular well-defined directions, we become confident that in similar directions other means will follow, tending to other similar purposes. In brief, what Nature points out to us that God now is, may be some indication of what God will for ever be. Prophetic Nature will address herself to Faith rather than to Knowledge; but as the ages roll on, Faith will give place to Knowledge, and Knowledge will store up accomplished ends as cumulative proofs of the goodness of the Omnipotent.

VII.

THE INFINITE—THE ABSOLUTE BEING.

ALTHOUGH this subject is remote from common thought, and demands mental discipline for its apprehension, yet it possesses so much importance that a brief consideration of it cannot be dispensed with ; and so earnest a controversy has been maintained upon it, that to pass by it because of its inherent difficulties would be an unwarrantable omission.

We have briefly treated of the Divine Designer, the Supreme First Cause, who is at the same time the Infinite and the Absolute One. We presume that we can acquire sure and increasing knowledge of Him from Nature, and we are now directly brought to this philosophical question—is it possible to learn anything or form any conception of the Absolute or the Infinite—does He in such characters necessarily transcend all comprehension, all mental apprehension, and all reasoning? If he does transcend them entirely and hopelessly, if no concept of the Absolute or Infinite is possible to us, then all Religious Philosophy and all definite Natural Theology must in this world be impracticable; or in other and perhaps preferable terms, we are led to reason in one direction by Nature and in another by Metaphysics, the latter being the negation of the former. Abstruse as the enquiry necessarily is, it may, nevertheless, be intelligibly stated and in some measure popularly expounded. Those who desire to investigate it more fully can refer to the authors noticed in this chapter.

It is to the high reputation and influence of the late Sir William Hamilton that the frequent prevalence of views respecting our necessary ignorance of God as Infinite is due, though, probably, he himself would have recoiled from some of the applications now made of his doctrine. Hamilton, indeed, has explicitly declared that philosophy must erect her altar to the Unknown and Unknowable God.

The manner in which this doctrine has been adopted and applied by Dr. Mansel in his Bampton Lecture, though acceptable to many, has called forth strong remonstrances from several able thinkers, and especially Mr. John Stuart Mill and the Reverend F. D. Maurice. The aim to demonstrate the necessity of a Divine Revelation to man from the impossibility of his forming any conception of the Absolute One without it, was no doubt well intended, but does not appear to be well-founded. It is not needful for us to point out the disastrous consequences of such a doctrine if it were carried to the extreme.

In his "Philosophy of the Unconditioned" Sir William Hamilton has affirmed, and with all his power endeavoured to establish our necessary ignorance of the Absolute. We shall endeavour to present his views in a few sentences, which may be taken as a simplification of the whole doctrine. The Absolute is thus defined by Sir William Hamilton "*Absolutum* means that which is freed or loosed," in which sense the Absolute will be that which is aloof from relation, comparison, limitation, condition, dependence, etc."

Dr. Mansel thus more plainly defines the word—"By the Absolute is meant, that which exists in and by itself; having no necessary relation to any other Being."

Sir William Hamilton's views may be thus epitomized under three heads:—

1. The Infinite and the Absolute cannot be represented by the imagination, and, therefore, cannot be apprehended in thought.

2. In all attempts to reason about the Infinite we fall into contradictions and absurdities, from which it is to be inferred that our mental faculties are inadequate to such thinking.

3. All matter of thought must first be given to us from without, through perception; or, from within, by self-consciousness. But there is nothing infinite either in that which we experience, or in our own nature. Therefore, there is no source from whence a notion of the Infinite can be furnished to us.

In respect of the first statement, Hamilton declares that the Infinite is unimaginable, because "we cannot positively represent, or realize, or construe to the mind an infinite whole; for this could only be done by the definite cognition in thought of infinite wholes—which would itself require an infinite time for its accomplishment. Nor for the same reason can we follow out in thoughts an infinite divisibility of parts. The result is the same, whether we apply the process to limitation in *space*, in *time*, or in *degree*. The unconditional negation and the unconditional affirmation of limitation —in other words, the infinite and the absolute, properly so called, are thus absolutely inconceivable to us. (Discussions, p. 13.)

Dr. Mansel adopts the same opinion, and carries it to his favourite theological issue. In opposition to both, and to the one radical doctrine which both maintain, let us cite the clear counter-statement of a writer who has no theological leanings whatever, and who merely speaks as a metaphysical critic in objecting decidedly to this tenet.

" Besides that *definite* consciousness of which logic furnishes the laws, there is also an *indefinite* consciousness which cannot be formulated. Besides complete thoughts, and besides the thoughts which though incomplete admit of completion, there are thoughts which it is impossible to complete; and yet which are still real, in the sense that they are normal affections of the intellect.

Observe in the first place, that every one of the arguments by which the relativity of our knowledge is demonstrated, distinctively postulates the positive existence of something beyond the relative. To say that we cannot know the

Absolute is by implication to affirm that this is an Absolute. In the very denial of our power to learn *what* the Absolute is, there lies hidden the assumption that it is; and the making of this assumption proves that the Absolute has been present to the mind, not as a nothing but as a something. Strike out from the argument the terms Unconditioned, Infinite, Absolute, with their equivalents, and in place of them write " negation of conceivability " or " absence of the conditions under which consciousness is possible," and you find that the argument becomes nonsense. Surely to realize in thought any one of the propositions of which the argument consists, the Unconditioned must be represented as positive and not negative. How then can it be a legitimate conclusion from the argument, that our consciousness of it is negative? An argument the very construction of which assigns to a term a certain meaning, but which ends in showing that this term has no such meaning, is simply an elaborate suicide. Clearly then the very demonstration that a *definite* consciousness of the Absolute is impossible to us, unavoidably presupposes an *indefinite* consciousness of it." *

" First Principles," by Herbert Spencer, 1867.

It has also been well observed by Dr. Noah Porter respecting the statements of Hamilton and Mansel, "When these statements are closely scrutinized, it will be seen that this so-called negative thinking is simply a peculiar method of knowing or believing which is unlike, and so the negative of another particular way of thinking or believing. That the Absolute is believed to exist, is affirmed by both Mansel and Hamilton, as well as by Kant. They contend that it is not known under the limitations or relations which are appropriate to thought. Let this be allowed; it does not prove that what is known is therefore negatively known, or that the process by which it is known is a "*process of negative thinking.*"

It is expressly contended by Dr. Porter, that when we have properly defined the term *Absolute*, then the absolute is knowable—that man can both know *that it is* and *what it is*. It cannot be known by the imagination either as representative or creative—for the imagination can only picture that which is limited by space and time, and which is possessed of limited powers of matter or spirit. While it is necessary to use the imagination in order to know the absolute, because it pictures the finite objects which suppose and require the infinite and absolute; yet the imagination cannot in any useful or proper sense picture the absolute itself.

Further, the absolute though knowable, is not a notion which is the product of reasoning inductive or deductive, or that can be defined in a system of logical classification. But it can be and is known as the *correlate* which must be necessarily assumed to explain and account for the finite universe. We cannot know *that it is*, without to a certain degree knowing *what it is*. If it is necessary to the mind to assume the absolute in order to explain the finite, then the finite is certainly explained by those relations which it holds to the absolute. Those relations must be real, else our knowledge is a fiction.*

A formal opponent of the doctrine of the unknowable absolute is Mr. Calderwood, who in his "Philosophy of the Infinite," has brought the subject under deliberate and decisive discussion. His views may be thus condensed :—

1. Man does realize a positive notion of the Infinite.
2. This is not realized by any course of addition or progression either in space or time,

* "The Human Intellect," by Dr. Noah Porter, 1868.

which starting from the finite seeks to reach the infinite; and it is not the result of any logical demonstration.

3. This notion of the infinite is in fact an ultimate datum of consciousness, involved in the constitution of the mind, and arising in various relations.

4. This notion of the infinite, though real and positive, is only partial and indefinite, capable of enlargement, but not of perfection.

It will hardly be denied by those who have thought on these subjects, that the simple idea of God is native to man's soul, and is the result of a prompt and universal exercise of the understanding. In all such inquiries we must accept the testimony of consciousness as a revelation of the facts relating to our inward being, and such testimony must be accepted unconditionally; otherwise no philosophy is possible. Universal consciousness testifies to the existence of God. From the spiritual nature within ourselves, we reason to the spiritual nature above and over all. Although we may not form a mental image of spirit as distinguished from matter, we have a clear fixed idea of a spirit dwelling within us, which is the residence of spiritual attributes, and the source of a spiritual life and energies. The mind of man is a reflected ray of illumination from the Mind above all minds. We do not adequately know our own minds, and therefore cannot expect to form any other than a most inadequate idea of God. Still this idea is positive and impressive. It leads also to positive conclusions, such as that God is infinite. But infinity is not all that constitutes God; if it were, He would be, strictly speaking, incognizable, although we form some notion of infinity, however indistinct. The human mind knows that there is such a thing as infinitude. It is the idea of Universal Being, which includes all beings in itself. Our minds form an idea of infinity, yet know that they cannot fully comprehend it. We are first conscious of the existence of the infinite, and then we narrow the conception and make it finite. Our idea does not represent the Infinite Being as He is, and we know this well; nevertheless it represents to us something determinate. We are ever conscious that actual infinity is really beyond the grasp of our conceptions; but we know that there is an infinite God, and what is important, that He is something more than infinity.*

* See Dr. John Young's "Province of Reason," in reply to

That we may determine what our knowledge of the Infinite Being is, we must first determine the characters and degrees of knowledge in general; and we cannot do this better than in the terms of Leibnitz, who classifies these degrees as follows: "Knowledge is either obscure or clear; and clear, again, is either composed or distinct; and distinct is either inadequate or adequate; also either symbolic or intuitive; and if it be at the same time adequate and intuitive, it is perfect."—(Medit. de Cognitione, etc.) Now, in relation to this classification, it has been well observed, that our knowledge of the Infinite God is a *clear* knowledge; that is, we clearly distinguish the object of knowledge from any other existence; and our knowledge is *distinct*, inasmuch as we are able to distinguish from each other the various attributes of the Divine Nature; but while it is distinct, our knowledge is *inadequate*, because our power of knowing is insufficient to embrace the Infinite in the fulness of His immensity.

Dean Mansel's Bampton Lecture, where he says that the failing which vitiates that book is that infinity *constitutes* God, and that since that which is *infinite* is inconceivable, therefore He is only and wholly inconceivable and unknowable.

We make, however, an important advance in the same direction of thought, by adding that, while our knowledge of the Absolute Being here, by the exercise of unaided reason, is limited, it is nevertheless expansive. The finite cannot fully comprehend the infinite; but it can gradually comprehend more and yet more; and all can clearly understand that, though the term finite is proper in comparison with the infinite, there is no warrant for concluding that the soul of man is incapable of such an enlargement of comprehension as that when compared with his present limitations, it may not be considered as relatively unrestricted. Who can determine the limits of the future expansion of immortal mind ? In this conviction we avail ourselves of the language of Mr. Calderwood:

" Our knowledge of the Infinite Being, while limited and indefinite, is capable of continuous expansion. As we are conscious of no limits in the Deity, but rest in the certain assurance of His infinitude, we are conscious of no restraint, such as would finally terminate our advancement in the knowledge of His boundless excellence. We discover no impassable barrier to further progress, staying us in our contemplations, and saying, ' Thus far shall ye go and no farther,—thus much shall ye know and nothing more.' We are, indeed restricted by the conditions which have been attached to the operations of our cognitive powers, and which it is necessarily impossible for these powers on any occasion to overleap; but these are no hindrance to continuous progress. In harmony with these conditions, we find that persevering contemplation and study secure for us continuous progress in knowledge; ever as we return to renewed effort, we find the same freedom granted to us for the enlargement of the sphere of our acquaintance with the Divine excellence; and still as we advance, we see more and more clearly before us the soul-inspiring prospect of the indefinite expansion of this form of knowledge, which to an intelligent creature, bearing the image of God, must ever seem transcendently attractive. With eternal existence before us, the prospect is intellectually, morally, and spiritually, a glorious one. The conditions which the Creator has attracted to our cognitive powers, serve only to guide and not to hinder them in their exercise; and if the restraints of a feeble body, the distractions of manifold cares, and the darkness of a sinful condition be only taken away, we have faculties which fit us for ceaseless progress in the sublimest of all human studies." *

The most elaborate and vigorous assailant of Sir William Hamilton's doctrine is Mr. John Stuart Mill, in his volume specially devoted to an "Examination of Sir William Hamilton's Philosophy." In its pages the writer takes the same direction of thought as that just stated, and argues most earnestly against Dean Mansel's application of Hamilton's doctrine, pronouncing it to be the most pernicious current doctrine of the day. His language is strong, and in one often-quoted passage (from page 103) has been held to be very objectionable, but Mr. Mill's conviction of the dangerous consequences of Dean Mansel's distinctions is so profound, that strong denunciation might be expected from him. All who wish to pursue this important inquiry, and who feel perplexed by the applications made of Hamilton's doctrine, should read that portion of Mr. Mill's volume which relates to this subject, and they will perceive how logically baseless is the argument that would exclude us from all natural conceptions of the absolute, and the infinite; more especially the opinion that the attributes

* "The Philosophy of the Infinite," p. 234.

of God are essentially different from the like qualities manifested in a limited degree in man. The latter view is quite untenable in any true philosophy or theology.

With relation to Hamilton's theory, we should be glad to introduce more detailed counter-statements from the writers referred to, but it is sufficient perhaps simply to indicate the sources in which they may be found.

Another celebrated philosopher, Victor Cousin, whose views were opposed by Sir William Hamilton in his principal essay, has stated them apparently in a somewhat modified form in one of his latest works, and they are here cited not more on account of their near approach to what we hold to be the truth than for their felicity of expression. Victor Cousin observes:

"We say, in the first place, that God is not absolutely incomprehensible, for this manifest reason, that being the cause of this universe, He passes with it, and is reflected in it as the cause in the effect; therefore, we recognize Him. 'The heavens declare His glory, and the invisible things of Him from the creation of the world are clearly seen, being understood by the things that are made.'—His power in the thousands of worlds sown in the boundless regions of space; His intelligence in their harmonious laws. Finally, whilst there is in Him, all that is most august in the sentiments of virtue, of holiness, of love, which the heart of man contains, it must be that God is not incomprehensible to us; for all nations have petitioned Him since the first day of the intellectual life of humanity. God then, as the cause of the universe, reveals Himself to us; but God is not only the cause of the universe, He is also the perfect and infinite cause, possessing in Himself not only a relative perfection, which is only a degree of imperfection, but as absolute perfection as infinity; which is not only the finite multiplied by itself, in those proportions which the human mind *is* able always to enumerate, but a true infinity that is the absolute negative of all limits, in all the powers of his being. Moreover, it is not true that an indefinite effect adequately expresses an infinite cause; hence it is not true that we are able absolutely to comprehend God by the world and by man, for all of God is not in them. In order absolutely to comprehend the infinite, it is necessary to have an infinite power of comprehension, and that is not granted to us. God in manifesting himself retains something in Himself which nothing finite can absolutely manifest; consequently it is not permitted us to comprehend absolutely. There remains, then, in God, beyond the universe and man, something unknown, impenetrable, incomprehensible. Hence in the immeasurable spaces of the universe, and beneath all the profundities of the human soul, God escapes as in that inexhaustible infinitude, whence he is able to draw without limit, new worlds, new beings, new manifestations. God is to us, therefore, incomprehensible; but even of this incomprehensibility we have a clear and precise idea; for we have the most precise idea of infinity. And this idea is not in us a metaphysical refinement, it is a simple primitive conception which enlightens us from our entrance into this world, both luminous and obscure, explaining everything, and being explained by nothing, because it carries us at first to the summit and the limit of all explanation. There is something inexplicable for thought,—behold then whither thought tends; there is infinite being,—behold then the necessary principle of all relative and finite beings. Reason explains not the inexplicable ; it conceives it. It is not able to comprehend infinity in an absolute manner ; but it comprehends it in some degree in its infinite manifestations, which reveal it and which veil it ; and further, it has been said, it comprehends it so far as incomprehensible. It is therefore an error to call God absolutely comprehensible, and absolutely incomprehensible. He is both invisible and present, revealed and withdrawn in Himself, in the world and out of the world, so familiar and intimate with His creatures that we see Him by opening our eyes, that we feel him in feeling our hearts beat, and at the same time inaccessible in His impenetrable majesty; mingled with everything and separated from everything, manifesting Himself in universal life, and causing scarcely an ephemeral shadow of his eternal essence to appear there ; communicating Himself without cessation, and remaining incommunicable, at once the living God and the God concealed. 'Deus vivus et Deus absconditus.'" *

I add a few observations upon our apprehension of the moral attributes of God, which are surely not beyond our grasp, any more than

* Cousin's Works, First Series, vol. iv., sec. 12, quoted by Professor A. C. Fraser.

the spiritual nature in which wisdom and moral attributes dwell. It is true that the Divine attributes in their greatness and infinitude far transcend our comprehension, but their actual existence does not transcend it. Our perception of the display of the Divine attributes in the natural world should be as certain and clear as our perception of light. We feel that our own moral attributes are as sparks of those glorious Divine attributes which go forth from God to enlighten and bless all created beings wherever they may dwell in the universe.

Dean Mansel combats the notion "that the attributes of God differ from those of man in degree only, not in kind, and hence that certain mental and moral qualities of which we are immediately conscious in ourselves, furnish at the same time a true and adequate image of the infinite perfection of God." (The word *adequate*, as Mr. Mill observes in quoting this passage must have slipped in by inadvertence, otherwise it would be an inexcusable misrepresentation) and he identifies it with "the Vulgar Rationalism which regards the reason of man, in its ordinary and normal operation, as the supreme criterion of religious truth." He declares the principles of this vulgar

Rationalism to be that "all the excellence of which we are conscious in the creature, must necessarily exist in the same manner, though in a higher degree in the Creator. God is indeed more wise, more just, more merciful than man; but for this very reason his wisdom and justice and mercy must contain nothing that is incompatible with the corresponding attributes in their human character."*

Objecting *in toto* to this view, Mr. Mill says: "Here, then, I take my stand on the acknowledged principles of logic and of morality, that when we mean different things we have no right to call them by the same name, and to apply to them the same predicates, moral and intellectual. Language has no meaning for the words Just, Merciful, Benevolent, save that in which we predicate them of our fellow creatures, and unless that is what we intend to express by them, we have no business to employ the words. If in affirming them of God, we do not mean to affirm these very qualities, differing only as greater in degree, we are neither philosophically nor morally entitled to affirm them at all. If it be said that the qualities are the same, but that we cannot con-

* Bampton Lecture, "Limits of Religious Thought," p. 28.

ceive them as they are when raised to the infinite, I grant that we cannot adequately conceive them in one of their elements, their infinity. But we can conceive them in their other elements, which are the very same in the infinite as in the finite development. Anything carried to the infinite must have all the properties of the same thing as finite, except those which depend on the finiteness. What belongs to it (goodness) as Infinite (or more properly as Absolute) I do not pretend to know, but I know that infinite goodness must be goodness, and that what is not consistent with goodness, is not consistent with infinite goodness." *

* "An Examination of Sir William Hamilton's Philosophy," 1865, p. 100, etc.

VIII.

THE INFINITE AND THE PERSONAL GOD.

A CONCEPTION of God as the Infinite, so far as it is attainable by us, may be employed in two opposite directions, one being that of repression, and the other that of elevation of thought. In the former case, it may be menacingly though fallaciously pointed towards the extinction of a consistent idea of God in the human mind, by showing the supposed incompatibleness of an infinite with a personal being. It may be argued that the one conception destroys the other, and that either God is not personal or not infinite. An infinite personality may be said to be contradictory and unthinkable, since personality has conditions, while infinitude can have none. It is vain to affirm that this consideration forms no barrier to our thoughts; for it is marked, and in our present state insuperable. The unbeliever, therefore, readily avails himself of this weapon of attack. On the other hand, the conception of infinitude, at least as the opposite of finitude, may be employed in the elevation of our thoughts to God. In a devout mind, influenced by faith as well as metaphysical knowledge, the aforesaid difficulty is at once confessed, and rightly attributed not to the actual, but to the apparent incompatibleness of some kind of personality with infinitude. In nature the Creator and the Preserver is displayed to us as infinite, for seemingly, the universe, which is His handiwork, is infinite; and when we realize Him as the Creator, we conceive of Him as coextensive with creation. As the Creator of an apparently infinite universe, He cannot be less than His own work. Yet as distinct Creator, He must of necessity be a separate personality. If we refuse personality to Him, we relapse into Pantheism; if we doubt His infinity, He ceases to be the Creator, in not being coextensive with creation.

Admit, however, His infinite personality as a great truth, although a great mystery; regard and worship Him as a person, while you reverence Him as infinite; believe in His dealings with you individually as the Undivided One; in your responsibility to Him as a son is responsible to a father, or a servant to his master. Foster within your heart and soul the love awakened by His benevolence as a person, and the awe inspired by His infinity as Creator, and then you gain the redoubled blessing which the contemplation of God in His mysterious twofold character should afford you. Confess the mystery, for you cannot solve it; admit it, for you are not compelled to solve it. Be not impatient under your limitations, and above all, do not, because of those limitations, doubt His existence; and do not diffuse your conceptions of it into an indefinite Pantheism. This by liberally placing God everywhere, places Him in particular nowhere. It grants Him omnipresence, but it denies Him personality. He is everywhere merely because He is everything, and everything is equally Divine. This destroys separate existence by merging all individual distinctions. It enthrones humanity by dethroning divinity.

If we analyze our own profoundest religious meditations, or examine those which have been recorded of the highest minds, we shall discern how these two apparently irreconcilable conceptions of God have ministered to pure and elevated devotion. The devoutness of contracted and uncultivated understandings must necessarily be restricted to a low level, by limiting the character of God's dealings with them to a narrow sphere of thought, and often, alas! to a painfully unworthy notion of his greatness; but what is painful and plainly unworthy in this respect, should not be allowed to repress our attempts to ascend to and commune with the awful yet merciful King, who, while He bears a regal relation to all existence, condescends to bear a personal relation to our humble individuality. It is a postulate of enlightened consciousness that He must be infinite; it is a prompting of enlightened consciousness that He must be also personal. By all the metaphysical analyses of which my mind is capable, I cannot find him out to perfection. By all His spiritual communications of which I am the recipient, I cannot doubt His real and influential personality. Although I decline to accept the representations and superstitions of undisciplined minds as suitable illustrations of His character and His conduct, I am not to be thereby deterred from regarding Him as emphatically my Father, and when humanly conceived, as my Friend. Assure me, if you will, that Infinity cannot philosophically be my Friend and Father; that the great Unconditioned Being cannot actually bear a definite relation to my conditioned humanity. Against this assurance I bring my most refined and elevated consciousness. If you object to theological language, I will abjure its phraseology: but still the fact, the consciousness of divine communication remains, however it may be phrased. In my inmost solitude, in my most complete retiredness, in my entire isolation from dogmas and systems, from creeds and customs, in my fullest recognition of the requirements of logic and metaphysic, in my most subservient obedience to the necessary laws of thought, I feel confident that my own personality possesses a distinct relation to the Divine personality; and that the expansiveness of my capacities progressively bears a certain, though an unknown, and at present unmeasured, proportion to His infinity.

Under many feeble and impoverished conceptions of His presidence and governance on the part of others, I still recognize a substratum of undeniable truth which beyond and above passing forms remains as an abiding experience.

If the appeal to *enlightened* consciousness be the confessed test of metaphysics, it is equally and indeed more strictly the test of *our experimental* knowledge of God. We lay stress upon the qualification *enlightened*, because he who does not seek enlightenment from Nature as well as from Scriptural Revelation, cannot reap the full benefits of all that is divinely offered to him. In Scripture we have a personal Jehovah, a personal Father, an Almighty Friend, pervading all its history; dealing indeed with men quite anthropologically, because in no other way could the men of past ages apprehend him. If He there and then condescends to reveal Himself under images and limitations, which in our later times of highly educated societies appear circumscribed, let us only be thankful that we live in a period when such limitations are less needful. Yet even in believers in the views of those ancient times we occasionally perceive a transcendence of the conditional anthropomorphism of their obscure day. With a longing though indefinite anticipation of higher and future revelations, they look beyond the present, and with an unspeakably ardent yearning they antedate the Divine glory that is to be revealed even in the present world. They delight themselves in the present, and also prospectively in the future. They are assured of the shining of a brighter glory, although they know that they must pass away ere it appears. Many doubts hang like dark clouds over them, but they are nobly confident that their posterity will look on the sun when those clouds have been dispersed. The great Father talks with them, as it were face to face, but at the same time He points to the stars very high above them; and in like manner the incomprehensible Father still points to the stars very high above us. We are indeed no nearer to them even now, yet to us they shine with a brighter light; we view them through more perfect instruments; we have catalogued their names, we have calculated their courses, we have observed their orbits, and we have heard some strains of their mysterious harmony.

In rising above much of early anthropomorphism have we dispelled human ignorance of God as he is essentially? Perhaps but little; still we do not now so commonly apprehend Him as a mere superior Lord and fellow-being. Certainly we do conceive of Him as beyond all explanation and all really visible shaping. In our modern conceptions He is more awful, but therefore at the same time less familiar and less sensibly present with us. We remove him further from us by our baffled attempts to apprehend Him; while we place Nature nearer to us, and as a veil through which we can bear to gaze. We see more of effects, and feel less of Himself as the personal and primary cause. We recognize the omnipresence and omnipotence of Law, but lose sight of the omnipresence and omnipotence of Love. We feel more of reverence, it may be, and less of trusting friendship. Our philosophical gains are compensated by sensible losses. The world, the universe, is still His, but He is less clearly manifest in all outward things. The elements, the winds, the storms, the magnificent and ever-changeful phenomena of the scenes in which we live are traced to physical causes, and are rightly dissociated from ideas of an anthropomorphic superintendence, from humanly capricious changefulness and passionate interference. We mount in every successive age another step of those endless stairs which, ascending from the level plains, go mysteriously upwards to the Throne of the Almighty. We look down and contemn our forefathers who placed their feet only upon a lower stair than ours. We stand higher and we feel prouder; we count the steps by which we have mounted, and we boast that by so many advances we are nearer to truth. Alas! they who stood on the lower steps, while inferior in position, were often superior in holiness; while lower in place, they were loftier in expression. We may ascend to the top of the highest mountain and breathe a keener air, and behold a vastly wider panorama of form and beauty: heights which appeared grand to our less instructed forefathers are dwarfed to us, and things are indistinct to us, which were impressive to them. But we have gained in altitude and lost in power; we are scientifically nearer to truth, yet at the same time sensibly further from God. We can indeed speak of Him, but our words are less sonorous in the more rarefied air. Where we now are it is harder for us to breathe, and we are disinclined to praise. Who that loves God does not at such an elevation feel the beauty of one of those grand hymns of the Old Hebrew Psalmists which savour so little of the science of our day, but preserve so preciously the piety of their day? Although chargeable with an antique anthropomorphism, although so replete with what are now regarded as unphilosophical conceptions, and so full of discarded forms and unfelt aspirations and lamentations, nevertheless, who does not feel that those Psalmists worshipped the Divine Father with a deeper devoutness and a more exuberant gladness of soul, or besought Him with a more sorrowing wail of humble penitence, than we who stand high above them in knowledge, but far beneath them in holy experience and in force and fervour of expression? We are aiming to grasp the conception of the Infinite, and have lost the sense of the Personal Father.

Should we then gain by returning to the unphilosophical ignorance of those inspired singers? Ought we to strive to retrace our steps and to reduce our conceptions to the dimensions of theirs? No right-thinking man can suppose that we should. But our constant and vigorous effort should be, to increase our religious feeling in due proportion to our increased knowledge. Our duties are wider as our position is higher. The eye takes in more, and the heart ought to feel more. And as we are now inheritors of an ampler and an accumulated wealth of ideas and observations, so are our responsibilities the greater and the more pressing. The boundaries of our estate of knowledge have been continually enlarged, and by so much the heavier has become the burden of our stewardship.

It must be clearly set before men that only upon the belief in a personal God can any sound superstructure of religion be raised. What love can we cherish for an impersonal universal substance? Before we can feel real human love for God we must assuredly apprehend Him as love personified. Not only must we believe that "God is love" abstractedly, but likewise love in the relationship of person. In like manner we cannot fear to offend Him in any other light. Pursue in thought the entire series of religious acts and meditations of which any human being is capable, and they all tend towards a divine *person*. The moment you dissipate that into infinite extension, at the same moment you dissipate religion into an unmeaning generality. Send the galvanic current of your thoughts throughout the entire universe, and there are but two points which can meet and give out a spark of light and heat, and those two points are the Divine and the human personalities.

We are not chargeable with irrational faith because we cannot define the nature of the

Divine personality. It utterly transcends language, and therefore any approach to verbal definitions. In an ordinary view personality implies limitations which cannot exist in God. We should require a superhuman language to express this Divine thing, but we can only ascribe spiritual existence, reason, freedom of action, knowledge, power, and other qualities to Him as a person. Without distinct personality God can possess no comprehensible attributes. Apart from Divine personality, Justice, Wisdom, Love, and Mercy are inapplicable names. Infinity is grand beyond expression, but it is insufficient to overmaster the idea of the personal, unless its vague grandeur resembles that of a dark, mysterious tomb in which all the life of particularity moulders away.

It may be presumed that the Divine personality is of so much higher an order than our own, that while its character is preserved, its conditions are wholly different. It must assuredly be transcendently higher. It may be wholly indescribable in human language, without being inconceivable by human thought. It may be the one Eternal Insoluble Mystery —beyond the ken of men, and angels and archangels. It may be the dazzling sun ever luminously veiled within its own glorious photosphere. Language utterly fails to expound it; but it certainly exists. It is a revealed truth, and an essential element of enlightened consciousness. It is the bright and morning star that is reflected in the pure depths of every regenerate soul. In its reflection in these depths it is contracted to a distinct and visible image of that which we know to be, in the infinite heights above us, a vast and immeasurable orb—immeasurable by any created understanding, nevertheless capable of being reflected in a single clear wave.

Let no man therefore consent to be bewildered by the impossibility of representing or conceiving of this Divine personality as really and truly infinite. He believes without conscious effort in the enormous dimensions of a remote planet, whose diameter of thousands of miles comes within the few actual inches of his telescopic glass. He beholds with ready credence the direct but infinitely diminished reflex of an immense world in a little pool at his feet; but he doubts and despairs of believing that the Infinite Orb can be reflected in his own soul as that which is truly personal.

Yet this is and must be the truth which is propounded to his faith, and while its difficulty cannot be evaded, its reality cannot be denied. He who once allows himself to be mastered by the admitted difficulty sees the basis of all practical religion crumble away. Even then he is not delivered from difficulty, which is as inherent in Pantheism as in personal Theism. Nothing but the kind of difficulty is varied, and he who rejects the only possible foundation for a practical religion, has to find another foundation, which may indeed satisfy him, while it appears thoroughly unsatisfactory to thinkers of at least equal vigour and penetration to his own.

The idea of a Divine impersonality may be held in different forms, and possibly in some such forms as to lead the holders of them to disavow a gross Pantheism; but our prime duty is not to admit the conception of infinity into the mind as predominant over, and exclusive of God's existence in some personal mode. No man who acquaints himself with the views of certain naturalists and evolutionists of the present age can fail to perceive that the extinction of the idea of a personal Creator and Governor of the universe is either complete or tending to completion in their minds, and that in days to come impersonalism may be more plainly and authoritatively proposed to general acceptance than at present. The ultimate object and the actual tendency of some increasingly favoured schemes of naturalism, is to extirpate the belief in a specific Creator, and in a distinct and avowed creation. An infinite power—a kind of Divine Omnipotence, may be admitted as in accordance with such schemes, but the infinity will always suppress the active divinity, and the result will either be some modification of Pantheism, or if we may employ a new term for the occasion, of *Anthropotheism.* This latter is indeed the existing outcome of Comte's Positivism, and the worship of humanity is that philosopher's highest form of faith, of which as exemplified in his own and in recent practice, a serious consideration is totally out of place. The world has heard and read what the Comtean worship of humanity is, or if any one be ignorant of it let him consult the Catechism of Positive Religion, of which an English version has been published, and likewise the circular of M. P. Lafitte, the supposed head of Positivism. In the circular for 1867 M. Lafitte announces the death of Martin Thomas, the husband of Comte's adopted daughter, and after stating that a commemorative service had been held, he announces that seven years afterwards, that is in 1874, he will confer on Martin Thomas the Sacrament of *Incorporation*. By this, which is the last of the Positive Sacraments, all who are accounted true servants of humanity are, seven years after death, incorporated with the *Grand Etre*. Meantime the image of M. Thomas would be placed in the building consecrated to the religious meetings of the Positivists.

In the foregoing observations no attempt has been made to deny the inherent difficulty of realizing the Divine personality in conjunction with infinity. It has been fully and fairly confessed. The term *personality* implies to us a person in whom as such there is the mind of a conscious being with a bodily form, the latter being essential to the simplest idea of personality. If we affirm that God is incorporeal, we seem at the same time to affirm that he is impersonal. If we declare him to be infinite, we know that the infinite mind transcends the limits of any finite personality. The conclusion must be that the words we employ entangle us or do not sufficiently express our thoughts. Every Theist who forms any conception of God attaches to it the idea of personality. How we acquire the idea, or whence it originally came to man it is impossible to decide. Possibly it is implanted in his mind; possibly it was originally a tradition handed down through the earliest ages and derived from an early revelation. Certainly it is now a revealed truth, and those who accept it purely as a revealed truth may refuse to be troubled with the philosophical difficulties associated with it.

All who accept Jesus Christ as the Divine Son of God at once find a living testimony to the truth of a Divine personality in His sacred incarnated person. For them the difficulty seems overcome, not by philosophical conciliation, but by belief in Him. They receive and worship Him as a person; they attribute a distinct personality to Him now that He is ascended up on high, and all their thoughts, prayers, and adorations proceed to Him as the same personality, though in what form and under what conditions they cannot attempt to realize.

There are some feeble aids of another kind which will perhaps assist reflecting minds in their endeavours to distinguish the personal Deity from the world He has created, and is sustaining. Such helps are necessarily derived from our present life and the objects before us, and one such is the following, as it has presented itself to the mind of the writer.

We contemplate Nature as the work of a great artist. Nature in its totality is a magnificent work of the Divine Artist, who must necessarily be as distinct from it and as separably personal in relation to it, as must be any great painter from the picture which he paints. Let us suppose that we inspect an imposing picture in the absence of, and without personal knowledge of the painter. We feel instinctively that *some* painter has been previously present, and has painted this picture, which though embodying his very self as to his thoughts, is yet not himself, but so distinct from him that he may be distant by any space from it, and yet be intimately related to it.

If the picture be an unfinished work, but approaching to its completion, and if we inspect it daily during its progress without ever encountering the artist himself, still we feel quite confident of his personality, and watch the progressive marks of his activity continually as the painting advances. We trace by degrees the conception of the worker, we note his silent yet manifest purposes, we discern his adaptation of lights and shades to an ultimate harmony of effect. We see his very soul in the painting, and in every part of the work, as much so as though we should see him face to face and talk with him, and listen to his exposition of his own ideal, and witness the touches of his own hand.

In like manner, he who studies Nature as the great work of the greatest Artist, he who contemplates it daily and lovingly, he who stands before it with reverence and sympathy, feels as assured of the separate existence and personal working of God, as the supposed spectator of a great picture. One can no more confound the work with the worker than one can confound Raffael or Titian, or Rubens or Rembrandt with their wonderful paintings.

IX.

PANTHEISM AND SPINOZISM.

PANTHEISM is essentially, as well as etymologically, the opposite to Personal Theism, for it postulates that the Infinite and Unconditioned must be impersonal, and all that is associated with personality must be logically deducted from the idea of God. Consequently, understanding and will, as we are conscious of them, are detached by the Pantheist. There are, indeed, attributes in God, but they are not personal attributes, for Spinoza's definition is this: " God is an infinite substance, constituted by an infinite number of attributes, infinitely infinite." A strong fascination has led many minds to Pantheism, and it is little known that even Leibnitz himself confesses that he once " leant to the side of the Spinozists, who, he adds, leave to God nothing but an infinite impotence."

To trace the rise and currency of Pantheistic views is interesting and instructive. They are much older than is commonly supposed, and much more subtle than many theologians believe. We here omit to dwell upon the great oriental systems of Pantheism, which have deluded and still delude millions of our race, but we briefly revert to an ancient school of philosophers, the Eleatics, who appear to have anticipated modern views on this and on collateral subjects.

In this school—whose metaphysics were inherited by the Megaric succession—we find the principle openly stated that the sensible world is purely phenomenal, accidental, apparent; in contradistinction from that substantial world of Reason which alone descries the little real existence. When considered by the intelligence, the world of existence becomes subordinated to the laws and forms of intelligence; it is a world of which we have an interpretation in our own reason, there alone, and there perfectly. As it is the undoubted character of these laws of intelligence that they regard the Necessary, the Unconditional, the Absolute, so it is certain that this absolute thing, thus contemplated by intellectual intuition—it being the common foundation and essential reality of all things, and of all things equally—cannot but be one and ever identical with itself. Thus to the eye of reason there is no plurality, no change. One Being not merely supports, but is the universe; and all that reveals itself in the lower world of sense is but the external manifestation of this Absolute Unity. Of anything which that mutable world includes, it cannot be said that it *is*—it *becomes*; for its property is incessant change, and of that which incessantly changes, as on the one hand there can be no assured science, so on the other there cannot be any true and proper *reality* predicated. It is in vain to affirm, with the short-sighted Ionic school, that it is sufficient for us to trust the regulated sequences of Nature; for if these sequences be casual, not even the shadows of science can regard them; if they be arbitrary but believed to be invariable, this again is not science, but faith; if they be necessary and unalterable, then are they what we affirm them to be, the mere manifestations in the world of sense of the necessary attributes of a necessary and eternal thing. They are, as it were, the Absolute contemplated by the eyes of sense; and all the scientific reality of such laws is only the reality of the Absolute Being that exhibits itself in them. The Universe, then, is One, to the total exclusion of superior, inferior, or equal.

Such is the Eleatic principle of unity, and are there not in this very ancient Greek philosophy the same prevalent ideas as abound in much of modern philosophy; such as that of Schelling and his followers, who affirm the identity of subject and object in that Absolute Unity of which nothing can be determined; for determination of itself supposes limitation, but which the reason directly contemplates by an exclusive privilege, and because it can in truth directly contemplate nothing else.*

The formulated dilemma then of the Eleatics is this—"either God is all or nothing; for if there be any reality beyond Him, that reality is wanting to His perfection."

To pass by the Pantheism of Plotinus and his followers, and omitting to specify its influence upon the mediæval scholastics, we only name John Scotus Erigena as a singular instance of the combination of Pantheistic opinions with a reputation for great Catholic

* W. A. Butler's "History of Ancient Philosophy," 1856.

sanctity. That once famous, though now forgotten thinker, seems to have entertained views almost identical with those of later Pantheists, and to have maintained, like some of our contemporaries, that God is unknown and altogether unknowable.

We now proceed to offer a summary of the doctrine of Spinoza respecting God, gathered from his works and his expositors, as succinctly and clearly as the subject will allow.

The absolute existence is God.—There is but one infinite substance, and that is God.—Whatever is, is in God, and without Him nothing can be conceived. He is the universal Being of which all things are the manifestations. From Him all individual and concrete existence arises. He is the sole substance; everything else is a mode, yet without substance mode cannot exist. God, viewed under the attributes of infinite substance, is the *natura naturans*—viewed as a manifestation, as the mode under which his attributes appear, he is the *natura naturata*. He is the cause of all things, and that immanently but not transiently. He has two infinite attributes, Extension and Thought. Extension is visible Thought, and Thought is invisible Extension: they are the objective and subjective of which God is the identity. Every *thing* is a mode of God's attribute of extension; every *thought*, wish, or feeling, a mode of His attribute of thought. That Extension and Thought are not substances, as Descartes maintained, is obvious from this: that they are not conceived *per se*, but *per aliud*. Something is extended; but what is? Not the extension itself, but something prior to it, viz. substance. Substance is uncreated, but creates by the internal necessity of its nature. There may be many existing things, but only one existence; many forms, but only one substance.*

The ordinary acceptance of the term *substance* as something material may account for the long and persistent imputations of Atheism

---

* For Spinoza's doctrines and life, see " Biographical History of Philosophy," by G. H. Lewes. In the enlarged editions of this work Mr. Lewes gives at length the words of the form of a Jewish excommunication, which may have been pronounced against Spinoza on his public expulsion from Judaism. Those, however, who desire to study Spinoza systematically, should peruse the Essays of Mons. Emile Saisset, who published a French version of the works of Spinoza. The criticisms upon, answers to, and essays relating to Spinoza are numerous, and come down to the present time. It is remarkable that this short-lived recluse, with apparently no outward help, should have thought out a system which has interested so many and such different minds. A Lutheran minister, Colerus, has left an interesting sketch of Spinoza's life and death.

to Spinoza. "But," says Mr. Lewes, "No one could ever have read twenty pages of Spinoza without perceiving that this was a misunderstanding; for he expressly teaches that God is not corporeal, but that body is a mode of extension. Nay, God is not the material universe; but the universe is one aspect of his infinite attribute of extension: he is the identity of the *natura naturans*, and the *natura naturata*. It is a mere verbal resemblance, therefore, this of Spinozism to Atheism."

Much depends upon our granting to Spinoza what he demands for the word *substance*. He himself defines it thus:—"By substance I understand that which is in itself, and is conceived *per se*; that is, the conception of which does not require the conception of anything else antecedent to it." By the term *attribute* he understands "that which the mind perceives as constituting the very essence of substance." By *modes* he understands "the accidents of substance; or that which is something else, through which also it is conceived." "By *God*," defines Spinoza, "I understand the Being absolutely infinite, *i.e.*, the substance consisting of infinite attributes, each of which expresses an infinite and eternal essence." Bayle, who was at one time generally considered to have refuted Spinoza, disregarded the philosopher's own definition of substance, and proceeded to show that everything has a substance of its own. Voltaire, suspecting that Bayle did not quite understand Spinoza's substance, adopts the following argument in refutation of the latter:—Spinoza erects a theory on the mistaken maxim of Descartes, that nature is a *Plenum*. But as every motion requires empty space for itself, where is Spinoza's one and only substance? For how can the substance of a star, between which and man there is so vast a void, be precisely the substance of this earth, or the substance of a fly eaten by a spider?"

However strict in form and logical in construction the theory of Spinoza may appear to be, if you will grant to him his premises, yet he by no means satisfactorily solves the problem of the relation of God to the universe. In his view, God is the infinite substance of which bodies and souls are merely the modes, and there is no real and practical distinction between God and the universe. We may conceive of them as separate, but only by abstract effort. Without the universe God is not a being possessing determinate existence, but simply substance without its modes, or, in other words, pure and undetermined being. He is then conceived abstractedly without the determinations which to us make up His reality and life. Then, again, the universe becomes as necessary as God, being not merely a manifestation of God, but His act and His life, and in effect God Himself.

We cannot speak of the Creator and the creature consistently with this philosophy, since, according to it, God is a cause absolutely incapable of going out of and beyond itself, for it comprehends as a part of itself every possible existence. "God," says Spinoza, in his *Ethica*, "is the immanent cause of all things, not indeed the transient cause." In place of God and the universe he substitutes his *natura naturans* and *natura naturata;* and these terms express the identity of one and the same existence, though decomposed by abstraction, and alternately regarded as substance and mode, infinite and finite, fundamentally undetermined and determined in its necessary forms.

Schelling, in laying down the distinction between Pantheism and Atheism, thus exposes one fundamental error:—"God is that which exists in itself, and is comprehended from itself alone; the finite is that which is necessary in another, and can only be comprehended from that other. Things therefore are not only in degree, or through their limitations different from God, but *toto genere*. Whatever their relation to God in other points, they are absolutely divided from him on this: that they exist in another, and he is self-existent or original. From this difference it is manifest that all individual finite things taken together cannot constitute God, since that which is in nature *derived*, cannot be one with its original, any more than the single points of a circumference taken together can constitute the circumference, which, as a whole, is of necessity prior to them in idea."

If we endeavour to form a clear conception of God according to Spinoza, it must be owned that such a being is a mere idol of reason, and only so far superior to lower forms of ideality in that it is not an idol of sense or mere imagination. The unique substance God is all. Without this substance neither the world nor man exists. Creation is a myth, because what is, is, and there is no other existence than God. A tissue of contradictions is involved in the consequences of the Spinozistic idea of God, who is extended and yet incorporeal; who thinks and yet has not understanding; who is free, and yet possesses not will. God is but one substance, and yet is not a personality. God, who is the most desirable and the most to be loved of all beings, is at the same time the unknown supreme. He is infinite yet finite. All proceeds from God as all has proceeded, and therefore all is good, while at the same time much is evil—or rather there are no such things as good and evil, just as there are no such things as beauty and ugliness. Well may a French critic ask, "Who shall unmystify for us this chaos? who shall explain these enigmas? who shall reconcile these contradictions? Can it satisfy us still to receive the monotonous and derisive affirmation, that all is one, and that in this all things conciliate themselves. Spinoza, wrote Leibnitz, decisively has pretended to demonstrate that there is but one substance in the universe, but his demonstrations are pitiable and unintelligible."*

Nevertheless the highest encomiums are sometimes bestowed upon Spinoza's system as mathematically rigorous. Thus Mr. G. H.

* Nourrisson. "Spinoza, et Le Naturalisme Contemporain," 1866.

Lewes regards Spinoza's system as being "one of the most extraordinary efforts of the speculative faculty which history has revealed to us. We have witnessed the mathematical rigour with which it is developed; we have followed him step by step, dragged onwards by his irresistible logic; and yet the final impression left on our minds is that the system has a logical but not a vital truth. But," Mr. Lewes adds, "the conclusions are repugned, refused; they are not the truth the inquirer has been seeking; they are no expressions of the thousand-fold life, whose enigma he has been endeavouring to solve."

"It is our firm conviction," says the same critic, "that no believer in metaphysics as a *possible* science can escape the all-embracing dialectics of Spinoza. To him who believes that the human mind can know *noumena* as well as *phenomena*—who accepts the verdict of the mind as not merely the *relative* truth, but also the *perfect, absolute* truth—we see nothing, humanly speaking, but Spinozism as a philosophical refuge."*

M. Saisset has made a careful and comprehensive study of Spinoza and his system, and has

* Op. cit., iii, 148—9.

published some valuable criticism upon it. He defines its leading idea to be the essential and necessary *consubstantiality*—of the finite and the infinite—of Nature and God—of human persons and the Divine. The religion and the habits of life of Spinoza were continual meditation on God, and he thought he had obtained tranquillity and happiness in his knowledge of God,—who, as he declared, is the One God, the only Substance, the Perfect, the Absolute. Since He must be the only Power, no other power can subsist, or conflict with Him. Men are only powers in and through His operations in them. The more fully and freely we exercise ourselves in the development of our highest faculties, the nearer do we approach to that perfection which consists in identification with God. We shall be freed from the impediments to a happy life when we have risen above the objects of sense, and are, through reason, united in life to the Infinite and Eternal.

All this seems good, and has the appearance of religiousness. But then what is the character of God in Spinoza's system—what does the word *God* mean in his conception? If God be the only substance, there is universally but one substance, which itself is God. This one substance or power has attributes, and these attributes have modes. The former are infinite, the latter finite. The known attributes of substance are extension and thought. God is known to us as absolute but incorporeal extension, and absolute but unconscious thought. The absolute extension and thought, of which God's existence is the common ground, are expressed in persons and things. These constitute Nature, and are the *natura naturata*. Absolute extension and thought, or the essence and power of nature, are the *natura naturans*. Though there is really nothing in common between these two, they cannot be separated. Therefore what we call creation, cannot be separated from what we call God, because God is perfect, and that which is perfect cannot be other than what it is. The universe must simply be what it is.

It was supposed that by maintaining this uniting conception absolute and intact, two difficulties could be escaped which are alleged to be so fatal to the consistency and completeness of other systems; so that we neither deny the Infinite and religion as do atheistic materialists, nor imitate the mystical idealists in their denial of finite persons and things. But by conceiving God and nature (including material things and men in the term *nature*), as two faces of one sole and self-same existence, God becomes Nature fastened to its immanent principle, and nature becomes God considered in the evolution of His power. There is not on one side a solitary God, and on the other an isolated universe, for the Creator is incessantly incarnated in each of His creatures, and becomes each of them in turn. Under this conception it may be said that God sleeps in the mineral, dreams in the animal, and wakens into consciousness in the man. This continuous evolution of the Divine —this eternal progress in which Deity passes through changes that are always new—is the supreme law, is reality, is life, in the view of Spinoza. Such is M. Saisset's abstract.

Besides, to be consistent, a Spinozist must suppose that the great Substance is constrained by law of some kind in all its evolutions, and the same must be supposed in any system of material Pantheism. Now when constrained by law, this law must have operated on substance from without, or otherwise substance must have bound itself. If operating from without, then there is a power above substance. If substance bound itself by law, then substance is intelligent, capable of willing, and so far as self-bound by law, is continually willing;—all which is contrary to and destructive of the hypothesis of Spinoza.

It has been observed that even Calvin displayed a leaning to Pantheism; but while representing God as the absolutely determining principle of the world, he was preserved from Spinozism in refusing to represent God as under a necessity of nature to determine as he actually does determine. Calvin, on the contrary, maintains that God is "*Liberum Arbitrium*," and thus he was kept from Pantheism. He saw that God is the absolutely supernatural being, and in his essence separated from the world: the apparent unity of the two consisting solely in the fact of the determination of the latter by the former.

Several interesting particulars of certain early followers of Spinoza have been published by Van der Linde, and the decisive influence which Spinozism exercised on theologians is made manifest in the tenets of some forgotten ministers and religious mystics. The instance of Pontian Van Hattem, who lived from 1641 to 1706, is the most remarkable. So influential was he over some minds as to originate a heresy called Hattemism—which is evidently a Spinozistic theology. He affirms that the capital error of the vulgar is to represent God and man as separate beings, so that man is made to exist outside of, and apart from God, and in like manner, God apart from man. He affirms this objective idea of God, as the separately perfect, most wise, and omnipotent being to be an idol—to be in fact Satan. The true conception is the perfect union of man by faith with Christ or God. The believer cannot correctly regard himself as self-complete and self-contained, but only as a part of that whole of which Christ is the head, for Christ also is the foundation of all existence. The natural issue of such a system was that Van Hattem was led to assert that the only sin is believing in sin. Nor on the same ground can there be any personal virtue. Such ideas are a revolt against the necessity of things, which necessity is the Holy Spirit. The only sin is the vulgar idea of the separate existence of God and man, and this error leads to the further errors of personal independence and responsibility.

It is not difficult to trace similar influences of Spinozism in certain, once famous mystics, such as Eckhart, Tauler, and Suso. A kind of mystic Pantheism became endemic in Holland and Flanders, and Poiret and Antoinette Bourignon held only in different forms a belief in the substantial unity of God and man. So dangerous had Spinoza's principle proved in its fructification. In one aspect it seemed likely only to grow outside the sphere of religion; in another we find it vigorous even in the higher regions of enthusiasm, and potent to contemplative mystics who had acquired a reputation for unusual faith. To trace the various ramifications of Spinoza's principles in different times, creeds, and countries, would indeed be interesting, and also instructive, as demonstrating how perilous it is to depart from a clearly conceivable distinctness between God and man.

In our own country we even now occasionally see the direct and paramount influence of Spinozism, both speculative and practical.

One instance of this will suffice. In a work recently published, and entitled "Benedict De Spinoza, His Life, Correspondence, and Ethics," Dr. R. Willis notes (p. xxiii.,) as "one of Spinoza's special claims to the consideration of mankind, his broad assertion fo the eternal changeless character of the natural laws of God, accepted unconditionally now in the world of science, still very far, it is much to be deplored, from being admitted in the world of morals and religion. Well would it assuredly be for mankind were God preached to them as the author of eternal changeless and inexorable law, and neither a deity to be bought off from his resolves, by a price of any kind, even the sacrifice of that which is nearest and dearest, as the Jews of old conceived him; nor by lip-service, or even heart-felt repentance, to be induced to pardon sin, condone misdeed, and take the evil-doer into his favour, as the modern Christians hold. God never forgives transgression."

Spinoza himself in a letter to W. Van Bleyenberg, argues openly for the nonentity of Sin, and affirms that what we call such is only an imperfection, that it cannot exist positively, because it would be contrary to the will of God, and " it would imply great imperfection in God could anything be done contrary to His will. Further he adds, " Sins, inasmuch as they indicate imperfections only, consist in nothing expressive of reality; and of this nature were the determination of Adam to eat of the fruit, and his act of eating."

Buddhism.—A close resemblance may be traced between the systems of Buddha and Spinoza in some of their stronger outlines, and there is also some similarity between the two founders themselves.

According to modern students of Buddhism and its founder, he early retired from the world and betook himself to voluntary poverty and the elaboration of this system, until he died (as some say) in his forty-fifth year. At the same age died Spinoza, who had likewise led a life of voluntary poverty and meditative seclusion. Buddha had in effect taught the substantial unity of all existence, and thus destroyed all human individuality. So did Spinoza. The latter indeed supposed the existence of a God, but, as already shown, not the God personal, and not the Creator. Buddha taught no God, but the practical issue of both systems is nearly the same. We may even call Spinozism the Western Buddhism, and it is notable that the simple self-denying lives both of Buddha and Spinoza, though similar in character, have independently elicited like admiration from those who denounce their systems. So true is this that we find a recent student and expositor of Buddhism, namely M. Barthelemy St. Hilare, declares that with the single exception of Jesus Christ, he finds no character more worthy of admiration than that of Buddha. Yet this very critic strongly exposes the absurdity and wickedness of Buddhism.

The Buddhists of Nepaul, indeed, suppose that there is a supreme Creator whom they call "Adi Buddha;" but in Ceylon the same term would mean *ancient* or former, that is, one who existed previous to Buddha, but who was of the same order, and possessed the same attributes.

Assuming the fact of a continual succession of human transmigrations, Gotama Buddha taught as fundamental truths that wherever there is existence there is sorrow; that man's great object should be to free himself from sorrow by freeing himself from the various sequences of existence; that he destroyed himself by cleaving to sensuous objects; that only by freeing himself from the sequences of existence could he escape evil and attain to Nirvâna. This word is Sanscrit and may mean the "City of Peace," but however it be interpreted, in the Buddhist creed it signifies nonentity. The best authorities agree that it means total annihilation.

In Buddhism there can be no real individuality—no *ego;*—for it teaches that the supremely happy are those in whom the pride of *I am* is subdued. Things are not what they are commonly called. For example, the aggregate of a number of things, such as wood, leather, and brass, is called a *chariot*, yet this is but a name. So, likewise, the aggregate of a number of things, such as brain, blood, and flesh, is called a *man*, which also is a mere name, for, apart from the things aggregated, there is no man. There being, therefore, no real individuality, when a sentient being like man dies, all the elements of his existence are broken up and pass away, and exist no longer. His actions, however, still live, and possess a kind of potentiality. Nirvâna or nonentity, is the blessed end of all.

Never has there been a more rigidly atheistic system than this, which reduces man to a temporary organization, and refers all events, and all that we term creation and existence, to a non-intelligent power. It accounts for all existence without God; it requires no intervention but that of Nature. It begins in non-intelligence and ends in nonentity. No distinct trace of God is found in it from beginning to end.

This system has been by some much admired, partly because of its supposed originality and partly because of the virtues practised by its ascetic devotees; but it is really entitled to no such admiration, for under specious disguises it is, as one who has carefully studied it says, " nothing but a tissue of contradictions, and looking only at its best side it may be affirmed without calumniating it, that it is spiritualism without a soul, virtue without duty, morality without liberty, charity without love, a world without nature and God."

One ever-recurring difficulty in endeavouring to unfold such systems as Buddhism and Spinozism, or to exhibit their ultimate tendencies, arises from the incompleteness of the expositions of their respective founders. We have to gather up their systems from fragmentary statements, from imperfect and partial and separate expositions. Hence, at any stage a partisan may start up and say— " Sakya-Muni did not say this, or Spinoza did not say that. The one or the other is inaccurately explained by you; in this respect or in that you misapprehend his meaning." In reply to such objections it can only be said when propounders of systems declare them only piecemeal, and explain their views themselves only partially and progressively, leaving much to conjecture, and carefully guarding them by reserve, against opposition and confutation, giving forth portion by portion, position by position, the baffled expounder is justified in making the best he can out of an incoherent and uncompacted mass of materials, and must not be blamed for misapprehension.

X.

SPINOZA AND LEIBNITZ: THE SIGNIFICANCE OF THE INDIVIDUAL.

HAD it not been for a passage in one of the letters of Leibnitz, it would not have been known to us that he and Spinoza met once or oftener, and conversed for several hours on philosophic subjects. Such meetings would indeed be a good subject for a philosophical artist, who could fitly and expressively depict a humble Dutch chamber, poorly furnished, at the Hague, with two men engaged in earnest but calm conversation. One is a swarthy, slender, olive-complexioned, consumptive Jew, and is of Spanish aspect; having well-formed features, penetrating eyes, and dark hair,* who spends nearly all his time

---

* Some of these particulars of Spinoza's person are from Leibnitz's brief notice. It is uncertain how often Leibnitz visited Spinoza; we can be sure only of the one visit here mentioned.

solitarily in this forlorn apartment. What little money he requires for absolute necessities he earns by polishing lenses; yet he needs very little, for he lives whole days on milk soup, with an occasional pot of beer, or a pint of thin wine. He indulges in no luxury except a tobacco pipe; in no amusement but that of seeking out spiders, which he brings together for battle; or throwing flies into a spider's web, and contemplating the mortal struggle of the insects with a philosophical pleasure, which sometimes expresses itself in loud laughter. Yet this man's poverty was voluntary, for he courteously declined the offer of a large sum of money from a friend who desired to see him live in comfort. Nor would he allow the same friend to bequeath his property to him, but declared that it ought to go to his friend's natural heir. He was a Pantheist, but yet not a profligate, nor was he irreligious, but most religious after his own fashion. "Does *he* cast off religion," inquired Spinoza on one occasion, "who rests all he has to say on the subject on the ground that God is to be acknowledged as the Supreme Good, that He is with entire single-ness of soul to be loved as such, and that in loving God consists our highest bliss, our best privilege, our most perfect freedom; that the reward of virtue is virtue itself, and the punishment of meanness is baseness of spirit." Nevertheless, his devoutness seems to influence him rather in spite of his system than as the fruit of it. He reveres God in name; but while he preserves His name he abolishes His distinct personality. How can an individual man intelligently worship the God whom he refuses to individualize, and with whom he is abstractedly bound up in one universal substance?

The opposite of Spinoza in ultimate philosophical and religious tendencies, though at one time confessedly inclining to his doctrine, is the middle-sized, prosperous-looking German who now visits him, and converses with him for some hours. A faithful record of that conversation would have been precious indeed, but all we know of it is that Spinoza failed to see the force of some arguments urged upon him by his visitor. They parted never to meet again. Spinoza lived only for a short time afterwards, attempting to perfect his system of Pantheism. He died in his forty-fifth year, probably in the same poor room wherein he had talked with Leibnitz, and during the absence at church on a certain Sunday of the humble family in whose house he lodged, and with whom he was sometimes pleased to talk as a friend and counsellor. Who in that house and at that time could have supposed that this impoverished spectacle-maker had been writing books which were to be the subject of earnest controversy, and to make his name known over half of Europe? How could this be suspected when most of his works were unpublished, and appeared only in 1667, a few months after his death, under the obscure title of "B. B. S. Opera Posthuma." He had indeed published one work seven years before, but the storm of objections which it raised deterred him from a second and similar venture.

Yet this passing German visitor became his avowed philosophical opponent. While the Jew of the Hague laboured in his studious solitude to excogitate a logical system wherein the universe, including God and man, is but one vast consubstantiated existence, in which individuality is merged in a necessary unity, the Saxon metaphysician aimed to elaborate an equally vast and all-embracing system, which, though thrown out to the public piecemeal, may yet be gathered from his philosophical works when studied collectively, and which strives as clearly to establish individuality as Spinoza did to extinguish it.

Leibnitz sought to give to his philosophy a mathematical strictness and certainty, and at the same time to reconcile its doctrines with those of theology. By him the universe is contemplated in the threefold relation of (1) its elements; (2) their manner of connection; and (3) the end of their combinations. He names the doctrine of elements *monadologic*. He held the mutual relations of these elements to be developed in a pre-established harmony; while he represented the final end of creation to be *Optimism*. In his view the amazing variety of compound material bodies, by which we are surrounded, implies the existence of elements, of which these compounds are the results, and the nature of these elements is to be ascertained according to the laws of thought. By applying his fancied principle of the Sufficient Reason, it may be demonstrated that matter can consist neither of parts which are infinitely divisible, nor of atoms possessed of figure and extension. Its elements, therefore, must be simple, unextended forces, or *Monads*, in which we obtain the *à priori* idea of substance. The individuality of these monads must consist in the different series of internal change through which each one passes in the course of its existence. In these series each successive change is termed a Perception, and every monad is a living mirror, giving forth, after its own fashion, a picture of the universe, which is thus one vast collection of spiritual forces. These necessary elements of concrete existence cannot all be reduced to one class or order, but are distinguished by different degrees of perception and active power. Some are destitute of conscious perception, and these are the elements which form the material world. The animating principle of the lower animals comes next; and then the self-conscious souls of men, containing in themselves the fountains of necessary truth. These three classes of created forces or substances must have a sufficient reason for their existence. There cannot be an infinite series of contingents, and if there could be, still the final reason, even if such were infinite series, could be found only in a necessary substance. In this way creation must involve the existence of One Supreme Infinite, the *monas monadum*, from whom all that is finite has been derived, and in whose existence it all finds its due explanation. God, who is this Supreme Substance, is the fountain of all reality;

and the attributes of the created monads, as far as they are perfect, result from the perfection of God Himself; as far as they are imperfect, from the necessary imperfection of the creature.

In respect of the mutual relations of the elementary forces of creation, as the monads cannot have either figure or extension in themselves, their co-existence and relations must sufficiently account for the phenomena of extension, duration, and body. Thus space and time have merely an ideal and relative existence, resulting from the relation of monads, regarded as co-existing or in succession. God " in the beginning " launched the elements into being, having resolved for each one of them a determinate history throughout eternity, and a history which should harmonize with that of every other one. From the given state of any monad at any time, the Eternal Geometer can find the state of the universe, past, present, and to come. The apparent action of finite monads upon each other is not the result of mere intercausation, but of that original harmonious arrangement of God, in virtue of which He secures without failure, those ends which he contemplated when the universe came from His hands. The phenomena attendant upon the union of soul and body—of the self-conscious monads and the related monads of an inferior order, are counted as capable of explanation on the same general principle. The successive changes of the soul must exactly tally with those of the body, yet without any mutual action. They are related as two clocks, of which the one points to the hour exactly as the other strikes; or else as separate parts of the same clock.*

Upon the *end* of this combination of monads it is sufficient to add that the pre-established harmony is a revelation of Divine perfection in a scheme of Optimism. Every possible universe was conceived in the mind of God from eternity; but as one of these only can be translated from potential into actual existence, that one must be the best: although this best universe includes moral and natural evil in itself, the latter is the harmonious consequent of the former, and a reaction against it. The mystery of sin is not to be explained by the resolution of evil into good, for sin is essentially evil. But sin is necessarily involved in the *idea* of this best possible of universes, which it is better, notwithstanding its evil, to translate out of the possible into the actual, than to have no uni-

* North British Review, No. IX., article "Leibnitz."

verse. Thus the created universe must be the harmony of one great theocracy, expressive of the attributes of the one Perfect Being.

Brief and inadequate as this epitome is, it is sufficient to show the main object of Leibnitz, viz., to refute Pantheism by Monadology,—and to indicate the metaphysical and moral relations of the Divine Being with the universe as His creation; and it is here noticed as an elaborate scheme of individualism in opposition to all leading to the extinction of the individual. However illusory it may be, it is unquestionably more acceptable than Spinozism, and at least equally well constructed. Indeed as a mere philosophical structure it may claim our consideration and admiration while we have fears for its stability. It may be resolvable into idealism, and there may be truth in the objection that " by his subtle process of reasoning, Leibnitz virtually excludes the possibility of an external world. The last result of his analysis is a created aggregate of unextended spiritual forces, of various orders, of which the mutual relations, as collocated in bodies, originate the phenomena of the visible creation. The demonstrative metaphysic of Leibnitz has parted with body and extension before it has resolved nature into its elements; while the experimental philosophy of Berkeley fails to extract from the phenomena of perception the evidence of a substance different in kind from the self-conscious spirit which perceives them. Nevertheless we could name at least two German philosophers of very recent date and considerable influence, who are disposed to place faith in the Monadology of Leibnitz, and to think it worthy of serious study.

What we have to maintain as a superstructure upon our present and conscious personality as men is—the significance of every individual of our race. This is both *natural* and *moral*; —natural in relation to surrounding nature simultaneously existing with us, and moral in relation to our spiritual existence present and future. Blot out the *moral*, and man is merely a superior animal, and significant only in proportion to his structural and social superiority to the various living creatures of his era. Blot out the *natural* significance of individual man and the moral seems to want a basis—combine the two and you have his twofold pre-eminence, the one visible, the other inwardly conscious.

No philosophical scheme can be held consistently with Christianity which does not admit and support our individual significance; for our idea of responsibility, of future judgment, of a high and conscious immortality—in short, all our hopes and joys are built upon this foundation; and therefore it is assumed and enforced in Holy Scripture. Limit man to a mere natural significance, and we flutter for a time and then fall like the fowls of the air. But "ye are of more value than many sparrows,"—although both bird and man are cared for by the paternal Provider. And our significance is *individual* in its strictest sense, for it is undivided and indivisible. It springs up into existence in time, it spreads and grows out with all eternity. It is personal responsibility allied to personal identity. That something undefinable by us in words, but of which we are continually conscious—that identity which every man is confident he possesses in the midst of all surrounding changes;—that one fixed central point around which the whole circumference of things turns in relation to self; yes, that one thing is intimately associated with our individual significance for all time and all states of being. The Almighty Father in the highest sense manifests individual significance to every individual creature, while He has created us to possess an individual significance in relation to Him. He is the central sun, which divinely and diversely radiates light and heat to every one of his creatures who star-like revolve around him. Confound them with him—consubstantiate your substance with his, and there can be no distinct system of divine and human beings, for in such case you make sun and stars to be one and the same; you destroy all significance of separate courses or orbits. There can be nothing of diverse natures when all is lost in one central and universal substance.

There is a place and purpose marked out for every man by his Creator, and the manner in which action and feeling are developed in him in relation to a particular place and purpose, constitute the significance of his individuality. An analogical illustration of this truth may be drawn from a theory which Mr. Darwin has recently proposed as a provisional hypothesis to account for certain observed phenomena, under the name of *Pangenesis*. He assumes that the germ-cells of animals and plants are capable of generating minute bodies, named cell-gemmules, which become diffused through all parts of an organism, and are capable of multiplying and uniting with others like themselves, and that when

SIGNIFICANCE OF THE INDIVIDUAL. 185

this union does not take place, they may remain in a dormant state. In this state they may be compared to seeds lying dormant in the earth, and such cell-gemmules may remain undeveloped for many generations. The number of cell-gemmules in an undeveloped embryo may be almost infinite in number, but each one has a potential development. At one time, it was thought a microscopic cell was quite small enough for our observation and theorizing; but now we are called upon in addition to imagine that there are numerous minuter molecules in each germ or ovule, in which the characteristics of remote progenitors may be always present and some day powerful.

Here then, whether Pangenesis shall be proved by further observation to be a truth, or a mere imagination,—here at least we have an available suggestion in relation to our present doctrine. In every man morally viewed there may be a Spiritual Pangenesis. He may be created not simply as a natural individual, like any one of the inferior animals which he beholds; but he may be primarily endowed with an almost infinite number of germs which may lie dormant in him for centuries of his existence. Yet each one of these numberless gemmules may carry with it a particular potentiality of unlimited development—may carry such potentiality through death and the grave, and though lying dormant there yet not be dead. Each gemmule may mysteriously enfold some principle of the individual which imparts to him a distinct personality ; thousands of such gemmules may preserve and impart his entire personality to the man, and in them may lie sleeping his individual significance through ages of eternity. If through centuries of earthly time an unsuspected and invisible gemmule preserves for the body hereditary characteristics of a remote progenitor ; if in human successions there be present some such physiological persistence as this ; surely it is not unnatural to presume that there is a spiritual persistence of a like kind. Every part of the human body periodically changes, but yet the gemmules are supposed to remain in being through all corporeal changes. The forces of Nature do not destroy them; they are unharmed by the powers of chemistry, and invulnerable to all the quick agents of decay which abound in air, and sea, and earth. Where then is the improbability of a perpetual individual significance founded upon undeveloped and inherent germs, and developed in successional lines through incalculable periods? The human totality may carry with it its mysterious multitude of thought germs, and wherever and whenever some one or more of these becomes operative and powerful, a wonderful growth and unfolding may take effect, which may prolong and continue the significance of an individual who once dwelt for a few years upon this earth, little knowing at that time his unbounded capacities for the growth of good—or alas, it may be—of evil!

A remarkable distinctive feature of the teaching of Jesus Christ and of the Gospel of Grace, is the significance therein of every individual of our race. If we look at man apart from his relation to God, and his possible participation in the Gospel personally revealed by Jesus Christ, he seems to possess no marked, and certainly no abiding significance. The Ministry of Nature to man is, not one of Grace but of Law. By nature man stands structurally highest, intellectually noblest; but if he have no superiority beyond that of structure and natural capability, he must inevitably pass away into the ultimate insignificance of all that is of the earth earthy. For of all the enormous mass of extinguished vitality which composes the substrata upon which man now walks and labours, no fossil creature ever possessed more than the simple significance of its little hour and partial relationship to its kind. When its life was over, it went into dust, and now takes its place only in the constituency of earth and the chronology of ancient existences.

The same holds true of the human race apart from its possible becomings in the Divine economy of Grace. Substract these possibilities, and the history of ancient man is simply geological or historical—simply his relation to prehistoric or else historic times. And this kind of history is that of races, not of individuals: it is the significance of the genus not of the individual. Millions of mankind may have lived, and probably have lived on this earth, of whom we know nothing, and at present possess not a relic. They may or may not have flourished before or shortly after the great Glacial Period. We may conjecture or deny their existence; we may speculate on the possibility of their living, or on the probability of their sudden destruction by the cold desolation of a reign of life-destroying ice. To our knowledge the result of their existence in incalculable ages of the geological past is of no value except as a question of scientific discovery and climatic relation. The great glacial winter was the same in all its intensity and rigidity whether man felt it or felt it not.

The essential difference lies in the existence of man as known to us in the Kingdom of Grace, and contemplated by us as an immortal being destined to the everlasting enjoyment or loss of God's favour. Jesus Christ saw and taught the vastly superior importance of man as based upon his individual significance. He saw man not merely as he was, but as he might be, and as he would be. Think only of the helpless cripple, the wretched outcast, the blind and the palsied, the suffering and the sinful, the poor fisherman and the humble mechanic as they are, and as they will be in a few years of misery and obscurity; and what are they more than the worm that crawls, the insect that hums away its hour, and the bird that falls an easy prey to the fowler? Take them in the unsightly and corrupting mass, and what is earth the worthier for them, what are they the better for earth? For a time they cumber the ground, and then the ground covers them. Of whole generations of such human beings, it can only be said as of old, "Like sheep they are laid in the grave; death shall feed on them."

On the other side, contemplate all these beings as having a personal and endless significance in the eyes of their Creator; each one as possessing in himself the germ of an eternal unfolding of life and character, every germ known and appreciated by Him who imparted it—all its possibilities foreseen,—all its actualities anticipated. Contemplate man thus, and temporal distinctions pass into nothing. Man is man, not in his pomp or in his poverty, not in his vigour or in his infirmity, but he is man in the countless contingencies of his everlasting being. He is man in his capability of rescue from death of the spirit; man in his relation to the Redeemer of his race; man in his opportunity of restoration to God; man not as clothed in purple and fine linen, or in rags and shame, but man as one day to be "clothed upon" with garments beyond the fabrication of his own hand; to be clothed with a deathless life and unaging incorruption.

The spiritual significance of every one of us constitutes his heritage in Jesus Christ. In this lies his individual importance, that Christ died for him as though he were all, and for all our race as though they all were one. In this too lies the unspeakable blessing that every one of us may feel his particular significance to God in Christ. Death-doomed dust as we all are by nature, we are by divine favour in a higher sense, deathless, and our deathlessness will confer importance upon what would be naturally insignificant. When I regard with astonishment the perfection of parts in the minute polyzoön under the microscope, and when I see it perishing even while under observation, I lament its loss and wonder why such beauty of form and such marvellously adapted vital mechanism should be so frail, and so elusive. But were I to suppose for a moment that the race to which I belong, is only by so much the more complex in organization as I find it, and so much the longer in duration as I see it, and yet nothing more, nothing higher, nothing nobler than earthly clay; I should more bitterly mourn over his loss than over that of all the marvellous creatures in the inferior kingdoms of nature, and I should mourn over man the more bitterly in proportion to his bodily superiority and his far higher intellectual capacity. When, however, I superadd his future hopes to his present superiority, he transcends the dominion of outward nature and becomes a child of God and an inheritor of the Kingdom of Heaven.

Pantheism and Optimism.—If we reluctantly decline to accept the Optimism of Leibnitz, we decidedly reject the pessimism of Spinoza. If we seriously doubt whether we live in the best possible of all worlds, we altogether deny that we live in the worst. And a worse world than that of Spinozism it is difficult to conceive, unless it be one of avowed and complete Atheism. The difference indeed is only small, and chiefly verbal, in any form of material Pantheism. As already stated, Spinoza himself was not without a God and a religion of his own fashion; insomuch that he has been called the God-intoxicated philosopher. He was indeed, in one sense, full of God, since his God was all fulness and all existence. But the grandeur with which he seems to invest his God was vague and visionary, and to agree with him in his conclusions we have to condone his *petitio principii* respecting Substance. We do not allow that all substance is one; there may be innumerable substances or modes of substance. In the world of spirits who will believe that all substance is one? In that world there may be grade after grade of spiritual substance, almost infinite kinds of corporeality, as well as another mode of personality.

Pantheism, then, is radically and resultingly unsound. Spinozism is unsound in its logical root, and unhealthy, as well as unchristian, in its practical fruit. All the momentous consequences of individual significance are lost in its cold grasp. The human soul is in each man's esteem the most invaluable of his possessions, but upon Spinoza's system, man is merely a soul united to a body. As a soul, he is a mode of the thought of God. As a body, he is a mode of his extension. Man is the identity in God of the human soul and the human body. The human soul is nothing but a mode of that Divine substance. So in another way is the human body. As a general result of Spinoza's psychology, to use his own words, "the human soul is a spiritual automaton."*

Were such the truth, there could be no individual responsibility or significance; hence our aim to set forth the importance of these principles in opposition to Pantheism.

But some may ask, "Why dwell so long

---

* Spinoza de Intell. Emen. ii., p. 306. Saisset on Religious Philosophy, vol. i.

upon Pantheism? It is a slain foe, long since dead and entombed, and no sensible man now heeds or adheres to Spinoza, or to any form of Pantheism." " Why, then, it may be questioned in reply, " are the works of Spinoza re-edited and republished? Why do they offer a commercial reward to publishing enterprize? So far from being a forgotten and abandoned dream, there are around us too many and too painful proofs that in certain adaptations and disguises the Pantheistic doctrine reappears, and as of old strives for the mastery. There are so many and such subtle modifications of it that it sometimes appears to have taken hold even of professedly Christian writers. The author of the only extensive essay on Pantheism in the English language is the Rev. John Hunt, "curate of St. Ives," and he declares in his book (p. 374) that " Pantheism is on all hands acknowledged to be the theology of reason—of reason it may be in its impotence, but still of such reason as man is gifted with in the present life. It is the philosophy of religion, the philosophy of all religions. It is the goal of Rationalism, of Protestantism, of Catholicism, for it is the goal of thought."

Of what other character than materially

Pantheistic are the current theories that deny or render needless continuous Creation, and attribute all we see and are to a nebulous evolution? What is Mr. Darwin's theory but an avowed negation of specific creation? What are his Natural and Sexual Selection but applications, under some modifications, of Spinoza's "Natura naturans?" In his general summary at the end of his work on the "Descent of Man," (pp. 385-6) Mr. Darwin assures us that the main conclusion arrived at in that work is that man is not specially created by God, but descended from some less highly organized form. "The grounds," says he, "upon which this conclusion rests will never be shaken, for the close similarity between man and the lower animals in embryonic development, as well as in innumerable points of structure and constitution, both of high and of the most trifling importance,—the rudiments which he retains, and the abnormal reversions to which he is occasionally liable—are facts which cannot be disputed. They have long been known, but until recently they told us nothing with respect to the origin of man. Now, when viewed by the light of our knowledge of the whole organic world, their meaning is unmistakeable. The great principle of evolution stands up clear and firm, when these groups of facts are considered in connection with others, such as the mutual affinities of the members of the same group, their geographical distribution in past and present times, and their geological succession. It is incredible that all these facts should speak falsely. He who is not content to look, like a savage, at the phenomena of nature as disconnected, cannot any longer believe that man is the work of a separate act of creation. . . . All (facts) point in the plainest manner to the conclusion that man is the co-descendant with other mammals of a common progenitor."

As it now devolves upon us to consider the bearing of such teaching upon the accepted view of Divine Creation, we shall aim at the same time to show the tendency of the purely naturalistic doctrines of our day. This will render desirable a concise exposition of Mr. Darwin's theory of the Origin of Species, first, in its zoological and scientific merits, and afterwards in relation to its conflict with religious opinions, not simply with particular creeds professed by some divisions of the Christian Church, but in its presumed warfare with many of the first principles of the Christian Faith.

XI.

THEORIES AND IDEAS OF SPECIES. THE HYPOTHESIS OF MR. DARWIN.

THE very limited knowledge which even otherwise highly educated persons possess of Natural Science, is a formidable impediment to the full and critical consideration of any theory relating to it. If we assume the existence of even some acquaintance with its elementary principles, we fee' that we may assume too much, while it is impossible to afford adequate information in such a volume as the present without disproportionate treatment of one subject.

Moreover, when advocates of a particular hypothesis, like Mr. Darwin and Mr. Wallace, enter the arena, they are furnished with an amount of special knowledge which can only be the fortune of a few; and it would not only require a knowledge equal to theirs, but a number of volumes likewise as great as theirs, to answer them in detail, and even in part to controvert their theories.

All, then, that can be accomplished within a few pages is to state these theories as plainly as we are capable of stating them, and to supply a little elementary information in order to their comprehension, while presenting our objections, if we entertain them, in such a form as that they may be generally understood. Such a treatment excludes the application of many strictly scientific objections, restricts us to a few of easy apprehension, and confines us to what may be appreciated by the majority of the reading public. This preliminary impediment places the objector at a great disadvantage, and renders him liable to charges of incompetence and inconsideration, to which he must submit as he best can. Over him the theorists themselves have obvious and numerous advantages, independent of the truth of their theories. Mr. Darwin's views are especially difficult to estimate, since they are manifestly incomplete in his own mind, and are professedly put forth as hypothetical. Four works of his are now before the author, who has endeavoured to give them all, as they appeared, careful consideration. But in these volumes the indecisions and fluctuations of Mr. Darwin's mind are undeniable. He himself, with a most praiseworthy candour, confesses as much. No special theorist is more ready to acknowledge mistakes, modifications, and corrections; yet, while in this respect he wins our esteem, and gains a large amount of public credit, we must not on this account be precluded from weighing his hypotheses in the balance, and directing attention to their ulterior tendencies.

Animals and plants are arranged in groups distinguished summarily as Branches, Classes, Orders, Families, Genera, Species, and Varieties. But the vast number of organisms, when studied very carefully, occasion considerable difficulty in attempting to form a complete and accurate classification of them. Species in particular have been multiplied immensely, and sub-species and varieties have been added beyond measure. It is not easy to draw a distinct line between species and sub-species, between species and varieties; and again, between varieties and individuals. Lines have been sometimes drawn arbitrarily, and have seemed so questionable, that naturalists have denied their correspondence with actual natural distinctions. Many have denied all but individuals. This is the source of several theories of the transmutation of species, inclusive of the latest, namely that of Mr. Darwin.

It is important to possess as clear a conception as possible of what is meant by the term *Species* in Natural History. Without some aid, however, the reader will not easily form such a conception, as few who have employed the term have properly defined it. Cuvier explains it as meaning the collection of all the beings descended the one from the other, and from common parents, and of those which bear as close a resemblance to these as they bear to each other. De Candolle includes under one species all the individuals which bear to each other so close a resemblance as to allow of our supposing that they have proceeded originally from a single pair. Both of these definitions assume continuous descent from a primal pair, or protoplast; and Dr. Morton defines species in the same manner, as "a group of individuals descended from a primordial organic form." In this definition he has a special reference to man and his descent from a common pair. Professor Dana defines the term as "a specific amount or condition of concentrated force defined in the law or act of creation."

Many still believe, and perhaps until of recent years most naturalists believed, that each species is definable, and also permanently reproductive, though variable within narrow limits, and incapable of intermixture with other species. In this view, Species is not merely a designation of convenience, like many terms in Natural Science, but an actual existence. "The species," says Dr. Dawson in his Archaia, "is not merely an ideal unit; it is a unit in the work of creation. Creation refers to certain original individuals, protoplasts formed after their kinds or species, and representing the powers and limits of variation inherent in the species—the potentialities of their existence. The species, with all its powers and capabilities for reproduction, is the Creator's unit in his work, and our unit in study. The individuals are so many masses of organized matter, in which for the time the powers of the species are embodied, and the only animal having a true individuality is man, etc. The species is different, not in degree, but in kind from the genus, the order, and the class. We recognize a general resemblance in a series of line engravings representing different subjects, but only a specific unity in those struck from the same plate. The species differs from all other groups in not being an ideal entity, but consisting of individuals struck from the same die, produced by continuous reproduction from the same creative source."

According to Flourens, that which determines species is not the form, but its interior characteristics, especially fecundity. Continuous fecundity principally characterizes the Species, limited fecundity the Genus, and the absence of fecundity characterizes the Order. Species are distinct from genera, for the decisive reason that they have but a limited fecundity beyond themselves. Buffon had shown that the comparison of the resemblance of animals is but an accessory idea, and often independent of the constant succession of individuals by generation—for the ass is more like the horse than the water spaniel is like the greyhound; yet the two latter are but one species, since they together produce individuals which can themselves produce others in the same way, whereas the ass and the horse produce together only faulty and sterile animals.

Perhaps the clearest and most correct statement of the bearing of those conceptions of species is found in Sir Charles Lyell's recapitulation of inquiry into this subject, in his "Principles of Geology," where he has devoted three chapters to it:

"*Recapitulation.*—For the reasons, therefore, detailed in this and the two preceding chapters, we may draw the following inferences in regard to the reality of *species* in Nature.

"1st. That there is a capacity in all species to accommodate themselves, to a certain extent, to a change of external circumstances, the extent varying greatly, according to the species.

"2nd. When the change of situation which they can endure is great, it is usually attended by some modifications of the form, colour, size, structure, or other particulars; but the fluctuations thus superinduced are governed by constant laws, and the capability of so varying forms part of the permanent specific character.

"3rd. Some acquired peculiarities of form, structure, and instinct are transmissible to the offspring; but these consist of such qualities and attributes only as are intimately related to the natural wants and propensities of the species.

"4th. The entire variation from the original type which any given kind of change can produce, may usually be affected in a brief period of time, after which no further deviation can be obtained by continuing to alter the circumstances, though ever so gradually; indefinite divergence, either in the way of improvement or deterioration being prevented, and the least possible excess beyond the defined limits being fatal to the existence of the individual.

"5th. The intermixture of distinct species is guarded against by the aversion of the individuals composing them to sexual union, or by the sterility of the mule offspring.

"It does not appear that true hybrid races have ever been perpetuated for several generations, even by the assistance of man; for the cases usually cited relate to the crossing of mules with individuals of pure species, and not to the intermixture of hybrid with hybrid.

"6th. From the above considerations, it appears that species have a real existence in Nature, and that each was endowed at the time of its creation with the attributes and organization by which it is now distinguished."*

* "Principles of Geology." Eighth edition, pp. 588—9. This author's views are now entirely changed.

In direct opposition to these views of the distinctness of species, and of their individual creation, stand all those theories which, in one form or another, may be ranked under the general terms of Transmutation or Development. It is not easy to extract from the various advocates of such hypotheses, precise and defined views, but the leading supporters of them have advocated opinions which may be thus simply expressed. (1.) That all the genera of future plants, organized bodies of all kinds, and the reproducible parts of them were really contained in the first germ. (2.) That species were not produced by independent creation, but that, under the operation of a general law, the germs of organisms produced new forms, different from themselves when particular circumstances called the law into action. (3.) That these evoking circumstances have occurred in definite order, and in conformity with a great preordained form, whereby the scheme of life has ever been kept in harmony with the ordinal rank which now prevails among plants and animals.

The most distinguished exponent now living of such a theory, is Mr. Charles Darwin, whose work "On the Origin of Species," has been warmly welcomed by those who hold to transmutational development. In this interesting volume Mr. Darwin introduces a large number of natural phenomena which he claims as supports to his hypothesis. Disentangled from many circumlocutions and much obscurity, when stated as concisely as possible, the views advocated by this eminent Naturalist are these :—

Species are not fixed and distinct, but mutable, and there has been, and now is, a gradual evolution of one species out of another. Two great causes or laws effect this evolution.

(1.) *Natural Selection*, or the law of the conservation of the favourable variations of beings and the elimination of injurious deviations—in other words an incessant and inherent power of Nature to reject that which is bad, and to preserve and assist that which is good.

(2.) *The Struggle for Existence*, or the perpetual contest which all living beings wage with each other for the means of existence, from the carnivorous animal which devours its prey, to the plant which chokes its neighbour.

The law of Natural Selection is founded on the supposition that each new species forms and maintains itself by the help of some advantage which it possesses over those with which it meets, and from which inevitably results the destruction of forms less favourable. This law Mr. Darwin believes to have been in operation from the time of the first appearance of life on our earth.

The Struggle for Existence comes in aid of Natural Selection, by destroying the weaker and rejected creatures. This, indeed, is only a generalization of the law of Mr. Matthews and the application of it to all organic existence.

Endeavouring further to simplify and represent fairly Mr. Darwin's hypothesis, it is considered that the following is a plain and concise statement of it in connection with the operation of the main causes just specified.

Looking at our entire fauna and flora, or animal and vegetable kingdoms, the whole are bound together in one continuous series, and in such unbroken continuity that it is impossible to decide where one species ends and another begins, and that therefore there does not exist a multitude of distinct species as commonly supposed. To account for this continuity of animate beings, Mr. Darwin supposes that they all sprang from one or a few primordial forms—at most perhaps eight or ten, because we can discern some eight or ten unbroken series of animate beings, if the missing links in each chain be allowed to have existed, although there are no actual proofs of their having existed. In all these chains one being succeeds to another by almost insensible variations, or changes of structure, but organs found, in the process of these changes, to be rudimentary in one being, are seen in perfection in another being lower down in the same chain.

The continuity in each chain is the result of the descent of all its links from one common ancestor. The differences between any two members of each living chain are due to a law that any attributed change of structure in plant or animal is transmissible to its offspring. If favourable, it will be advantageous in the struggle for existence, and be perpetuated until again improved by accident. This hypothesis is thought sufficient to account for all the varieties in nature, and for the formation of every organ, however complex, of animal or vegetable. Mr. Darwin has even carried his views to the extreme of saying:—"Therefore I should infer from analogy that probably all the organic beings which have ever lived on this earth have descended from one form, into which life was breathed by the Creator."

It is not practicable or desirable in this

volume to enter either fully into Mr. Darwin's scientific details, or those of his opponents, for besides the space and time demanded for a full discussion of the hypothesis, it has been discussed by many writers, with various degrees of merit and at various lengths. The present author's principal aim in these pages is briefly to notice the assumptions on which the theory rests, to show its tendencies, and to advert to some radical objections to its truth. It is indeed but one of several theories of development, but claims special attention, since for some time past it has excited a wide and deep interest. We may observe that so many things are pure assumptions in this hypothesis, and so much is brought forward which is merely conjectural, that it is at best only tentative, and Mr. Darwin has made several candid admissions of the difficulties which may prevail against its general reception.

Of the numerous objections which lie against Darwin's hypothesis, it is sufficient to select some that are most forcible and readily intelligible. Flourens declares his conviction after long reflection, that Mr. Darwin confounds variability with mutability.

A very formidable objection against Darwinism is that a vast number of *transitional forms* should be apparent as the necessary consequence of the gradual passage of one species into another. Any reader will perceive on reflection that an universal and continuous development of organic beings through a long series of forms, must, if it has been in actual operation, disclose numerous mutations at its various stages, or show the existence at various stages, of forms intermediate between two species. Otherwise the connecting links in the living chain would be wanting. Yet there neither is in the organic beings now known to be living on earth, nor in the remains of animals as yet exhumed, a single decided and incontrovertibly admitted instance of a transitional variety.

The reply made to this serious objection is that the Geological Record is so imperfect—that we have so few fossils from out of the vast mass of ancient life—and that we at present know so little concerning the fulness of life in geological epochs, that in truth all conclusions drawn from what we now discover, must be insufficient. There may have been numerous transitional forms though we have not found them. Of the many volumes of palæontological history we have but, as it were, the last volume, and even that in an imperfect state.

The objection mentioned is regarded as weighty by Mr. Darwin himself, although he and his friends employ the answers just adverted to. A recent attempt to lighten it shapes itself into the assertion, "that Nature can produce a new type without our being able to see the marks of transition, and she can alter a whole race simultaneously without its passing through the phase of development from an individual in whom the entire change was first produced."* If Nature *can* do this, it remains to be shown that she ever *has* done it, and if she can do it without our seeing it, how are we to know that she can do it?

In conjunction with these objections, another may be offered to the hypothesis of a persistence of *profitable* variations in every species of plants and animals.

The hypothesis of Mr. Darwin absolutely requires that every variation or modification of an animal or plant, in order to become permanent, must be an *improvement*, whereby it is fitted for its existing condition. We can understand how

* "Geographical Distribution of Mammals." By Andrew Murray, 1866.

certain organs might become lengthened or modified by efforts towards their advantageous applications, upon such an hypothesis; but there are other organs which can be of no use whatever, until they obtain a certain degree of development. For example, until a bird's wing is sufficiently developed to enable the animal to lift itself in the air, it is absolutely useless. The partial development—the incomplete organ would be an impediment, so that whether the bird with perfect wings were developed from a fish or a quadruped, the intermediate stages would have greatly impeded the intermediate creatures. And that there must have been many such intermediate creatures is manifest, if we look at the great differences between birds, and all other vertebrate animals. So great are these that Mr. Darwin remarks, " We may account for the distinctness of birds from all other vertebrate animals by the belief that many ancient forms of life have been utterly lost."

But where could these lost forms have been, granting that they ever existed? They must have been intermediate, and must have borne organs in many intermediate and imperfect states; whi'e any animal approaching to a bird, yet not a bird, any animal with a half developed wing, together with or without other half developed organs at the same time, must have been a monstrosity, and either in respect of easy motion on the ground or any motion in the air, an inconvenient and painfully existing monstrosity. A creature between any known vertebrate animal and any known bird, in many and perhaps every preceding stage of development, could not have moved without difficulty or failure; and such failure must, in most cases, if not in all, have prevented the perfection and completeness of the after growth and structure. All such imperfections of structure must have been hindrances to freedom of action, and thereby to fulness of growth, and thereby again to success.

The more this objection is regarded, the more formidable, I think, it will probably be found. Not only have we no known intermediate forms, but if we had, we should see many of them labouring under a burden of half developed impediments to motion and improvement. Organs which are useless till perfect, must be long in coming to perfection, and just so long, a great inconvenience to the wearer. They would not be known to be improvements.

until they had begun to discharge their definite functions, or, if they were foreknown to be improvements, then every other variation must have been destroyed. By the hypothesis there have been no specific creations except a few primary forms in the far beginning, but all life has been an extremely slow development, and every result has come into existence by very small and very gradual additions or modifications. Therefore, for equally long periods, there must have been great transitional imperfections, and in the case of many organs useless until quite perfect, great transitional hindrances, extreme awkwardness of locomotion, and, as it must be confessed, continually increasing awkwardness until the rudimental became the perfect structure.

Assume various transitional developments for the purpose of illustration, and then the extreme difficulty, or clumsiness or inconvenience of existence in the intermediate stages will be apparent. It is manifestly impossible that in and during all such stages, every variation should have been an improvement to the animal exhibiting it, or could have been foreseen to tend to ultimate improvement by any conception which we can form of Nature or Natural Selection.

If with such ideas we look at the state of the organic world of life around us, and apply the Darwinian hypothesis to it, we must suppose ourselves to be living at some one stage of developed life, a stage which is not final but only transitional. We are not supposed to be now living at the ultimate epoch of perfect Nature, but only in one of the periods which lead towards it. All living creatures upon our earth, are, by hypothesis, developed from other forms in the past, and all are passing on by descent with modifications to higher forms in the future. Hence there should now be numerous and minute variations which clearly display every intermediate degree of transitional improvement; and further some other variations which are not beneficial, and which should therefore be in course of suppression and destruction. Where are these, and what indicates them?

The *facies* of every order of living things displays the contrary. In each order such transitional imperfections are wanting, and no naturalist points out their existence. By hypothesis, the *facies* of the total earthly fauna or flora ought to display them.

Furthermore not only ought the total terrestrial fauna and flora to have displayed them, plainly, but likewise most numerously and most minutely, for the transitions must have been at least as numerous as the individuals, and this in all biological time. If an appeal be made to Palæontology, then the absence of transitional links is not due to the casual imperfection of the record only, for strangely enough the Geological Record appears purposely to have omitted the preservation of these, and purposely to have preserved only the untransitional. The destructive probabilities were surely as great against the one as the other. If we discover fossils only by accident, at wide distances, and at considerable intervals, almost inevitably we should have discovered some of the one kind, as well as of the other. Granted that some parts of the ancient earth are better explored than others, nevertheless many parts have now been industriously explored, and yet of all the indefinitely numerous and of all the excessively various transitions which must by hypothesis have existed, none have been brought to light *in transitu*. What has been said of the fossil Archæopteryx, and other forms, allowing all to have its full weight, does not invalidate the general force of the preceding observations.

While the hypothesis advocated by Mr.

Darwin supposes an indefinite number of variations, and a ceaseless struggle for existence, we ask, what is the balance of probabilities in favour of the preservation of some over the extinction of others? If there be a ceaseless struggle amongst all, the consequences of the struggle must frequently be as disastrous against the one as the other; otherwise the continual survival of the fittest would amount to a certainty, and exclude probabilities. If all variations have to contend with repressing powers, it is hard to see upon a correct theory of probabilities, why useful variations alone in every case prevail. If they do in every instance so prevail, then their perpetual prevalence must be beyond any natural principle, and can be due only to some supranatural control. Assume an unintermitting action of destructive forces as operating in Nature against organic life, then how can we at the same time admit an unintermitting and concurrent action of opposingly conservative powers, the latter being always conservative in a particular direction, but yet recognized as only natural? Mr. Darwin says that in the struggle for existence a grain may turn the balance in favour of a particular structure which will thereby be preserved. Why, however, is the grain always found in one scale, and never in the other? Can any natural power always place this preponderant grain in one scale in order to outweigh another natural power in the other? When a house is divided against itself it must fall. Can Nature when divided against itself certainly stand?

In Mr. Darwin's subsequent work entitled "The Variation of Plants and Animals under Domestication," he assumes the same ground, but does not really strengthen his position. "If," says he, "organic beings had not possessed an inherent tendency to vary, man could have done nothing." To this we may reply, that man has done almost nothing. He has never originated a species, and he has never permanently varied a species. The tendency in animals and plants is not to vary, and if odd breeds be produced, still there is an inherent disposition to return, and not permanently to vary. "The immutability of species," says an anonymous writer concisely, "is maintained by two unconquerable laws—the ultimate sterility of breeds, and their reversion to the type when let alone. Man can influence size, which is a variation of individuals and not of species.

Man can modify the flowers and fruits of plants within certain inexorable limits, and obtain size, or flavour, or varying blooms, but specific characters elude his power entirely. Permanent reproduction is the fundamental idea of species, and there is no continuous fecundity in breeds, their sterility or reversion being inevitable. What man seems to be most able to transmit through several generations is diseases." This subject of fecundity is carefully and freely treated by M. Flourens in his refutation of Mr. Darwin's theory.

Another line of objection has been adopted by several critics, to the effect that the arguments for Darwin's theory are chiefly derived from the variations to be met with in animals and plants, which seldom occur in the wild state, but only after subjection to the control of man. Whenever under human control such variations do occur, they result in a weakening of the animal in respect of those qualities which render it most fit to maintain the struggle for life; and after a return to the wild state, the animal loses those qualities which it had acquired, and merges into the common stock. Were the theory of progressive and profitable development true, this result could not follow, but the animal would impart its own acquired properties to its descendants. Similar consequences may be witnessed in plants, as for instance in the rose and pine-apple, which, while by cultivation they gained properties agreeable to man, on the other hand lost the power of reproduction, and thus became weakened in the so-called struggle for life.

Much remains to be said in relation to the stability of species in the intervals of change, to the extent of specific stability, and several allied topics, but the discussion of them would be out of place in these pages and exceed their limits. Reference may be made for some of these considerations to the excellent recent book of Mr. St. George Mivart, on the Genesis of Species, (1871), and to an able critique of the Darwinian theory in the " North British Review" (June, 1867). To both of these I am indebted, and they are well worth attentive perusal. The Reviewer has dealt clearly and fairly with this theory, and concludes that " the chief arguments used to establish the theory rest on conjecture;" and after specifying the principal conjectural arguments, he adds, " We are asked to believe all these 'maybes' happening on an enormous scale, in order that we may believe the final Darwinian 'maybe,' as to the origin of species. The general form of his (Darwin's) argument is as follows:—'All these things may have been, therefore my theory is possible, and since my theory is a possible one, all those hypotheses which it requires are rendered probable.' There is little direct evidence that any of these maybes actually *have been*."

"What can we believe," he concludes by saying, "but that Darwin's theory is an ingenious and plausible speculation, to which future physiologists will look back with the kind of admiration we bestow on the atoms of Lucretius, or the crystal spheres of Eudoxus, containing like those some faint half truths, marking at once the ignorance of the age and the ability of the philosopher. Surely the time is past when a theory unsupported by evidence is to be received as probable, because in our ignorance we know not why it should be false, though we cannot show it to be true. Yet we have heard grave men gravely urge that because Darwin's theory was the most plausible known, it should be received." Let this be added, and many readers may have read it, as the assertion of a popular naturalist of our day, that to reject Darwin's theory is to reject all worthy of the name: that our choice lies between that and nothing.

Over and above the strictly scientific objections offered by disbelievers in the efficiency claimed for Natural Selection, there is one of the most menacing character, and at the same time readily comprehensible. This is strongly and I think successfully urged by the Reviewer above cited, and might even be enlarged, and so enforced as almost to overthrow the assumptions of Darwin in favour of Natural Selection. It is based upon Time. Mr. Darwin himself candidly confesses that he " who does not admit how incomprehensibly vast have been the past periods of time" may at once close his volume, thus acknowledging that an indefinite, if not infinite, time is demanded for his theory. Now, in point of lapse of time, the theory transcends all our knowledge and all probability. If we regard a period of two or three thousand years we are certain that no great change has been made in men or animals during that time, for the figures in Egyptian and other very ancient monuments display the same forms as now exist. Whatever unimportant change might be found within such a period, a very large number of years must be necessary to magnify this into an important change. Imagine twenty or thirty thousand years to be necessary to convert the unimportant into the important, still the animal would not greatly differ from its primeval form. Since the changes by hypothesis are immeasurably small and slow, we may go back to three hundred or four hundred thousand years, and even then discover essentially the same animal. How many hundreds of thousands or millions of years then would be required to discover an essentially different form —to convert a monkey into a man? Furthermore, when we take the extreme terms of transmutation, how many millions upon millions of years are indispensable for the agency of natural selection in converting a fly into an elephant, or a stickleback into a whale? Lastly, will any conceivable lapse of time suffice for transmuting a primordial germ into a perfect man?

Past time may for aught that is told us be indefinite in quantity, but as a fundamental element the rate of change should not be equally indefinite. Geology bears an adverse testimony, for it shows that innumerable ages have elapsed, each bearing countless generations of creatures, and none differing in a very great degree as to its physical conditions from those of our own age. In order to empower Natural Selection sufficiently, we must go back to ages even antecedent to observable geological evidence; and thus in respect of immensity of time we are wholly at fault.

Suppose that the probable time of the beginning of the very ancient Cambrian deposits was (as Mr. Wallace assumes) something approximating to twenty-four million years ago—we have that length of ages for the duration of the known fossils; and that confessedly is altogether insufficient for the great alleged changes by transmutation. Sir William Thomson of Glasgow has advanced arguments drawn from three distinct lines of scientific inquiry—(1) the action of the tides upon the earth's rotation; (2) the probable length of time in which the sun has illuminated our planet; (3) the temperature of the interior of the earth. The conclusion at which he arrives, as the result of his calculations, is that life on the earth, geological history, and the visible state of things must be brought within some such approximate point as one hundred millions of years.

Few adherents to Mr. Darwin would presume that the extensive effects attributed to Natural Selection could be accomplished within any such period. We must therefore postulate a vastly longer period, and refute the conclusions of Sir William Thomson, and show by others that many more millions of years have elapsed in terrestrial life-history. The theory of the gradual dissipation of energy is available against the immense time required by Darwin's Natural Selection; and is well applied by the writer of the review article above alluded to. A brief summary in his own words will be interesting:—"Darwin's theory requires countless ages, during which the earth shall have been habitable, and he claims geological evidence as showing an inconceivably great lapse of time, and as not being in contradiction with inconceivably greater periods than are even geologically indicated,—periods of rest between formations, and periods anterior to our so-called first formations, during which the rudimentary organs of the early fossils became degraded from their primeval uses. In answer, it is shown that a general physical law obtains, irreconcileable with the persistence of active change at a constant rate; in any portion of the universe, however large, only a certain capacity for change exists, so that every change which occurs renders the possibility of future change less, and on the whole the rapidity or violence of changes tends to diminish. Not only would this law gradually entail in the future the death of all beings and cessation of all change in the planetary system, and in the past point to a state of previous violence equally inconsistent with life, if no energy were lost by the system, but this gradual decay from a previous state of violence is rendered far more rapid by the continual loss of energy going on by means of radiation. This general conception points either to a beginning, or to the equally inconceivable idea of infinite energy in finite materials."

Although we have partly included Natural Selection in the foregoing considerations respecting the theory before us, we have not adverted so specially to that supposed agent as we now proceed to do. Its alleged effects have been estimated, but we here desire to inquire what the principle itself is; whether it be mere words, or a metaphor, or a personification, or anything that is clearly definable.

Natural Selection. All readers know that this is Mr. Darwin's chief factor in numerous changes, preservations, and transmutations. Human Selection brings about in animals the attributes most useful to man, or most admired by man. Natural Selection secures the attributes most useful to the animal. The question is not whether or not there be in Nature some such principle as this, since there plainly is, and in continual operation; but to admit thus much is very different from adopting the view of Darwin, that by processes like those of human selection, differences may be accumulated, though far more slowly, yet so surely, that these additions may be carried in the course of vastly long periods of time to so great an extent as to produce every known species of animal from one or two pairs, and perhaps from organisms of the lowest known types.

A patient examination of the book "On Origin of Species," is required in order to arrive at what the author himself appears to mean by this term. In one page he says, "The preservation of favourable variations, and the rejection of injurious variations, I call Natural Selection;" in another page this is called "Nature's power of selection." In the fourth chapter he remarks, "It has been said that I speak of Natural Selection as an active power or Deity, but who objects to an author speaking of the attraction of gravity as ruling the movements of the planets? Every one knows what is meant and is implied by such metaphorical expressions, and they are almost necessary for brevity. So, again, it is difficult to avoid personifying the word Nature; but I mean by Nature only the aggregate action and product of many natural laws, and by-laws the sequence of events as ascertained by us."

So far this is clear enough, and we learn that Natural Selection is merely a metaphorical expression; but we are not told for what. Yet the principal agent in an enormous series of long-continued operations must be surely something more than a metaphorical expression. Some power is said to operate universally and uninterruptedly. That power has wrought through countless ages, and has changed the face of the organic world. What, then, is it? What underlies the metaphorical expression?

But wonderful attributes are given to this metaphorical expression. Whatever it be, it is more, for it exercises a prescient and elective will; it chooses and rejects; it preserves the good and the ornamental; it passes by the weak, the ugly, the sickly, the useless. What can that be which affects this choice, and succeeds unerringly in securing it? " Natural

Selection," we are assured, "can only act through and for the good of each being." Here indeed is a great difficulty—a something, or some agent, foresees and employs means, works the greatest results in Nature, finds out and appreciates the good, and acts only for the good of each being. Nevertheless, the author is displeased when he is charged with using it as an active power or Deity." If it be neither, it does the work of both. Stranger still, the very author who seems to disclaim the employment of this metaphor as intimating an active power or Deity, elsewhere informs us that "Natural Selection is a power incessantly ready for action, and is as immeasurably superior to man's feeble efforts, as the works of Nature are to those of Art!"

If the expression, the Survival of the Fittest, be substituted for Natural Selection, some of the preceding discrepancies would disappear; but then the former expression would only indicate a result, and not an agent; and Mr. Darwin's distinctive factor would nearly disappear at the same time. I do not see how the conclusion can be evaded, that if Natural Selection is merely a metaphorical expression, the whole of what is attributed to it is attributed to a metaphor, which must be a veil for some unexpressed reality; and if the whole result be not metaphorical, yet it is certainly attached to what confessedly is so.

A similar objection does not lie against the use of the word Nature, when we adopt that as a *professedly* metaphorical expression, and when we do not set up Nature as an agent in the place of Deity; but on the other hand, plainly affirm that Nature is the work of God, though He is distinct from it, and is not to be confounded or consubstantiated with it.

If Natural Selection be employed as a Pantheistic term, we can understand its use, and place it in the same rank as Spinoza's *Natura naturans*. But if the Creator is occasionally referred to as some power and existence distinct from Natural Selection, as remote from it, as not necessarily connected with it, our perplexity remains.

Upon the perusal of Mr. Darwin's "Descent of Man," I find no deliverance from this perplexity. The term still appears to be a metaphorical expression. Far wider use indeed is made of it in the two volumes of the new book, and another great power is associated with it; but what it really signifies, presuming that the author would still be disposed to disown it as an active power or Deity, is uncertain. Truly has the author confessed "in the literal sense of the word, no doubt, natural selection is a false term."

One thing, however, is apparent, and that is that Mr. Darwin now materially limits the influence of this metaphorical principle, even while he endeavours to extend it other than to man. These are his words (vol. 1, p. 152). " Thus a very large and undefined extension may safely be given to the direct and indirect results of natural selection, but I now admit, after reading the essay by Nägeli on plants, and the remarks by various authors with respect to animals, more especially those recently made by Professor Broca, that in the earlier editions of my 'Origin of Species' I probably attributed too much to the action of Natural Selection or the Survival of the Fittest. I have altered the fifth edition of the Origin so as to confine my remarks to adaptive changes of structure. I had not formerly sufficiently considered the existence of many structures which appear to be, as far as we can judge, neither beneficial nor injurious, and this I believe to be one of the greatest oversights as yet detected in my work. I may be permitted to say as some excuse, that I had two distinct objects in view, partly to show that species had not been separately created, and secondly, that natural selection had been the chief agent in the change, though largely aided by the inherited effects of habit, and slightly by the direct action of the surrounding conditions . . . . If I have erred in giving to natural selection great power, which I am far from admitting, or in having exaggerated its power, which is in itself probable, I have at least, as I hope, done good service in aiding to overthrow the dogma of separate creations."

In this his new work on the Descent of Man, Mr. Darwin has introduced a new metaphorical character under the name of Sexual Selection. We feel precluded by the nature of the subject from writing about it as freely as Mr. Darwin has done, because we here address general readers of both sexes, and possibly Mr. Darwin is not supposed to address them, but to confine himself especially to naturalists. We may, however, venture to speak of the extent and efficacy of the principle as Mr. Darwin employs it, and to enquire as to its real value, and as to what conception its propounder appears to form of it.

In reference to extent of efficacy it appears to be a rival of Natural Selection; one of two Consuls in conjoined power; either a king or a queen, when both are co-regent. The efficiency of Sexual Selection must be great indeed, for it extends over the larger portion of Mr. Darwin's new work, occupying nearly the whole of the second volume and almost one-half of the first. It "appears to have acted as powerfully on man, as on many other animals." "Yet," says Mr. Darwin, "I do not pretend the effects of Sexual Selection can be indicated with scientific precision; but it can be shown that it would be an inexplicable fact if man had not been modified by this agency which has acted so powerfully on innumerable animals, both high and low in the scale." To treat the subject in a fitting manner, the author passes the whole animal kingdom in review in connection with this new and potent agent. Although, however, its operation is coextensive with, it is stated that it "acts in a less rigorous manner than Natural Selection. The latter produces its effects by the life or death at all ages of the more or less successful individuals. Death, indeed, not rarely ensues from the conduct of rival males. But generally the less successful male merely tries to obtain a female, or obtains, later in the season, a retarded and less vigorous female, so that they have fewer, or less vigorous, or no offspring."

As we proceed in these volumes, we are more and more surprised at the activity of this newly introduced factor, and we are the more impatient to demand what it essentially is. The only answer to this inquiry discoverable in the book is that it is an agency. Well then, if an agency, there must be an agent who employs it, and upon whose mode of employment the whole effects of the agency depend. If an agency, it cannot properly be said to do anything independently; therefore as an original principle, it has no tangible existence. Assuredly these inferences cannot be denied, they are to all plainly logical. The conclusion we draw from the author's admission of mere agency, and his confessed inability to indicate the effects of Sexual Selection with scientific precision, is that a mode of action and its effect are in this instance indefinitely illustrated. In short, while there are many results in Nature which exhibit the influence of sex, and which always have exhibited it to every careful observer, there are likewise more things which Mr. Darwin has industriously accumulated, and borrowed from various naturalists, all of which simply corroborate the same influence. Wherever there is sex, there are sexual attraction, and sexual conditions and consequences. But that Mr. Darwin has overstrained this principle in his late publication, even his warm friends acknowledge. Let any scientific man only attempt to state what Sexual Selection essentially is, as introduced in the book before us, and he must certainly add something of his own, or diminish or modify what Mr. Darwin has said.

No naturalist, no common observer of Nature denies the vast influence of sex; it is a truism to say that it is coextensive with the existence of sex. Wherever there is sex, there is sexuality. The Creator designed it to be so, and it is so. The Creator employs it, and it fulfils His purposes. It is nothing more or less than an instrument in His hand—a powerful and perfectly adapted instrument—and when it secures all the results He intended, it is after all nothing more than an instrument. It would have effected nothing without Him, and without Him it would not have been in operation.

Precisely the same is predicable of Natural

Selection. Join it with Sexual Selection, and we have two instruments instead of one. Neither of them is self-sufficing—neither is more than an agency. To these two effective instruments others may in time be added by other naturalists. Others indeed come under Mr. Darwin's view. They all have their appropriate spheres of operation, and the theme for perpetual admiration is that they are so wonderfully and perfectly adjusted to each other. In this opens a new field of research and of approach towards the Divine Being. We discover His methods in Natural and Sexual Selection, Heredity, Equilibrium, and other agencies to which distinctive names are given. In the same manner a human artificer may distinguish his tools; but who expects the tools, however named, to perform the work of the artificer who uses them? Or, if these things be represented as parts of a complicated machine, and if therefore by its complexity we are hindered from regarding them in their simplest significance, nevertheless the most complex machine requires its prime mover, and apart from that, complexity is only hopeless confusion, and multiplicity of parts only a bar to efficiency.

Mr. Darwin before the publication of his work on Man, had several expounders of his views, who were also apologists for them. One of the ablest of these, Mr. A. R. Wallace, arrests our attention by the fact of his having been a co-discoverer with Mr. Darwin of the agency of Natural Selection. The course of our immediately preceding observations brings us to Mr. Wallace's statement of Mr. Darwin's views, which is here introduced.

XII.

METHOD OF DIVINE OPERATIONS.—CREATION, OR CREATION BY LAW.

MR. DARWIN'S work, says Mr. Wallace, has for its main object to show that all the phenomena of living things—all their wonderful organs and complicated structure, their infinite variety of form, size, and colour, their intricate and involved relations to each other,—may have been produced by the action of a few general laws of the simplest kind, laws which in most cases are mere statements of admitted facts. The chief of these laws or facts are the following:—

1. *The Law of Multiplication in Geometrical Progression.*—All organized beings have enormous powers of multiplication. Even man who increases slower than all other animals, could under favourable circumstances double his number every fifteen years, or a hundred-fold

in a century. Many animals and plants could increase their numbers from ten to a thousand-fold every year.

2. *The Law of Limited Populations.* — The number of living individuals of each species in any country, or in the whole globe, is practically stationary; whence it follows that the whole of this enormous increase must die off almost as fast as produced, except only those individuals for whom room is made by the death of parents. As a simple but striking example, take an oak forest. Every oak will drop annually thousands or millions of acorns, but till an old tree falls, not one of these millions can grow up into an oak. They must die at various stages of growth.

3. *The Law of Heredity, or Likeness of Offspring to their Parents.* — This is a universal, but not an absolute law. All creatures resemble their parents in a high degree, and in the majority of cases very accurately; so that even peculiarities, of whatever kind, in the parents, are almost always transmitted to some of the offspring.

4. *The Law of Variation.* — This is fully expressed by the lines:—

> " No being on this earthly ball
> Is like another, all in all."

Offspring resemble their parents very much, but not wholly—each being possesses its individuality. This variation itself varies in amount but is always present, not only in the whole being, but in every part of every being. Every organ, every character, every feeling, is individual; that is to say, *varies* from the same organ, character, or feeling, in every other individual.

5. *The Law of increasing change of Physical Conditions upon the surface of the Earth.*—Geology shows us that this change has always gone on in times past, and we also know that it is now everywhere going on.

6. *The Equilibrium or Harmony of Nature.* When a species is well adapted to the conditions which environ it, it flourishes; when imperfectly adapted, it decays; when ill-adapted, it becomes extinct. If *all* the conditions which determine an organism's well-being are taken into consideration, this statement can hardly be disputed.

" This series of facts or laws are mere statements of what is the condition of Nature. They are facts or impressions which are generally known, generally admitted, but in discussing the subject of the Origin of Species, as generally forgotten. It is from these universally admitted facts that the origin of all the varied forms of Nature may be deduced by a logical train of reasoning, which is, however, at every step verified, and shown to be in strict accord with facts ; and at the same time, many curious phenomena, which can by no other means be understood, are explained and accounted for. It is probable that these primary facts or laws are but results of the very nature of life, and of the essential properties of organized and unorganized matter." *

" The question then is," continues Mr Wallace, " Whether the variety, the harmony, the contrivance, and the beauty we perceive in organic beings can have been produced by the action of these laws alone, or whether we are required to believe in the incessant interference and direct action of the mind and will of the Creator ? It is simply a question of how the Creator has worked. The Duke of Argyll, (and I quote him as having well expressed the views of the more intelligent of Mr. Darwin's opponents), maintains that He has personally applied general laws to produce effects, which

* A. R. Wallace. "Contributions to the Theory of Natural Selection," 1870, p. 265.

these laws are not in themselves capable of producing; that the universe alone, with all its laws intact, would be a sort of chaos, without variety, without harmony, without design, without beauty; that there is not (and therefore we may presume that there could not be) any self-developing power in the universe. I believe, on the contrary, that the universe is so constituted as to be self-regulating; that as long as it contains Life, the forms under which that life is manifested have an inherent power of adjustment to each other and to surrounding Nature; and that this adjustment necessarily leads to the greatest amount of variety, and beauty, and enjoyment, because it does depend on general laws and not on a continual supervision and rearrangement of details. As a matter of feeling and religion, I hold this to be a far higher conception of the Creator and of the Universe than that which we may call the "continual interference" hypothesis; but it is not a question to be decided by our feelings or convictions, it is a question of facts and of reason. Could the change, which Geology shows us has ever taken place in the forms of life, have been produced by general laws, or does it imperatively require the incessant supervision of a creative mind? This is the question for us to consider, and our opponents have the difficult task of proving a negative, if we show that these are both facts and analysis in our favour."

So far the difference is clearly stated, and the reader may choose his own views. But we are here led to consider what a law of Nature means, and on the determination of its significance depends that of Creation by Law. Now the expression Law of Nature means nothing more than the *method of intelligent agency*. As a law, it is the product of a lawgiver, and as a law of Nature it is an evidence of his governance. Wherever there are many such laws, his intelligence is seen to be manifold; where they operate irresistibly and continually, his power is added to his intelligence, and these combined cannot fall short of Deity. The existence and the operation of these laws enable us to understand that the God of Nature is actually present in controlling Nature.

Men speak of the Laws of Nature as if they really intimately knew them as independent activities. Yet what are they to us except formulæ? what but expressions of the constancy of phenomena? We are unable to comprehend one Law of Nature in its entirety. We cannot grasp its application, its extent, its unity Only in some of its effects do we see it, and only in some of our symbols do we express it. Who shall say where one single law begins and ends its sway, where it is interwoven with another law, and where limited and modified by that other? Nature, Man, all created things, exist, it is true, under the dominion of Law, in the sense that they are all governed. There is not, there cannot be an ungoverned thing in the universe; but it is only the Administrator of all who discerns all those laws in their remotest reach and their entire influence.

"Creation by Law," is the title of a considerable chapter in Mr. Wallace's book, and as it is reprinted " with improvements," in his book, after having originally appeared in the *Quarterly Journal of Science*, we conclude that its author has thoroughly considered and elaborated it; but he does not clearly define what he understands by its title. What, we repeat, is the strict meaning of Creation by Law? What is a creative law? If it means anything philosophical, it must be supposed to signify the law, or rule, or method which the Creator has prescribed to Himself in the act of creating.

The act of creating exhibits the method or law which, apart from such act, can have no existence. If it have, where does it exist? where does it operate? Its appearance, its existence is witnessed only in creation. Is it an activity impressed upon matter? Then matter becomes creative. This is a result to which unhappily much of the current physical teaching appears to lead; but Mr. Wallace is not, as I read him, a materialist, but rather the extreme opposite.

Now if matter have not impressed upon it any creative law, and if, therefore, there be no inherent creative activity in matter, the law exists outside of matter; but outside of matter whatever still acts upon matter, is surely something else, is something higher, and must be Spirit; and if spirit, and possessing the power to produce effects which all but Atheists acknowledge to be the works of Omnipotence, then we arrive at the identification of the imaginary self-existing law with Divine energy. Creation by law, therefore, can be nothing less nor more than creation by the Creator. There cannot be two essentially different kinds of creation, one by the Creator himself directly, and another by law, except mediately. Our imperfection may justify us in using the term Law, but we must always bear in mind that it really means method, or rule of acting.

I venture to submit that not only this particular phrase "Creation by Law," but also many similar phrases, as I have shown in reference to Natural Selection, are thoroughly and injuriously illusory. When phrases respecting the Deity and His actions are confessedly inadequate to the truth they shadow forth, the case is very different, and no injury follows. For example, when we speak of the *hand* of God, no one is deluded by the word *hand;* and so of a hundred phrases employed by reason of human impotence. But when any symbolical expression is used to support a theory, and to form an important theological or antitheological or philosophical distinction, inadequacy cannot be pleaded; and the evil effect of proposing a broad distinction between Creation by Law and other creation, is an illustration to the point. The one allows the Creator to be immediately present, the other seems to suppose that He is in some manner absent; that Law takes His place in His absence, and creates without Him, as a vicegerent; that Law receives and remembers and accomplishes His commands.

The inveterate habit of opposing law to perpetual Divine action, and government by law to government in person, and operations by law, to operations in person, does appear to me to be productive of much mischief and much confusion. If this view be correct, then we need not be perplexed by the reproach of "incessant interference."

No intelligent Christian entertains an idea of a continual "interference" of Divine power; the imputation originates with opponents. *Interference* is a term utterly inapplicable to Omnipotence, utterly incompatible with Omnipresence, and quite as much so with Omniscience. The Being who foresees all, who is present with all, and who can do all, can never, in any sense, interfere with Himself. Never can He come between the sequences which He himself has pre-ordained; never can there be any necessity for interference—less still for incessant interference—when the Omnipotent is executing by law His own designs, and accomplishing His ulterior purposes. To apply such a term to Him as interference arises from a fundamental misconception of His character.

Were this line of argument generally understood and admitted, it appears to me (though it may not so appear to others), that we should escape these and other difficulties to which certain traditional phraseology exposes us. To the Divine Being Himself there can be no such distinction as Natural and Supernatural. To attempt to draw such a distinction is pardonable on the part of a creature, but it has no underlying reality. In sailing over the ocean of far-stretching life, our vessel makes a mark which to us seems strong and decisive, but which he who looks upon it a little longer discerns to be speedily obliterated. All our provisional laws of science are as quickly obliterated when we regard them from a higher point than conventional phraseology. There doubtless are laws which pervade and regulate the whole ocean of existence, inorganic, organic, and spiritual. These do not interfere, but co-operate with each other. They are graduated, fitted, and appropriately applied. A perpetual Divine supremacy secures the graduation, the aptitude, and the successful application of them all. The Divine Unity effects uniformity in their operations. In respect of physical law, all physical phenomena are evidences of the uniformity of its operation. This, indeed, is what men in science so zealously contend for. Well, then, establish it generally, and all created things are not the mere result of the operation of law, but primarily the result of the action of the Divine Being immediately and perpetually acting by law, never for a moment absent from the exercise of law, never for an instant leaving it to itself, even if it could exist by itself. If we could conceive of a single active atom of creation apart from the control and influence of its Creator, we could conceive of an atomic interference, and thence ascend to a massive interference. But as this is inconceivable by any man who acknowledges God's omnipresence, as well as His omnipotence, the entire charge of invoking continual interference falls to the ground. Our opponents attempt to impale us on one horn of a dilemma which is of their own making. Recognize the Christian's conception of God and His attributes, and it is not *we* who have to prove a negative, but *they*.

In considering creation, it must be remembered that many think its explanation to be beyond the reach of all natural science. Mr. Mivart puts forth a caution of this kind when he writes:—"It may be well to remind some readers that belief in the existence of God, in

His primary creation of the universe, and in His derivative creation of all kinds of being, inorganic and organic, do not repose on physical phenomena, but on primary intuitions. To deny or ridicule any of these beliefs on physical grounds is to commit the fallacy of *ignoratio elenchi*. It is to commit an absurdity analogous to that of saying a blind child could not recognize his father because he could not see him, forgetting that he could *hear* or *feel* him. Yet there are some who appear to find it unreasonable and absurd that men should regard phenomena in a light not furnished by, or deducible from the very phenomena themselves, although the men so regarding them avow that the light in which they do view them comes quite from another source."

Of the right bearing of these observations no Christian reader will entertain much doubt, and so soon as it is admitted that this class of truths rests not on phenomena, but on our primary intuitions together with Revelation, other formidable difficulties disappear. Mr. Spencer regards the conception of God as the absolute originator of the universe without the employment of any pre-existing material or means, as a wholly illegitimate symbolic conception, as much so as the atheistic. He estimates as equally difficult of belief the idea of the self-existent Creator and a self-existent universe. To this Mr. Mivart properly replies, "both of course are equally *unimaginable*, but it is not a question of facility of conception—not which is easiest to conceive, but which best accounts for and accords with psychological facts; namely with the above-mentioned intuitions. It is contended that we *have* these primary intuitions, and that with these the conception of a self-existing Creator is perfectly harmonious. On the other hand, the notion of a self-existing universe—that there is no real distinction between the finite and the infinite—that the universe and ourselves are one and the same things with the infinite and the self-existent; these assertions in *addition to* being unimaginable, *contradict* our primary intuitions."

We have the testimony of Biblical revelation and its accordance with our primary intuitions. "In the beginning God created the heaven and the earth." Here original creation is declared to be directly and immediately the act of God. This is the assertion of a fact which no human science could have discovered, and which none can ever disprove. It lies out of the sphere of science, and is antecedent to it. We now come to secondary acts of creation. " Much confusion," says Mr. Mivart, " has arisen from not keeping clearly in view this distinction between absolute creation and *derivative* creation. With the first physical science has plainly nothing whatever to do, and is impotent to prove or refute it. The second is also safe from any attack on the part of physical science, for it is primarily derived from psychical, not physical phenomena. The greater part of the apparent force possessed by objectors to creation, like Mr. Darwin, lies in their treating of the assertion of derivative creation, as if it were an assertion of absolute creation, or at least of supernatural action."

So far I agree with Mr. Mivart, but must partly differ from him as to the necessity of drawing a strong line where he draws it; and more largely if not entirely from Mr. Darwin's method of viewing the subject. If what I have previously advanced be justified, then the term " Special Creation " is not strictly appropriate, for nothing can be special which may be universal under the same actor, and nothing can be exceptional which with him may be uniform and continuous.

If there be an omnipotent Creator, who can create at all, the same Being can create all. With Him speciality is not a distinction, while all creation is solely his own act. If it be unworthy of Him to act specially, it *may* be (not it *is*) equally unworthy of Him to create primarily. Allow that He has created one primordial germ, and why should He not create many—a multitude of germs? If the one act is not unsuitable to Him, why should many more of the same kind be so? In respect of unworthiness, the charge is plainly groundless, after the admission of any creation, even should that be limited to one primordial germ. This argument for unworthiness has been so strongly insisted upon by some, that it becomes desirable to show its total lack of force. In no measure can we apply it to the Divine Being on the grounds supposed; nor does it apply to a wise human constructor. A man constructs a single mechanism, and that is designed to execute certain ends. Who of his fellow-men will presume to say that this constructor acts unworthily in making many more similar machines, or in varying them, or in multiplying them with modifications, and particular adaptations? Does repetition render him unworthy, does multiplication lower his character? Is his genius less because he shows it more? Is the Deity then less adorable because he creates many creatures, and repeats, multiplies, and varies forms without end?

"Others," says the *North British* Reviewer, "seriously allege that it is more consonant with a lofty idea of the Creator's action to suppose that he produced beings by Natural Selection, rather than by the finikin process of making each separate little race by the exercise of Almighty power. The argument, such as it is, means simply that the user of it thinks that this is how he personally would act if possessed of Almighty power and knowledge, but his speculations as to his probable feelings and actions after such a great change of circumstances are not worth much." We are accused, it may be repeated, of anthropomorphizing the Deity by our attachment to him of design, and purpose, and contrivance. Verily equally guilty of humanizing Him, are they who build theories upon the supposition that He *does* operate in the way they *would*. A prophet of old time has already furnished an answer to them—in this, and in many other similar objections. "For my thoughts are not your thoughts, neither are your ways my ways, saith the Lord.

For as the heavens are higher than the earth, so are my ways higher than your ways, and my thoughts than your thoughts."—Isaiah lv. 8-9.

Some theorists, and notably Mr. Herbert Spencer, have reprobated as strongly, and in terms more severe than Mr. Darwin, the so-called dogma of Special Creations. Mr. Spencer argues that we have never seen Special Creations, that we have no testimony to their actuality, that our belief in them is the consequence of a certain kind of education—and that it will vanish before the progress and the process of perfecting Natural Science. It may vanish or it may not—but either result will not be the test of the truth—in any degree. Even if it should entirely vanish from the acceptance of physicists and naturalists, it may revive, and retain vitality in the minds of Christians—though I do not assert that it will. What, however, may be safely asserted is, that it does not, and will not necessarily rest upon a question of continual interference. What it must rest upon, is on questions of Evolution, or Pantheism, or Atheism. Recognize the Omnipotent as the Creator, and then it inevitably follows that He may create as He will, when He will, and how

He will. If we with limited faculties assign limits to His creative fiat, the limitation exists in our apprehensions, in our construction of Him, but not in Himself.

Evolution is regarded as opposed to Divine presence, and it is opposed to it by extreme Evolutionists. This opposition, however, belongs to and springs from them, and is not a necessary constituent of the hypothesis, as it may be materially modified.

The earnest and increased study of Nature in our day leads us to much broader views of Divine action than have been formerly entertained; and to these views Natural Science conducts us without really leading us away from the Deity. Just as we now discover more and more geographically, so we discern more and more theologically. The earth is far larger to us than to Herodotus; Columbus was a far better geographer than the Grecian; but the discovery of America did not annul the existence of England or Spain. The discovery of new stars does not extinguish the old stars, does not darken one beam of their light. In like manner, the discovery of Natural and Sexual Selection, or rather the application of them, does not limit the action of the Creator;

nor does the reproach of incessant interference in the least degree affect His operations. The shadows with which we darken or obscure Him are only those of our own projection.

What can we say of Evolution? If we treat it reverently, and not atheistically, we can only say that it presupposes an evolver, and that such an evolver must be Divine. The magnitude, the continuity, the certainty of Evolution, its progress and its results, must comprehend an evolver, and this again must comprehend God. Abolish, if you can, the dogma of Special Creation, and substitute for it what you name Evolution. Employ all the science at your command to establish it, and after all and by all you establish the Evolver. Of Him you cannot rid this earth, of Him you cannot rid the universe. All harmonious evolution, unspontaneous evolution, orderly, purposed, and planned evolution, must include the idea of God. Self-evolution, spontaneous evolution, evolution without personal will or previous plan of purpose, are each and all contradictory. The act of unfolding necessitates the existence or one who unfolds. The results of unfolding display his character, as well as his action.

The *manner* of his unfolding is the true and

limited province of physical inquiry; yet a noble province it is, rich in results, fair with flowers by the wayside, and abundant in promise for future ages. Men are observers of natural development, whether or not included in it; they watch its progress in other existences with deep interest. Every advance in it is fitted to impress the beholder with admiration, and to direct him not only to the advance itself, but to convert him from a mere interpreter of stage after stage into an obedient servant and reverent worshipper of the grand Evolver. While man acts merely as an interpreter and recorder, he will study the laws which regulate the methods of Evolution, and will see design in every method and contrivance, and adaptation in every stage. To discover and expound the methods of Evolution demands the utmost powers of physicists of all branches. Mechanicians, Electricians, Chemists, Biologists, Physiologists, and Geologists are all students of methods, or means. Every newly ascertained law, every more lucid definition of laws, all co-ordinations of laws, tend to the same desirable and valuable end. The exponent of them is an elucidator of their present stage, and of its connection with preceding stages of

Evolution. The entire Cosmos is an aggregate of combined evolutions. These are many to us, but one to the Evolver.

The more I can understand of the manner of Evolution, the more am I impressed with its unity of purpose, even in full view of its multiplicity of parts, and manifoldness of stages. From increase of such knowledge I rise into higher perceptions. I see rhythm in every motion on the earth, rhythm therefore in combined motions, a wonderful rhythm pervading the Cosmos. The manner is Nature's music. The end is Divine harmony.

All this, too, is not only consistent with strict physical science, but is a consequence of it; while there are other sciences and other consequences of which it takes no note. It records things and organisms in their several places and their natural order. It grows in comprehensiveness, it aims at the Cosmos—why not? The Cosmos is a magnificent manifestation of order.

In such a light, whatever title you bestow on the unfolding of the parts and purposes in the Cosmos, is of slight moment; whether you call it Creation, or Evolution, or Development, you do not change the phenomena, or alter the actual conditions. But if you confound a particular mean or method with the evolving power, with the acting and sufficient principle of the evolution, then you do alter the conditions; you substitute human figments for the Divine Being, and you make otherwise allowable names objectionable from the narrow and exclusive use to which you put them.

The most systematic builder of an Evolutionary Theory in the English language is Mr. Herbert Spencer. Unhappily his entire system is pervaded by views which positively oppose themselves to Christian tenets. When, however, he is read as a mere exponent of method, without regard to original principles, great advantage may be derived from his clearness and his firm grasp of the details of his subject. The unity of Evolution as comprehended by the Cosmos, is aptly described by Mr. Spencer, who shows the higher generalization of our knowledge concerning Evolution to be, —so far as we know the constitution of the world,—one unceasing and all perfecting system, advancing everywhere and in all.

After elaborately working out his own theory, Mr. Spencer suggestively intimates that the laws of Evolution, contemplated as holding true of each order of existence separately, hold true when we contemplate the several orders of existences as forming together one natural whole. While we think of Evolution as divided into Astronomic, Biologic, Psychologic, Sociologic, etc., it may seem to a certain extent a coincidence that the same law of metamorphosis holds throughout all its divisions. But when we recognize these divisions as mere conventional groupings made to facilitate the arrangement and acquisition of knowledge — when we regard the different existences with which they deal as component parts of one Cosmos—we see at once that there are not several kinds of Evolution having certain traits in common, but one Evolution going on everywhere after the same manner. While any whole is evolving, there is always going on an Evolution of the parts into which it divides itself. This holds true of the totality of things as made up of parts within parts from the greatest down to the smallest. We know that while a physically cohering aggregate like the human body is getting larger, and taking on its general shape, each of its organs is doing the same; that while each organ is growing and becoming unlike others, there is going on a differentiation and integration of its component tissues and vessels; and that even the components of these components are severally increasing and passing into more definitely heterogeneous structures. But we have not duly remarked that setting out with the human body as a minute part, and ascending from it to the greater parts, this simultaneity of transformation is equally manifest; that while each individual is developing, the society of which he is an insignificant unit is developing too; that while the aggregate mass forming a society is becoming more definitely heterogeneous, so likewise is that total aggregate, the Earth, of which the society is an inappreciable portion; that while the Earth, which in bulk is not a millionth of the solar system, progresses towards its concentrated and complex structure, the solar system similarly progresses; and that even its transformations are but those of a scarcely appreciable portion of our sidereal system, which has at the same time been going through parallel changes.

"So understood, Evolution becomes not one in principle only, but one in fact. There are not many metamorphoses similarly carried on; but there is a single metamorphosis universally progressing, wherever the reverse metamorphosis has not set in. In any locality, great or small, throughout space, where the occupying matter acquires an appreciable individuality, or distinguishableness from other matter, there Evolution goes on; or rather the acquirement of this appreciable individuality in the commencement of Evolution. And this holds uniformly; regardless of the size of the aggregate, regardless of its inclusion in other aggregates, and regardless of the wider Evolutions within which its own is comprehended."*

Quite apart from, or in entire opposition to Mr. Spencer's peculiar opinions, whatever may be the factors producing Evolution, the theory itself may be so modified as to express graduation, and thus may include creational action, purpose, and all that is associated with modern ideas of the Divine attributes in relation to Nature. It may be used as a term expressive on the largest scale of what we daily see displayed on a small scale. In Embryology, Evolution is the mode of educing the growth and completion of the individual, and it may be fairly applied to the growth and completion of a

* "First Principles." Second Edition, 1867, p. 546.

collection of individuals, always pre-supposing that neither could take effect without Divine, and therefore intelligent causation in continual activity.

Under such conditions many of the expositions of Darwin, Spencer, and their friends may rest on their proper merits. "It is interesting," says Mr. Darwin at the close of his 'Origin of Species,' "to contemplate an entangled bank clothed with many plants of many kinds, with birds singing on the bushes, with various insects flitting about, and with worms crawling through the damp earth, and to reflect that these elaborately constituted forms, so different from each other, and dependent on each other in so complex a manner, have all been produced by laws acting around us." And further:—"There is grandeur in this view of life with its several powers, having been originally breathed by the Creator into a few forms or into one; and that while this planet has gone cycling on according to the fixed law of gravity, from so simple a beginning, endless forms, most beautiful and most wonderful, have been and are being evolved."

"With the feeling expressed in these two sentences," said Professor Sir William Thomson, after quoting them in his presidential address at the last meeting of the British Association (in 1871), " I most cordially sympathize —I have omitted two sentences which come between them, describing briefly the hypothesis of the Origin of Species by Natural Selection, because I have always felt that this hypothesis does not contain the true theory of Evolution, if evolution there has been in Biology. Sir John Herschel, in expressing a favourable judgment on the hypothesis of Zoological Evolution, with, however, some reserve in respect to the origin of man, objected to the doctrine of Natural Selection, that it was too like the Laputan method of making books, and that it did not sufficiently take into account a continually guiding and controlling intelligence. This seems to me a most valuable and instructive criticism. I feel profoundly convinced that the argument of design has been greatly too much lost sight of in recent zoological speculations. Reaction against the frivolities of teleology, such as are to be found, not rarely, in the notes of the learned commentators on Paley's Natural Theology, has, I believe, had a temporary effect in turning attention from the solid and irrefragable argument so well put forward in that excellent old book. But overpoweringly strong proofs of intelligent and benevolent design lie all around us, and if ever perplexities, whether metaphysical or scientific, turn us away from them for a time, they come back upon us with irresistible force, showing to us through Nature the influence of a free will, and teaching us that all living beings depend on one ever-acting Creator and Ruler."

It is then manifest, that at least some of the most eminent men of science, who incline to Evolution at all, lean to it, not atheistically, but as consistent with intelligence, design, and benevolence. One other quotation to the same effect is appended from the book of an American author, which may not come before many readers in this country: " In the succession of beings from a lower to a higher type, and a consentaneous greater degree of complication, we have the strongest proof of an intelligent Being, designing, ordaining, and controlling. The laws of the older physicists were not claimed to be derived from an intelligence; they were deemed to exhibit the necessary operations of matter upon matter; but when we see that these laws have an order, and, as they are understood at the present day, a *rate* *of succession* in their operations, which have the stamp of thoughtfulness impressed upon them, it is impossible not to discover that they do not work of their own accord, but are controlled by a creative forethought and design. If the product of these causes was a heterogeneous mixture of beings, with no relation whatever among themselves, then one might more plausibly claim that the so-called physical causes had produced living creatures. As it is, though, we have before us animals allied to each other by progressive relations, which finally, if we follow them up, end in the highest forms of life at the present day, from having begun with the lowest, and ascended. What mere non-intelligent causation could produce the like?" *

With the opinions of Spencer and Darwin and others on the causes or factors of Evolution, the case is very different. When Mr. Spencer asks, and endeavours to answer the question, "How is Organic Evolution caused?" he assigns the causes to (1) External Factors, and (2) Internal Factors. Amongst the former there are astronomical and geological changes, meteorologic and organic agencies, and others all at work from without on each species

* "Mind in Nature," by H. J. Clark. New York, 1865.

of organization. Amongst Internal Factors are certain principal terms which cannot be popularly explained in a limited space—such as Direct and Indirect Equilibration. All the factors co-operate in effecting the evolution. Those universal laws of the re-distribution of matter and motion, to which things in general conform, are conformed to by all living things; whether considered in their individual histories, in their histories as species, or in their aggregate history." "The progressive inner changes, for which we find a cause in the continuous outer changes, conform so far as we can trace them, to that universal law of the instability of the homogeneous which is manifested throughout evolution in general. We see that in organisms, as in all other things, the exposure of different parts to different kinds and amounts of incident forces, has necessitated their differentiation; and that for the like reason, aggregates of individuals have been lapsing into varieties, and species, and genera, and classes. We also see that in each type of organism, as in the aggregate of types, the multiplication of effects has continually aided this transition from a more homogeneous to a more heterogeneous state. Finally, we have found that each change of structure, superposed on preceding changes, has been a re-equilibrium necessitated by the disturbance of a preceding equilibrium. The maintenance of life being the maintenance of a balanced combination of functions, it follows that individuals and species that have continued to live, are individuals and species in which balance of functions has not been overthrown. Inevitably, therefore, survival through successive changes of conditions, implies successive adjustments of the balance to new conditions. The actions that are here specified are in reality simultaneous; and they must be so conceived before organic evolution can be rightly understood." *

As to these factors, the same questions I have asked respecting Natural Selection, Sexual Selection, and Creation by Law, might be here repeated. What are these external and internal factors? What are Homogeneousness, Heterogeneity, Integration, Differentiation, Equilibration, and all the other terms which Mr. Spencer adopts and applies as factors in his great and all-embracing scheme of Evolution? Are they mere names, or are they objective entities? If the latter, what and where is

* "Principles of Biology," Vol. i.

their objective existence? It must be at once admitted that they have no objective existence, and that they are nothing more than verbal representations of Mr. Spencer's ideas. They may be apt or inapt, sound or unsound; they may express changes that really are exhibited in Evolution, and the impression derived from reading Mr. Spencer's book is that they are apt, relative terms, and do represent in some degree the manner in which Evolution may be supposed to take place. When, however, this is granted, little more can be said in their favour, while in respect of their being the causes, they are not the first or last conceivable causes in the vast scheme of Evolution. As to their being *factors* in the sense of *making* and progressively fashioning and perfecting Evolution—it seems hard to imagine that any intelligent person can so regard them. *

We know what factors are in mathematical language, viz., mere symbols or signs, *or elements of products*. Are they intended to be anything more in Spencerian or scientific language? If more, how much more? If the same, then

---

* With Mr. Spencer "the persistence of force is the deepest knowable cause of those modifications which constitute physiological development; as it is the deepest knowable cause of all other evolution."

we agree in the meaning of the words, but differ totally from all those who employ them even relatively, and as representing active entities—inherent, definite, causative entities—and as and by themselves, producing observed effects.

A reader of Mr. Spencer's or Mr. Darwin's books who accepts this limitation in relation to factors, need not be deluded by the manner in which they are used, or the hypothetical ends to which they are applied by these authors. Over and above their factors exists the controlling Prime Factor, who is employing such methods of action as these terms indicate, or methods similar to them, and who is energizing and combining, destroying and creating, distributing and redistributing—in one word *evolving*, or more plainly,—ceaselessly *unfolding*, fold after fold, form after form, age after age, world upon world, for His own grand purposes, of which we see but a small part; a glimpse, or a shadow, or a passing stage.

Some observations upon the current idea of Evolution, offered by Dr. Lionel S. Beale in a little book. termed "The Mystery of Life," which has come into my hands while I am writing these pages (1871), appear to be apposite.

"Man, as well as man's brain, we have been told, is formed by 'Evolution.' The organs result from 'Evolution,' and the higher mental faculties with which he is endowed, like the instrument of which these are the supposed function, are 'evolved' from the more simple. So that a complex structure may be 'evolved from a simpler structure, and a complex action from a more simple action. But 'Evolution,' like many other terms employed in the Science of our day for the purpose of accounting for phenomena, has had no definite meaning assigned to it. To say that a thing has been formed by 'Evolution,' conveys information less definite and less correct than is conveyed by the statement that it has been derived from a pre-existing living thing. The formation of tissue has been attributed to 'vacuolation' and 'differentiation,' and these polysyllables have lately been superseded by the still more vague terms, 'subtle influences,' and 'external conditions,' and 'sundry circumstances.' And it has been affirmed that, 'to the primitive properties of the molecules,' and 'Natural Selection,' may be referred all the varying forms and structures known to us, as well as the phenomena of the living world. But such terms explain nothing. By their use further inquiry is discouraged, and the mind bent upon investigating the secrets of Nature is misled at the very outset. Can any one of these very pretentious phrases be resolved into anything more than the statement of a fact or facts in the form and language of an explanation? Natural Selection is the formation of species, and species are produced by Natural Selection. Crystallization is the formation of crystals, and crystals are produced by the operation of crystallization. Tissues are formed by differentiation, and differentiation is the formation of tissues; and so on. But whether formation be attributed to 'subtle influences,' and 'sundry circumstances,' or to evil influences, witchcraft, or the influence of fairies, can surely be of very little consequence. By such explanations, especially if conveyed very emphatically, and with authority, the unlearned may be astonished, and pleased, and confused, and imposed upon, but those who put forward such explanations do not convey information, and instead of promoting the advance of Natural Knowledge, they retard real progress."

The truth is that the term 'Evolution,' together with others continually associated with it by current theorists, seems to have deluded many persons into the supposition that it and they represent some marvellous discoveries—new natural powers—new causes. After what has been already advanced, it must be manifest such a supposition is a specious delusion. The employment of new terms and a number of well or ill-formed words, in no way changes the original facts and phenomena. Evolution may be turned in any direction the supporter of it chooses. As you add, or subtract, or consubstantiate the Creator, you obtain the particular system you prefer.

Evolution maybe made Theistic, or Atheistic, Materialistic or Pantheistic, in accordance with the mood of its framer's mind. The same facts and phenomena may be so differently grouped, and so variously estimated as to appear to support any one of these systems. Although I believe that a truthful and scientific arrangement of facts conducts to Theism, and that the march of Science confirms Theism, still others believe differently. Darwinism, Spencerism, Comteism, are all said to be based on facts, and the advocate of each will say, "My theory is not a question of opinion, but of facts and phenomena." The adoption then of any hypothesis rests upon the proposer's way of contemplating things, and reasoning about them. Here responsibility forces itself upon us. If there be human responsibility for the influences and consequences of our philosophies and creeds, they become unspeakably momentous to *us*. If there be no responsibility, let us divert ourselves with any theory that interests men for the time. Seize the passing day, seize the prevalent philosophy. Whatever it be now, in the end it will be nothing, and the same holds true of ourselves.

Should the term Evolution be disliked, from its usual association with materialistic views, then another, Derivative Creation may be substituted. This has been used by Mr. Mivart in the Genesis of Species, where he has cited some doctors, or authorities amongst Roman Catholics, who have taken a like view of Creation. St. Augustine seems to have held such opinions of this kind, and a decided distinction was established between *formal* and *potential* creation. The *potentiality* or *derivation*, however, cannot be regarded as the same as Evolution. Mr. Mivart takes some pains to expose Mr. Darwin's misconceptions on creation, and he certainly places many topics in a clearer light. He also quotes these observations of Professor Huxley, which as coming from him are worth attention. "It is necessary to remark that there is a wider teleology, which is not touched by the doctrine of Evolution, but is actually based upon the fundamental proposition of Evolution." "The teleological and the mechanical views of Nature are not necessarily mutually exclusive; on the contrary, the more purely a mechanist the speculator is, the more firmly does he assume a primordial molecular arrangement, of which all the phenomena in the universe are the consequences; and the more completely thereby is he at the mercy of the teleologist, who can always defy him to disprove that the primordial molecular arrangement was not intended to evolve the phenomena of the universe." Professor Huxley proceeds to say that the mechanist may, in turn, demand of the teleologist how the latter learns that it was intended; to which question it may be replied, he knows this as a necessary truth of reason deduced from his own primary intuitions, which cannot be denied without absolute scepticism.

To the same effect Professor Owen is cited, who says that Natural Evolution "by means of slow physical and organic operations through long ages is not the less clearly recognizable as the act of an adaptive mind, because we have abandoned the old error of supposing it to be the result of a primary, direct, and sudden act of creational construction." " The succession of species," continues the Professor, " by continuously operating law is not necessarily a 'blind operation.' Such law, however discerned in the properties and successions of natural objects, intimates, nevertheless, a preconceived progress. Organisms may be evolved in orderly succession, stage after stage, towards a foreseen goal, and the broad features of the course may still show the unmistakeable impress of Divine volition."

These views though merely expressing commonly entertained opinions on one side, acquire some value as issuing from another side ; and so far as names are influential, confirm the views previously offered. I simply carry the same views onward to their utmost application, not only to the molecular, but to the entire constitution of the cosmical Evolution. Not merely do I think that "the broad features of the course," but likewise all the features, great and small, wherever they are recognized by us, show the unmistakeable impress of Divine volition.

Not here and there only are we to look for it, as if interruptive or exceptional, but everywhere and altogether—without limit and without end.

The Evolution of Man and his Faculties.—All systematic, materialistic, and rigid Evolutionists, all who carry out their principles irrespectively of any such modifications as just suggested, will include Man as one of the results or examples of the great natural operation. This Mr. Spencer and Mr. Darwin do, as a matter of principle; the former, not less pointedly, but only as forming a constituent of his system; the latter with fuller detail, with somewhat keener sense of difficulties, though with equal positiveness and occasional dogmatism. His details, indeed, fill the two volumes so widely known under the title of "The Descent of Man."

In our pages it would be quite inappropriate to enter upon a particular analysis, or deliberative estimate of Mr. Darwin's arguments, or upon a literary critique of his volumes. This, I trust, will be sufficiently done by others; certainly the book will be extensively read, at least as a collection of curious facts in support of a famous hypothesis. Some observations on fundamental questions will suffice for my purpose, and some extracts will exhibit Mr. Darwin's views.

He has no hesitation in assigning the whole Man from beginning to end, his body, soul, and spirit, to Natural Evolution, and to Evolution by the modifying action of Natural and Sexual Selection. Viewed in this light, Man falls to be considered under the divisions of Organic and Mental Evolution.

Dwelling for the present on Organic Evolution, we find Mr. Darwin elaborating his argument upon the basis he previously assumed in his "Origin of Species:"—Man and all other vertebrate animals have been constructed on the same general model, they pass through the same stages of development, and they retain certain rudiments in common. Consequently, we ought frankly to admit their community of descent: to take any other view, is to admit that our own structure, and that of all the animals around us, is a mere snare laid to entrap our judgment. This conclusion is greatly strengthened, if we look to the numbers of the whole animal series, and consider the evidence derived from their affinities or classification, their geographical distribution, and geological succession. It is only our natural prejudice, and that arrogance which made our forefathers declare that they were descended from demigods, which leads us to demur to this conclusion. But the time will before long come when it will be thought wonderful that naturalists, who were well acquainted with the comparative structure of man and other mammals, should have believed that each was the work of a separate creation."

The fourth chapter of the work treats "On the Manner of Development of Man from some Lower Form," and in preceding chapters, the same topic is further illustrated. His "Affinities and Genealogy" are detailed, and in a chapter devoted to them, we find depicted the structure of our early progenitors. This sketch is so characteristic that its quotation here (with some omissions relating to sexual conformation) will be highly interesting.

"We will now look to man as he exists; and we shall, I think, be able to restore during successive periods, but not in due order of time, the structure of our early progenitors. This can be effected by means of the rudiments which man still retains, by the characters which occasionally make their appearance in him through reversion, and by the aid of the principles of morphology and embryology. The various facts to which I allude have been given in the previous chapters. The early progenitors of man were once no doubt covered with hair, both sexes having beards; their ears were pointed and capable of movement; and their bodies were provided with a tail having the proper muscles. Their limbs and bodies were also acted upon by many muscles which now only occasionally re-appear, but are normally present in the Quadrumana. The great artery and nerve of the humerus ran through a supra-condyloid foramen. At this, or some earlier period, the intestine gave forth a much larger diverticulum or cœcum than that now existing. The foot, judging from the condition of the great toe in the fetus, was then prehensile; and our progenitors were then no doubt arboreal in their habits, frequenting some warm, forest-clad land. The males were provided with great canine teeth, which served them as formidable weapons.

"At a much earlier period the uterus was double; and the eye was protected by a third eyelid or nictitating membrane. At a still earlier period the progenitors of man must have been aquatic in their habits; for morphology plainly tells us that our lungs consist of a modified swim-bladder, which once served as a float. The clefts on the neck in the embryo of man show where the branchiæ once existed. At about this period the true kidneys were replaced by the corpora wolffiana. The heart existed as a simple pulsatory vessel; and the chorda dorsalis took the place of a vertebrate column. These early predecessors of man, thus seen in the dim recesses of time, must have been as lowly organized as the lancelet or amphioxus, or even still more lowly organized."*

Respecting the marked grades of man's descent this summary is sufficient:—

" The most ancient progenitors in the kingdom of the Vertebrata, at which we are able to obtain an obscure glance, apparently consisted of a group of marine animals, resembling the larvæ of existing Ascidians. These animals gave rise to a group of fishes, as lowly organized as the lancelet, and from these the Ganoids, and other fishes like the Lepidosiren, must have been developed. From such fish a very small advance would carry us on to the Amphibians. We have seen that

* "Descent of Man," Vol. i., pp. 206—7.

birds and reptiles were once intimately connected together; and the Monotremata now in a slight degree connect mammals with reptiles. But no one can at present say by what line of descent the three higher and related classes, namely, mammals, birds, and reptiles, were derived from either of the two lower vertebrate classes, namely, amphibians and fishes. In the class of mammals the steps are not difficult to conceive which led from the ancient Monotremata to the ancient Marsupials; and from these to the early progenitors of the placental mammals. We may thus ascend to the Lemuridœ; and the interval is not wide from these to the Simiadœ. The Simiadœ then branched off into two great stems, the New World and Old World monkeys; and from the latter, at a remote period, Man, the wonder and glory of the Universe, proceeded."[*]

Such is the result and such the course of the operations of Natural Selection, and Sexual Selection in slowly perfecting the wonder and glory of the Universe. This hypothesis evidently founds itself more on morphology than physiology, and is vulnerable at many points, as physiologists will perceive. All that

[*] Ibid. pp. 212—213.

is advanced in opposition to the origin of species applies equally to the case of the human organism. But the strength of the opposing arguments is greatly increased by the force of those to be directed against Mental Evolution.

It is very instructive to find that even Mr. Wallace, the anticipator of Mr. Darwin, or the co-discoverer with him of Natural Selection, hesitates when this principle is fully applied to Man, as he has shown in his chapter on " The Limits of Natural Selection as applied to Man" This is introduced at the close of the volume already mentioned, throughout which he has performed his utmost in endeavouring to show " that the known laws of variation, multiplication, and heredity, resulting in a ' struggle for existence,' and the ' survival of the fittest,' have probably sufficed to produce all the varieties of structure, all the wonderful adaptations, all the beauty of form and of colour, that we see in the animal and vegetable kingdoms. It will, therefore, probably excite some surprise among my readers to find that I do not consider that all nature can be explained on the principles of which I am so ardent an advocate : and that I am now myself going to state objections, and to place limits, to the power of "Natural Selection." I believe, however, that there are such limits; and that just as surely as we can trace the action of natural laws in the development of organic forms, and can clearly conceive that fuller knowledge would enable us to follow step by step the whole process of true development, so surely can we trace the action of some unknown higher law, beyond and independent of all those laws of which we have any knowledge. We can trace this action more or less distinctly in many phenomena, the two most important of which are—the origin of sensation or consciousness, and the development of man from the lower animals.

"In considering the question of the development of man by known natural laws, we must ever bear in mind the first principle of Natural Selection, no less than of the general theory of Evolution, that all changes of form or structure, all increase in the size of an organ or in its complexity, all greater specialization or physiological division of labour, can only be brought about, inasmuch as it is for the good of the being so modified. Mr. Darwin himself has taken care to impress upon us that Natural

Selection has no power to produce absolute perfection, but only relative perfection; no power to advance any being much beyond his fellow-beings; but only just so much beyond it as to enable it to survive them in the struggle for existence. Still less has it any power to produce any modifications which are in any degree injurious to its possessor; and Mr. Darwin frequently uses the strong expression that a single instance of this kind would be fatal to his theory. If, therefore, we find in man any characters which all the evidence we can obtain goes to show would have been actually injurious to him on their first appearance, they could not possibly have been produced by Natural Selection. Neither could any specially developed organ have been so produced if it had been merely useless to him, or if its use was not proportionate to its degree of development. Such cases as these would prove that some other law, or some other power than Natural Selection, had been at work. But if further we could see that these very modifications, though hurtful and useless at the time when they first appeared, became in the highest degree useful at a much later period, and are now essential to the full moral and intellectual development of human nature, we should then infer the action of mind, foreseeing the future and preparing for it, just as surely as we do when we see the breeder set himself to work with the determination to produce a definite improvement in some cultivated plant and domestic animal. I would further remark that this inquiry is as thoroughly scientific and legitimate as that into the origin of species itself. It is an attempt to solve the inverse problem, to deduce the existence of a new power of a definite character, in order to account for facts which, according to the theory of Natural Selection, ought not to happen. Such problems are well known to science, and the search after their solution has often led to the most brilliant results. In the case of man, there are facts of the nature above alluded to, and in calling attention to them, and inferring a cause for them, I believe that I am as strictly within the bounds of scientific investigation as I have been in any other portion of my work."

Mr. Wallace then proceeds to adduce these facts, the first of which is that the brain of the savage can be shown to be larger than he needs it to be. After exhibiting the proofs of this fact, and comparing the intellect of savages and animals, and considering them in proportion to their respective wants, he shows that whether we compare the savage with the higher developments of man, or with the brutes around him, we are alike driven to the conclusion that in his large and well-developed brain he possesses an organ quite disproportionate to his actual requirements—an organ that seems prepared in advance, only to be fully utilized as he progresses in civilization. " A brain slightly larger than that of the gorilla would, according to the evidence before us, fully prove sufficient for the limited mental development of the savage ; and we must therefore admit that the large brain he possesses could never have been developed by any of those laws of Evolution, whose essence is that they lead to a degree of organization exactly proportionate to the wants of each species, never beyond their wants— that no preparation can be made for the future development of the race—that one part of the body can never increase in size or complexity, except in strict co-ordination to the pressing wants of the whole. The brain of prehistoric and savage man seems to me to prove the existence of some power distinct from that which has guided the development of the lower animals through their ever-varying forms of being."

The Use of the hairy covering of Mammalia is the next difficulty specified. One of the most general external characters of the terrestrial mammalia is the hairy covering of the body, which, whenever the skin is flexible, soft, and sensitive, forms a natural protection against the severities of climate, and particularly against rain. Mr. Wallace adduces one or two striking evidences of design and contrivance in the adaptation of the their hairy coverings to the necessities of the animals provided with them. The hair, for instance, lies downwards on the limbs of all walking mammals, from the shoulder to the toes, but in the orang-utan it is directed from the shoulder to the elbow, and again from the wrist to the elbow, in a reverse direction. This correspondence to the habits of the animal, which, when resting, holds its long arms upwards over its head, or clasps a branch above it, so that the rain would flow down both the arm and fore-arm to the long hair which meets at the elbow. " In accordance with this principle, the hair is always longer or more dense along the spine or middle of the back from the nape to the tail, often rising into a crest of hairs or bristles on the ridge of the back. This character prevails through the entire series of the mammalia, from the marsupials to the quadrumana; and by this long persistence it must have acquired such a powerful hereditary tendency, that we should expect it to reappear continually, even after it had been abolished by ages of the most rigid selection; and we may feel sure that it never could have been completely abolished under the law of Natural Selection, unless it had become so positively injurious as to lead to the almost invariable extinction of the individuals possessing it."

Yet in man, hypothetically descended by Natural Selection from apes, the hairy covering of the body has almost totally disappeared, and what is very remarkable, it has disappeared more completely from the back than from any other part of the body. Bearded and beardless races alike have the back smooth, and even when a considerable quantity of hair appears on the limbs and breast, the back, and especially the spinal region, is absolutely free, thus completely reversing the characteristics of all other mammalia.

Furthermore, savage man actually feels the want of this hairy covering. One of the commonest habits of savages is to use some covering for the back and shoulders, even when they have none for any other part of the body. The Tasmanian savages, the Maories, the Patagonians, and the Fuegians, the Hottentots, the natives of Timor, have all used, or do use, cloths, cloaks, or mantles, small pieces of skin, and leaves of the fan palm, as more or less ample back coverings, while almost all the Malay races, as well as the Indians of South America make great palm-leaf hats, four feet or more across, which they use during their canoe voyages to protect their bodies from showers of heavy rain. Savages then, far and wide, so urgently need the use of a hairy covering, that they employ various substitutes for that which Natural Selection ought to have left them, by rule and right of heredity.

Mr. Darwin has said in reply—"No one supposes that the nakedness of the skin is any direct advantage to man, so that his body cannot have been divested of hair through Natural Selection. Nor have we any grounds for believing, as shown in a former chapter, that this can be due to the direct action of the conditions to which man has long been exposed, or that it is the result of correlative development.

The absence of hair on the body is, to a certain extent, a secondary sexual character; for in all parts of the world women are less hairy than men. Therefore we may reasonably suspect that this is a character which has been gained through Sexual Selection. As woman has a less hairy body than man, and as this character is common to all races, we may suppose that our female semi-human progenitors were probably first partially divested of hair, and that this occurred at an extremely remote period before the several races had diverged from a common stock. As our female progenitors gradually acquired this new character of nudity, they must have transmitted it in an almost equal degree to their young offspring of both sexes; so that its transmission, as in the case of many ornaments with mammals and birds, has not been limited either by age or sex." Those who desire more of this argument may refer to Mr. Darwin's Descent of Man (vol. ii., p. 377, etc.) It is clear that the concession is made respecting the inapplicability of Natural Selection, but when Mr. Wallace wrote, he knew not the wonderful power and possibilities which were about to be attributed by his friend to Sexual Selection. It should be observed that much of what makes against the one equally invalidates the other agency. Mr. Darwin's argument on this subject appears to amount to this—what Natural Selection could not do, and no one supposes that it did, Sexual Selection *probably* did; and there are various reasons for supposing that it did. But Mr. Wallace, the co-discoverer of Natural Selection, had really supposed that Mr. Darwin and his friends had all conceived our hairlessness to be due to Natural Selection.

"It seems to me then," says Mr. Wallace, "to be absolutely certain, that 'Natural Selection' could not have produced man's hairless body by the accumulation of variations from a hairy ancestor. The evidence all goes to show that such variations could not have been useful, but on the contrary, must have been to some extent hurtful. Two characters could hardly be wider apart, than the size and development of man's brain, and the distribution of hair upon his body; yet they both lead us to the same conclusion—that some other power than Natural Selection has been engaged in his production."

Other physical characteristics of man might be instanced for the same argument, particularly the Feet and the Hands of man. Throughout the whole of the Quadrumana, the foot is prehensile; and a very rigid selection must have been requisite to bring about that arrangement of the bones and muscles which has converted the thumb into a great toe; so completely has the power of "opposability" been totally lost in every race, whatever some teachers may say to the contrary. Nor is there any apparent reason why the prehensile power should have been taken away.

As to the powers of the human voice, they are only briefly adverted to by Mr. Wallace as another exception to the power of Natural Selection, bnt a very strong argument against the operation of that power or metaphor, might be founded upon this peculiarly human possession—and well founded in relation to Mr. Darwin's recently expressed views, which Mr. Wallace at the time he wrote had not before him.

The problem is simply this: In man, especially in the female sex, we have the larynx capable of producing not only articulate speech (which might be considered apart), but over and far above that, musical sounds of a wonderful and enchanting character. The flexibility, the compass, the magical achievements of the human voice are notorious and unfailing. Its highest achievements are exceptional, but they belong to the human race, and must be accounted for by any physical hypothesis which accounts for man. Mr. Wallace regards them as out of the power of Natural Selection to produce. "The habits of savages," he says, " give no indication of how this faculty could have been developed by Natural Selection, because it is never required or used by them. The singing of savages is a more or less monotonous howling, and the females seldom sing at all. Savages certainly never choose wives for their fine voices, but for rude health and strength and physical beauty. Sexual Selection therefore could not have developed this wonderful power, which only comes into play among civilized people. It seems as if the organ had been prepared in anticipation of the future progress of man, since it contains latent capacities which are useless to him in his earlier condition. The delicate correlations of structure that give it such marvellous power could not therefore have been acquired by means of Natural Selection."

Let us now hear Mr. Darwin: "The capacity

and love for singing and music, though not a sexual character in man, must not here be passed over. Although the sounds emitted by animals of all kinds serve many purposes, a strong case can be made out, that the vocal organs were primarily used and perfected in relation to the propagation of the species. Insects and some few species are the lowest animals which voluntarily produce any sound, and this is generally effected by the aid of beautifully constructed stridulating organs, which are often confined to the males alone. The sounds thus produced consist, I believe, in all cases, of the same note, repeated rhythmically, and this is pleasing even to the ears of man. Their chief, and in some cases exclusive use appears to be either to call or to charm the opposite sex.

"The sounds produced by fishes are said in some cases to be made by the males during the breeding season. All the air-breathing Vertebrata necessarily possess an apparatus for inhaling and expelling air, with a pipe capable of being closed at one end. Hence when the primeval members of this class were strongly excited, and their muscles violently contracted, purposeless sounds would almost certainly have been produced, and then, if they proved in any way serviceable, might readily have been modified or intensified by the preservation of properly adapted variations. In the class of Mammals, with which we are here more particularly concerned, the males of almost all the species use their voices during the breeding season, much more than at any other time; and some are absolutely mute excepting at this season. Both sexes of other species, or the female alone, use their voice as a love-call. Considering these facts, and that the vocal organs of some quadrupeds are much more largely developed in the male than in the female, either permanently or temporarily during the breeding season; and considering that in most of the lower classes the sounds produced by the males serve not only to call but to allure the female, it is a surprising fact that we have not as yet any good evidence that these organs are used by male mammals to charm the females.

"The perception, if not the enjoyment of musical cadences and of rhythm is probably common to all animals, and no doubt depends on the common physiological nature of their nervous systems. With man song is admitted to be the basis or origin of instrumental music. As neither the enjoyment nor the capacity of producing musical notes are faculties of the least direct use to man in reference to his ordinary habits in life, they must be ranked amongst the most mysterious with which he is endowed. They are present, though in a very rude and as it appears almost latent condition, in men of all races, even the most savage; but so different is the taste of the different races, that our music gives not the least pleasure to savages, and their music is to us hideous and unmeaning.... Whether or not the half human progenitors of man possessed, like the before mentioned gibbon, the capacity of producing, and no doubt of appreciating, musical notes, we have every reason to believe that man possessed these faculties at a very remote period, for singing and music are very ancient arts."*

In all the preceding observations, and in those which follow them in Mr. Darwin's pages, there does not appear any direct or even probable evidence that vocal, or the taste for instrumental music, has the slightest connection with Natural Selection, or any continuous connection with Sexual Selection. What is ad-

* " D scent of Man," Vol. ii., pp. 330—334.

vanced may be and apparently is true as to the animals referred to, but there is no kind of relation between their noises and our music; nor can the stridulation of beetles or other insects, or of crustaceans, or the cries of mammals, or even the rude shouts or songs of savages be compared with any seriousness to the singing of man. To attempt to establish a developmental connection between them seems to be simply ludicrous. The flexibility and extensive capacity of the human larynx are exclusively and peculiarly human. They are by no means mysterious when regarded as a particular endowment imparted directly by the Creator, but regarded in the light of development or selection from entomological sounds, they are mysterious beyond many mysteries, and could only be received as developmental, or sexually or naturally selected, upon the saintly principle of "*Credo quia impossibile est.*" Ridicule might be poured abundantly and easily on any such proposition.

But if the hypothesis breaks down upon so important a matter, and on one so readily apprehensible by all mankind, and if it likewise fails in respect of the other matters above named, and upon several which might be further instanced, what is its remaining validity?

On this subject of music Mr. Wallace is at issue with Mr. Darwin, and Mr. Herbert Spencer comes to an exactly opposite conclusion. The last-named theorist comes to the conclusion that the cadences used in emotional speech afford the foundation from which music has been developed; whilst Mr. Darwin concludes that musical notes and rhythm were first acquired by the male or female progenitors of mankind for the sake of charming the opposite sex. What then was the music of the transitional being depicted by Mr. Darwin in the passage previously quoted (p. 281)? It must by supposition have been a confused sound, if anything musical or rhythmical sounded from such a bisexual compound. But if this bisexual compound emitted no kind of musical sound, what becomes of the development of preceding entomological and crustacean stridulations?

Not only does Mr. Darwin adhere to such a theory, but he actually asserts that "the impassioned orator, bard, or musician, while with his varied tones and cadences he excites the strongest emotions in his hearers, little suspects that he uses the same means by which at an extremely remote period, his half human ancestors aroused each others' ardent passions, during their mutual courtship and rivalry." So that oratory, poetry, music, are nothing more than the issue of the crude dissonances of an hypothetical and incredible semi-humanity!

XIII.

MENTAL AND MORAL EVOLUTION.

IT will be advisable to cite Mr. Darwin's words on this subject:

"The greatest difficulty which presents itself when we are driven to the above conclusion on the origin of man" (in a remote aquatic animal), "is the high standard of intellectual power and of moral disposition which he has attained. But every one who admits the general principle of Evolution, must see that the mental powers of the higher animals, which are the same in kind with those of mankind, though so different in degree, are capable of advancement. Thus the interval between the mental forces of one of the higher apes and of a fish, or between those of an ant and scale-insect, is immense. The development of these powers in animals does not offer any special difficulty, for with our domesticated animals, the mental faculties are certainly variable, and the variations are inherited. No one doubts that these faculties are of the utmost importance to animals in a state of Nature. Therefore the considerations are favourable for their development through Natural Selection. The same conclusions may be extended to man; the intellect must have been all-important to him, even at a very remote period, enabling him to use language, to invent and make weapons, tools, traps, etc.; by which means, in combination with his social habits, he long ago became the most dominant of all living creatures.

* * * * * *

"The higher intellectual powers of man, such as those of ratiocination, abstraction, self-consciousness, etc., will have followed from the continued improvement of other mental faculties: but without considerable culture of the mind, both in the race and in the individual, it is doubtful whether these higher powers would be exercised, and thus fully attained."

" The development of the moral qualities is a more difficult and interesting problem. Their foundations lie in the social instincts, including in this term the family tie. These instincts are of a highly complex nature, and in the case of the lower animals, have special tendencies towards certain definite actions; but the more important elements for us are love, and the distinct emotion of sympathy. Animals endowed with the social instincts take pleasure in each other's company, warn each other of danger, defend and aid each other in many ways. These instincts are not extended to all the individuals of the species, but only to those of the same community. As they are highly beneficial to the species, they have in all probability been acquired through Natural Selection.

"A moral being is one who is capable of comparing his past, future actions and motives, —of approving of some and disapproving of others; and the fact that man is the one being who with certainty can be thus designated, makes the greatest of all distinction between him and the lower animals." *

Concerning this statement, which is quite sufficient, and explicit enough to represent the hypothesis, although much more might be quoted, let us briefly reason:—

It is plain that Mr. Darwin assigns both the intellectual and moral qualities of man to the power and process of Natural Selection, and he

* "Descent of Man," Vol. ii., pp. 390—2.

could not do otherwise consistently with his hypothesis. This appears to be a fundamental error; for intelligence as to the intellect, and the moral sense as to morality, are both incapable of being resolved into anything lower or simpler than themselves. They are *distinct*, *original*, and not DERIVATIVE endowments, and no multiplication of similitudes in the faculties of lower animals can abolish their originality and distinctness. The error arises from confounding resemblances with identity—and to an analytic and unbiassed reader of Mr. Darwin's instances and illustrations, it must appear that the resemblances are as far from identity as they can possibly be. Moreover, resemblances both mental and physiological pervade the organic world, because the Creator has acted upon a connected plan, call it type or evolution, or what we please. He has wrought and is still working upon a supremely-wise and long preconsidered plan, which displays to us the unity that characterizes Himself. He is one, and His plan is one. In its unity His plan is the reflection of the Divine unity.

Unity of plan, however, admits of multiform distinctions in execution, and just as a human architect or machinist works to his preconceived idea, with various differences of detail and with various evidences of intervention, so did the Creator, here introducing one kind of life, there another. Again he is discovered adding one distinctive element and then another. Such is the result not of Natural but of Divine Selection.

A like current of thought seems to have passed through the mind of Mr. Wallace, who, I may venture to say, appears to me a more philosophical and unprejudiced expositor of Natural Selection than even Mr. Darwin. Though Mr. Wallace cherishes a paternal affection for his own principle, his affection is not as blind as parental affection commonly is. He sees the shortcomings and failures of his own offspring, and will not through excess of the amiable weakness of natural paternity shut his eyes to what is wrong, or devote his advocacy to what is manifestly unreasonable. Hence we are disposed to listen to him when he confesses the inadequacy of his beloved progeny, Natural Selection.

"Turning to the mind of man," says Mr. Wallace, "we meet with many difficulties in attempting to understand how those mental faculties, which are especially human, could have been acquired by the preservation of useful variation. At first sight, it would seem that such feelings as those of abstract justice and benevolence could never have been so acquired, because they are incompatible with the law of the strongest, which is the essence of Natural Selection. But there is another class of human faculties that do not regard our fellow man, and which cannot therefore be thus accounted for. Such are the capacity to form ideal conceptions of space and time, of eternity and infinity—the capacity for intense artistic feelings of pleasure, in form, colour, or composition—and for those abstract notions of form and number, which render geometry and arithmetic possible—how were all or any of these faculties first developed, when they could have been of no possible use to man in his early stage of barbarism? How could Natural Selection, or Survival of the Fittest in the struggle for existence, at all favour the development of mental powers entirely removed from the material necessities of savage men, and which even now, with our comparatively high civilization, are, in their farthest development, in advance of the age, and appear to have relation rather to the future of the race than to its actual status?"

Then in respect of the origin of the moral sense, Mr. Wallace continues: "Exactly the same difficulty arises, when we endeavour to account for the development of the moral sense or conscience in savage man, for although the practice of benevolence, honesty, or truth may have been useful to the tribe possessing these virtues, that does not at all account for the peculiar *sanctity* attached to actions which each tribe considers right and moral, as contrasted with the very different feelings with which they regard what is useful. The Utilitarian hypothesis (which is the theory of Natural Selection applied to the mind), seems inadequate to account for the development of the moral sense. This subject has been recently very much discussed, and I will here only give one example to illustrate my argument. The utilitarian sanction for truthfulnesss is by no means very powerful or universal. Few cases enforce it. No very sure reprobation follows untruthfulness. In all ages and countries falsehood has been thought allowable in love, and laudable in war; while at the present day, it is held to be venial by the majority of mankind, in trade, commerce, and speculation. A certain amount of truthfulness is a necessary part of politeness in the east and west alike, while even some moralists have held a lie justifiable, to elude an enemy or prevent a crime. Such being the difficulties with which this virtue has had to struggle, with so many exceptions to its practice, with so many instances in which it brought ruin or death to its too ardent devotee, how can we believe that considerations of utility, could ever invest it with the mysterious sanctity of the highest virtue,—could ever induce men to value truth for its own sake, and practise it regardless of consequences?"

● ● ● ● ● ● ●

"It is difficult to conceive that such intense and mystical feeling of right and wrong (so intense as to overcome all ideas of personal advantage or utility), could have been developed out of accumulated ancestral experience of utility; and still more difficult to understand how feelings developed by one set of utilities could be transferred to acts of which the utility was partial, imaginary, or altogether absent. But if a moral sense is an essential part of our nature, it is easy to see that its sanction may be given to acts which are useless or immoral; just as the natural appetite for drink is perverted by the drunkard into the means of his destruction." *

We cannot dwell too emphatically on man's moral sense as one of his most distinctive peculiarities. It is not a mere product of cultivation developed by utilitarian considerations, but an innate or inherent principle, animating even savages. The Kurubars and Santals, barbarous hill tribes of Central India, are noted for veracity, for it is a common saying that "a Kurubar always speaks the truth," and Major Jervis says, "the Santals are the most truthful men I ever met with." As a remarkable instance of this quality, the following fact is given : "A number of prisoners taken during the Santal insurrection, were allowed to go free on parole, to work at a certain spot for wages. After some time cholera attacked them, and they were obliged to leave, but every man of them returned and gave up his earnings to the guard. Two hundred savages with money in their girdles, walked thirty miles to prison, rather than break their word!" "My own experience among savages," adds Mr. Wallace, "has furnished me with similar, though less severely tested, instances ; and we cannot

* "Contributions to the Theory of Natural Selection," p. 355.

avoid asking, how is it that in these few cases "experience of utility" have left such an overwhelming impression, while in so many others they have left none? The experience of savage men as regards the utility of truth, must in the long run be pretty nearly equal. How is it then, that in some cases the result is a sanctity which overrides all considerations of personal advantage, while in others there is hardly a rudiment of such a feeling? The intuitional theory, which I am now advocating, explains the supposition that there is a feeling, —a sense of right and wrong—in our nature antecedent to and independent of experiences of utility."

In this view Mr. Wallace will commend himself to most men, and it seems unaccountable that his friend and fellow naturalist, Mr. Darwin, after having read Mr. Wallace's statement, which however is only a repetition and enforcement of general opinion, should advocate one that opposes it. "I fully subscribe," says Mr. Darwin, "to the judgment of those writers who maintain that of all the differences between man and the lower animals, the moral sense or conscience is by far the most important." This sense, as Sir J. Mackintosh remarks, "has a rightful supremacy over every other principle of human action;" it is summed up in that short but imperious word *ought*, so full of high significance. It is the most noble of all the attributes of man, leading him without a moment's hesitation to risk his life for that of a fellow creature; or after due deliberation, impelled simply by the deep feeling of right or duty, to sacrifice it in some great cause. Immanuel Kant exclaims, "Duty! wondrous thought that worketh neither by foul insinuation, flattery, nor by any threat, but merely by holding up thy naked law in the soul, and so extorting for thyself always reverence, if not always obedience; before whom all appetites are dumb, however secretly they rebel ; whence thy original?"

This great question which has been discussed by many writers of consummate ability, and my sole excuse for touching on it is the impossibility of here passing it over, and because so far as I know, no one has approached it exclusively from the side of natural history. The investigation also possesses some independent interest, as an attempt to see how far the study of the lower animals can throw light on one of the highest psychical faculties of man.

The following proposition seems to me in a high degree probable, namely, that any animal whatever, endowed with well-marked social instincts, would inevitably acquire a moral sense or conscience as soon as its intellectual powers have become as well developed, or nearly as well developed, as in man.

Mr. Darwin proceeds to contend for this from several considerations : as these—(1) The social instincts lead an animal to take pleasure in the society of its fellows. (2) As soon as the mental faculties had become highly developed, images of all past actions and motives would be incessantly passing through the brain of each individual, and that feeling of dissatisfaction which invariably results from any unsatisfied instinct, would arise as often as it was perceived that the enduring and always present social instinct had yielded to some other instinct at the time strange, but neither enduring in its nature, nor leaving behind it a very vivid impression. (3) After the power of language had been acquired, and the wishes of the members of the same community could be distinctly expressed, the common opinion how each member ought to act for the public good would naturally become to a large extent the guide to action. (4) Habit in the individual would ultimately play a very important part in guiding the conduct of each member; for the social instincts and impulses, like all other instincts and impulses, would be greatly strengthened by habit, as would obedience to the wishes and judgment of the community.*

These propositions are discussed, some of them at considerable length, by Mr. Darwin in the chapter devoted to this subject. The whole discussion appears to take rather an apologetic than an elucidatory tone, and attempts to show how such things *may* be rather than why they *are* as we find them. Approached exclusively from the natural history side, the moral sense is viewed simply as a natural instinct, and by no means as moral and religious writers view it. Other purely naturalistic writers regard this principle in the same light. Thus Mr. Herbert Spencer (termed by Mr. Darwin, who quotes the following passage, " our great philosopher,") says, " I believe that the experiences of utility organized and consolidated through all past generations of the human race, have been producing corresponding modifications, which, by continued transmission and accumulation have

* "Descent of Man," Vol. i., p. 73.

become in us certain moral faculties of moral intuition—certain emotions responding to unjust and wrong conduct, which have no apparent basis in the individual experience of utility."

What is the value of this but a connection between mental and social phenomena which the authors themselves perceive or believe, but which has no foundation in the common opinion of mankind, and which is indeed contrary to our primary and our religious instincts. No considerations of utility answer to the solution of the problem, which is this—Present and operative the moral sense in man, even in many instances in his savage state :—that being given, how are we to discover its origin? There is nothing corresponding to it in the inferior animals, and we look to the human race for its first real manifestation. All the resemblances to it previously displayed by animals are so faint and so undefinable as to fall altogether short of derivative connection with it; when observed in the human race, it is plainly an initial and newly imparted principle. If founded upon the consolidation of an exceedingly long accumulation of experiences of utility, whence came the primary experience of utility? whence came the accumulative-growth? at what stage occurred the conversion of an accumulation of experiences of utility into that entirely different thing, the moral sense of man; which, as shown by Mr. Wallace, and as well known to all, in its nobler exercises utterly discards utility, openly rejects it as a principle of action, and looks fixedly to the good, and above the useful to the true and the self-denying? The moral sense of man, and the religious feeling associated with it in many exhibitions of its power, goes against all the accumulated experiences of utility of past generations. It wars against the world and its laws. Accumulated experiences, of mere utility in the present are opposed to it, and so far as their activity and power extend, would extinguish it. A sense of selfish or social utility may, and sometimes does, govern men so far as make them rebel against their moral sense; but selfish adherence to the idea of present utility is regarded as our bane, not as the conquence of the exercise of moral sense. If our moral sense and conscience be not directly and distinctively implanted in us by the Deity, then man has no principle directly derived from Him; the very result, however, at which naturalistic systems are designed to arrive by their advocates. Yet when they desire to bring us to this result, the burden of proof rests upon *them*. Faint adumbrations of animal intelligence, indistinct lines of supposed connection, and wholly imaginary deductions from a few selected phenomena of Natural History, are utterly inadequate to sustain a strong contradiction to our primary beliefs.

One additional extract from Mr. Darwin's new book will show how he regards some of the stronger feelings in man's moral nature.

"At the moment of action, man will no doubt be apt to follow the stronger influence, and though this may occasionally prompt him to the nobler deeds, it will far more commonly leave him to gratify his own desire at the expense of other men. But after that gratification, when past and weaker impressions are contrasted with the ever-enduring social interests, retribution will surely come. Man will then feel dissatisfied with himself, and will resolve with more or less force to act differently for the future. This is conscience; for conscience looks backward and judges past actions, inducing that kind of dissatisfaction, which if weak we call regret, and if severe, remorse.

"These sensations are no doubt different from

those experienced when other instincts are left unsatisfied; but every unsatisfied instinct has its own proper prompting sensation, as we recognize with hunger, thirst, etc. Man thus prompted will through long habit acquire such prompt self-command, that his desires and passions will at last instantly yield to his social sympathies, and there will no longer be a struggle between them. The still hungry, and the still revengeful man will not think of stealing food, or of wreaking his vengeance. It is possible, or, as we shall hereafter see, even probable, that the habit of self-command may, like other habits, be inherited. Thus at last man comes to feel, through acquired, and perhaps inherited habits, that it is best for him to obey his more persistent instincts. The imperious word *ought* seems merely to imply the consciousness of the existence of a persistent instinct, either innate or partly acquired, serving him as a guide, though liable to be disobeyed. We hardly use the word *ought* in a metaphysical sense, when we say hounds ought to hunt, pointers to point, and retrievers to retrieve their game. If they fail thus to act, they fail in their duty and act wrongly.

"If any desire or instinct, leading to an

action opposed to the good of others, still appears to a man, when re-called to mind, as strong as, or stronger than his social instincts, he will feel no keen regret at having followed it; but he will be conscious, that if his conduct were known to his fellows, it would meet with their disapprobation; and few are so destitute of sympathy as not to feel discomfort when this is realized. If he has no such sympathy, and if his desires leading to bad actions are at the time strong, and when recalled are not overmastered by the persistent social instincts, then he is essentially a bad man; and the sole restraining motive left is the fear of punishment, and the conviction that in the long run it would be best for his own selfish interests to regain the good of others rather than his own.

"It is obvious that every one may with an easy conscience gratify his own desires, if they do not interfere with his moral instincts, that is, with the good of others; but in order to be quite free from self-reproach, or at least of anxiety, it is almost necessary for him to avoid the disapprobation, whether reasonable or not, of his fellow-men. Nor must he break through the fixed habits of his life, especially if these are supported by reason; for if he does, he will assuredly feel dissatisfaction. He must likewise avoid the disapprobation of the one God, or gods, in whom, according to his knowledge or superstition, he may believe; but in this case the additional fear of Divine punishment often supervenes." *

Does not this read rather like an extract from Seneca or Plutarch, than from an accomplished author now living in England? Let these passages be carefully perused, and it will at once be seen that strict Naturalism here supersedes all religious impulses, and that the moral sense of man is placed on a level with the *ought* of dogs, who ought to hunt, point, and retrieve—and who, if they do not, fail in their duty and act wrongly, as man does when he does not perform what he *ought*. Here we have no higher appeal in one case than to the canine, and in the other than to the social conscience. Let the whole of these passages, and of the chapter of which they afford a fair specimen, be studied in the light of the recent tremendous events which have happened in France, and then let a just verdict be pronounced on the value of the canine, or Communistic, or social sense of *ought*.

* "Descent of Man," Vol. i., pp. 91—98.

Let also the reader of these extracts from Darwin afterwards turn to some clear and well-approved author who has written on mind and morals, and observe how little the one accords with the other. Turn for example to Thomas Reid on the " Active Powers of the Mind," and peruse the following :—

" The faculties of man unfold themselves in a certain order, appointed by the great Creator. In their gradual process they may be greatly assisted or retarded, improved or corrupted by education, instruction, example, exercise, and by the society and conversation of men, which, like soil and culture in plants, may produce great changes to the better or to the worse.

" But these means can never produce any new faculties, nor any other than were originally planted in the mind by the Author of Nature. And what is common to the whole species, in all the varieties of instruction and education, of improvement, and degeneracy, is the work of God, and not the operation of second causes.

" Such we may justly account conscience, or the faculty of distinguishing right conduct from wrong ; since it appears, and in all nations and ages, has appeared in men that are come to maturity. The seeds, as it were, of moral discernment are planted in the mind by him that made us." *

Without, for the present, pursuing the course of Mr. Darwin's arguments, or apologetic opinions, in this page, let us take a brief survey from the point at which we have arrived. From this summit-level we can clearly and comprehensively glance round at what Mr. Darwin has attempted and accomplished, or failed to accomplish. He has conducted his readers through the entanglements of the Origin of Species, and has attempted to show them that the effects which man brings to pass in the breeding of certain animals by means of the use of his knowledge of Selection, and by the exercise of his *will* in making such selection, is a ground for a theory of the Transformation of Species in Nature by something which has *no will*, no objective existence, and which is called Natural Selection. Necessarily a metaphorical factor has not personal will; necessarily inorganic matter can have no will; necessarily no "Law of Nature" can have a will, because the law itself is by hypothesis inflexible and unalterable, and if it had will, would cease to be so, because that will might change. There-

* Reid. Ed. Hamilton, p. 595

fore, we see that the Darwinian theory is based upon what man accomplishes by the exercise of choice and means, while the executive agent or agents in that theory cannot, in consistency with their impersonality, exhibit *will* in the manner of a human personality.

Yet, although they cannot exercise will, although they are merely metaphorical expressions for something else never explained, they, and especially the particular and chief agent, have been operating from the infinitely remote period of the creation of the first primordial germ or germs of organized existence. By selective, and intensely energetic selective action, this principal power or agency without personality has brought into existence a wonderful series of consequences, which, when contemplated altogether, astonish man, and would even astonish any higher beings, if there be such, than the human race, especially as the survey of existence by higher beings would be broader than the survey open to man.

But as man, and particularly higher beings than himself, exercise will to a great extent, and in the survey of Nature behold innumerable results which their united wills could not achieve, what would be their astonishment to learn that all these are brought to pass by something which subsequently evolves will, which unaccountably acts by it, and which, though acting from unreckonable time, through unnumbered ages, and acting always for the preservation of the beneficial and the extinction of the injurious and the weak, nevertheless is will-less and soulless, and possesses nothing more than a name?

Lo! here at the end of the series of natural marvels is Man—Man, the wonder and the glory of the universe! Emphatically he is so, and one of his principal claims to universal wonder and glory is that he exercises will, choice, and preference, and partly controls inanimate and animate Nature by them; and the higher he rises, and the more cultured and pronounced his intellectual power, the stronger, the nobler, the more dominant is his will. The will of man is indeed a wonderful power; how was it produced? by that which had no volition; yet that which has operated involuntarily has evolved him—man with his will as well as his moral sense; that is, some agencies metaphorically represented by Natural or Sexual Selection, which hypothetically and metaphorically can have no will, have evolved the highest embodiment of will known to our earth! In brief, No-Will has evolved Will!

Now a reader of the works of strict naturalists is accustomed to see scoffs at what are sneeringly called " Hebrew myths," particularly at the creation of matter out of nothing. Here, however, I find this very Hebrew myth equalled or surpassed in incredibility. No-Will has evolved human will. For this, I have no testimony but that of Mr. Darwin and other evolutionists, for the other I have a testimony at the least somewhat higher, and at the least accepted by a majority of cultivated mankind.

A " Hebrew myth " (it is Mr. Spencer's phrase) also informs me that God created man and woman, and I am led by this myth to suppose that such creation was special, whether so as to body and soul, or only as to soul, I am not about to discuss at this moment; but in distinct terms, the human creation is represented as a special or overt act of God. In contradiction to this Hebrew myth, Mr. Spencer ridicules in the most pointed terms the idea of any special creation, and Mr. Darwin congratulates himself that he has at least done something praiseworthy in overturning this dogma. How? By agencies deficient in personality, and to which nothing but a scientific myth gives a name! Of the two myths, which will men prefer? Assuredly the Hebrew myth is at least as credible as the Darwinian. Let us omit inspiration and authority, and confine ourselves to reasonableness and credibleness. If one be "unthinkable," (to borrow Mr. Spencer's favourite term) so is the other. Then if they are both and equally unthinkable, I take my choice, and I prefer the Mosaic or Biblical to the Darwinian myth. Suppose both to be myths, which of the two is the more acceptable myth?

But when we arrive at man's mind, psychology, and his moral sense, conscience, and duty, I find the Darwinian myth absolutely and hopelessly incredible. In trying to think it, I exercise that power of mine which is said to be in me the evolved product of another power, which, however, being merely a metaphor or name, could not think. My brain operates so as to impel me to a choice after full consideration. What influences me to this choice? Thought and reasoning. What evolved or made thought and reason in me? That which has neither; that which is nothing. Thus No-Thought has evolved my thought. *Ex nihilo nihil fit* has been the world-ruling apothegm, but it is false, for here behold *Ex nihilo aliquid. Ex nihilo Mens!* If this be not the Darwinian formula, I know not what to substitute in its place.

In reply to this formula, Mr. Wallace would probably say, " Natural Selection is only a means by which the Creator worked ; " if so, as before argued, our difference is chiefly verbal ; but this is apparently not the view of Mr. Darwin, as I gather from his books. It is the view of Mr. Wallace, and the consequence is that he is necessarily, though reluctantly, conducted to the belief that man is specially developed by a superior intelligence. " The inference " (to cite his own words) " I would draw from this class of phenomena is that a superior intelligence has guided the development of man in a definite direction, and for a special purpose, just as man guides the development of many animal and vegetable forms. The laws of Evolution alone would, perhaps, never have produced a grain so well adapted to man's use as wheat and maize, such fruits as the seedless banana and bread-fruit, or such animals as the Guernsey milch cow, or the London dray horse. Yet these so closely resemble the unaided productions of nature, that we may well imagine a being who had mastered the laws of development of organic forms through past ages, refusing to believe that any new power had been concerned in their production, and scornfully rejecting the theory (as my theory will be rejected by many who agree with me on other points) that in these few cases a controlling intelligence has directed the action of the laws of variation, multiplication, and survival, for his own purposes. We know, however, that this has been done, and we must therefore admit the possibility that, if we are not the highest intelligencies in the universe, some higher intelligence may have directed the process by which the human race was developed, by means of more subtle agencies than we are acquainted with. At the same time, I must confess that this theory has the disadvantage of requiring the intervention of some distinct individual intelligence, to aid in what we can hardly avoid considering as the ultimate aim and outcome of all organized existence, intellectual, ever-advancing, spiritual man. It therefore implies that the great laws which govern the material universe were insufficient for his production, unless we consider (as we may fairly do) that the controlling action of such higher intelligences is a necessary part of those laws, just as the action of all surrounding organisms is one of the agencies in organic development.*

This very instructive passage derives its importance from its author's claim before mentioned as the thinker who evolved from his own mind the idea of Natural Selection, and of which he is one of the foremost advocates and supporters.

If there be any advantage in continuing our retrospective survey of the Darwinian hypothesis from the summit level of man, the advantage will chiefly be found in an exposure of the dangerous and destructive consequences to Society which would follow from the universal reception of such a system of pure Naturalism.

Society cannot be kept together without religion, and this even Mr. Spencer admits very openly. Now the universal reception of the theory that man, body, soul, and spirit, is evolved by some such purely natural agencies as Natural and Sexual Selection—always remembering that they are represented *exclusively as natural* by Mr. Darwin; and quite apart from my admission that there are certain principles more or less closely corresponding to these,

* Wallace on Natural Selection, p. 360.

which are means by which the Creator creates and preserves, or evolves or derives, as respects the material world—the universal reception, I repeat, of pure, total, and exclusive Naturalism in relation to body and soul, matter and spirit, would evidently destroy the first principles of spiritual religion. The extracts from Mr. Darwin given in these pages sufficiently show this, but a perusal of his entire works would make it distinctly manifest.

Primarily, if man, as a whole, be nothing beyond the last trophy or climax of Natural and Sexual Selection, then (putting aside minor questions relating to the descent of man from the inferior animals) he is nothing more than the highest zoological organism, the last and best animal beyond beasts or brutes, these terms being here, of course, used in a zoological sense. He is not a distinct creation; by hypothesis he is determined not to be such, and all his hopes and fears, all his religion, all his art, poetry, music, and imagination, are the ultimate outcomes of supreme animality. He is as one of the beasts that perish, he came into existence as they do, and like them he goes out of existence.

Secondarily: If all his mental and moral and psychical faculties are simply evolutions of utilitarianism and sociology, if they have their origin and their ends as in Mr. Darwin's views above expressed, then there is no need of God to man, and no immediate use of God to man, and no obligation of man to God. His obligation, under such views, is to his fellow-men; his moral instincts spring from sympathy with his fellow-men; his regrets and remorse only apply to his failures of duty and sympathy towards them. Any other kind of remorse or regret has a reference to the fear of punishment by any God or gods in whom man may believe. Now it must be obvious that for those who hold such sentiments there can be no other religion than natural growth, no other motive than present utility, no further aim than this world and its sociology. What there may be of motive beyond these, springs from fear of punishment by some one God, or by many gods.

When a man is taught only to trace his moral and religious instincts downwards and reversely, he is not likely often to look upwards and prospectively. He will not, therefore, feel any obligation to worship the Spiritual Being known to Theists as God. His education and civilization will forbid him to worship animals, even the animals constituting his nearest ancestry. He may be averse to idolatry, but no appreciation of what Natural Selection has done for him will prompt him to share in anything that can bear the true character of religious worship. As an example, a full believer in the truth of Darwinism can scarcely ever, without the Darwinian amount of regret and remorse, employ one of the forms of prayer continually used in the Prayer Book of the Church of England; for instead of exclaiming, "We thank Thee for our Creation and Preservation, and all the blessings of this life," he *ought* to say, in all truthfulness, "We thank Thee for our Evolution, for Natural Selection, and all the blessings of Sexual Selection." It is manifest that the extreme application of the principles of this theory would lead to a burlesque of most forms of religious worship.

Without a much higher origin than Mr. Darwin allows to the moral sense and to regret and remorse, the principles of social Law would probably prove inefficient, and society would return to savagery. To Communism, indeed, strict Naturalism appears to be fully suitable. Immediate utility is its ruling principle, and so fear of God troubles it. No one can read the works, and regard the acts of Communists, especially in France, without observing that the Communists do act upon the most naked Naturalism, and the extremest views of utilitarianism. Let it be repeated that no fair opponent of Mr. Darwin will involve him personally in any extreme consequences of his theory, but when adverting to such consequences, the use of his name becomes unavoidable. I employ the term " pure naturalists" as frequently as possible, in order to escape the repetition of respected names. While, however reluctant to continue the use of this name, I cannot forbear continuing in a few paragraphs the same course of remark as to the effects of any such purely naturalistic hypothesis of the origin and psychical evolution of man. " The belief in God," says Mr. Darwin, " has been often advanced as not only the greatest, but the most complete of all the distinctions between man and the lower animals. It is, however, impossible, as we have seen, to maintain that this belief is innate or instinctive in man. On the other hand, a belief in all pervading spiritual agencies seems to be universal, and apparently follows from a considerable advance in the reasoning powers of man, and from a still greater advance in his faculties of imagination, curiosity, and wonder. I am aware that the assumed instinctive belief in God has been used by many persons as an argument for His existence. But this is a rash argument, as we should thus be compelled to believe in the existence of many evil and malignant spirits, possessing only a little more power than man ; for the belief in them is far more general than of a beneficent Deity. The idea of a universal and beneficent Creator of the universe does not seem to arise in the mind of man, until he has been elevated by long-continued culture."

If our belief in God be not instinctive or innate, if it be an exception to the power of the evolutionary agent, whether natural or other selection ; and since it is confessed that it follows only from a considerable advance in the reasoning power and other faculties of man, then it is surely imparted to man by a distinct power far above Nature. If so, why may not the other and allied human psychical principles, such as the moral sense, and such as belief in the soul's existence and immortality, be imparted to man by the same supernatural power? If our belief in God be not a consequence of Evolution, how can other beliefs be? How can our belief in utility, our belief in sympathy towards and from our fellow-man, our belief even in their existence, be evolved in us? If the highest of these beliefs be independent of derivative production, how can the lowest of the same nature be other than exceptions? and if all are exceptions to it, then why are not all our mental capacities and faculties equal exceptions? If long continued cultivation can originate and perfect one, and that one of the most important of our ideas, why not all? and if all, what does the human mind owe to Natural Selection, or any other similar agency? It is essentially distinct.

Again, no amount of culture can be conceived as capable of originating and advancing in any animal below that of man the idea of a universal and beneficent Creator of the universe. This will be at once admitted as an impossibility. But if so, it is a distinct belief or principle in man; therefore by so much is man a distinct species; and his possession of this belief is so special as to specialize him from all inferior animals, and hence no process of natural transition or evolution can account for his mental capacities.

Once more, "On the other hand, a belief in all-pervading spiritual agencies seems to be universal." It is not so in the lower animals, and does not so far as we can judge, exist in them at all. Therefore this also is a distinctly human and universally human belief, and thereby universally separates man from the inferior zoological organisms, and again implies his special creation, at least in part.

"I am aware," confesses Mr. Darwin, "that the conclusions arrived at in this work will be denounced by some as highly irreligious, but he who thus denounces them is bound to show why it is more irreligious to explain the origin of man as a distinct species from some lower form through the laws of variation and natural selection than to explain the birth of the individual through the laws of ordinary representation. The birth both of the species and of the individual are equally parts of that grand sequence of events which our minds refuse to accept as the results of blind chance. The understanding revolts at such a conclusion, whether or not we are able to believe that every slight variation of structure, the union of each pair in marriage, the dissemination of each seed, and other such events, have all been ordained for some special purpose." (Descent of Man, ii., 396.)

Surely the difference between the two processes cannot have escaped so acute a mind as that of Mr. Darwin. To explain the birth of an individual through the laws of ordinary reproduction, is to explain an undoubted and universally known phenomenon. To explain the origin of Man as a distinct species by descent from some lower form, through the laws of variation and Natural Selection, is to explain merely an *hypothesis*, not a *universally observed and accepted fact*. All the human world knows the one to be true; a very insignificant portion of that world believes in the other—and no mere belief can prove it to be a fact.

Whether the conclusions arrived at by the author of any book be irreligious must be judged not by the author's state of mind in making them public, nor by anything in his personal character or belief. The judgment must be founded on the consequences which would follow if his conclusions, when announced and published, should be universally adopted and carried out to their extreme length. Judged in this way a considerable number of persons must believe that Mr. Darwin's book has a decidedly irreligious tendency, and that his conclusions could not be generally adopted without the subversion of the religious principles which pervade and actuate the greater number of European societies. Further, as before intimated, so far as Religion cements and conserves society, and influences and controls it, so far the general reception of these conclusions would be subversive of the highest public principle. Subtract from any modern society a distinct belief in creation and the Creator, the certainty of the existence of a beneficent God and his continual connection with Nature, the belief of His spiritual accessibleness and nearness, man's instinctive conviction that he possesses a divinely given soul, its separation from all evolutions and developments of matter, its essential spirituality and immortality; and finally, subtract the conviction of the responsibility of all souls for deeds and thoughts to the arbitrament of the Deity. as absolutely distinguished from utilitarian and social arbitraments; subtract all these from any modern society, or weaken their influence by attributing them to Natural Evolution or to Natural Culture, then the result will speedily be social degradation or uncontrollable disorder. These beliefs have been subtracted or weakened aforetime, as French and other history informs us, and we know the sad consequences. These beliefs are subtracted in our day from small societies, and we feel the consequences too painfully. They may again be subtracted, and there is too much reason to fear that they will be from larger societies. The consequences can only be what they have been in the past. In such conditions of society—History will repeat itself.

Let the reader reflect for himself upon the doctrine that Natural Selection has evolved moral conceptions from numerous antecedent observations of what was useful or socially pleasant, by preserving a greater number of those which have been directed to the useful and the pleasant, than those which have not been so directed. Then let him attempt to derive from this supposition the moral idea of rectitude and duty, of *ought* or *should*, and substitute this for the Theistic origin of moral obligation and duty, and if not only the unphilosophical, but also the irreligious character of such a process, does not appear to him, then it is in vain to attempt to display to him the perniciousness of the theory, and its direct tendency to eliminate all the higher conceptions of God and responsibility, and sin, and crime, and obligation from human society.

It may be well to quote in this place Mr. Herbert Spencer's precise statement of his views on this subject, as they are evidently those of Mr. Darwin, in common with others of the same school—"Just in the same way that I believe the intuition of space possessed by any living individual to have arisen from organized and consolidated experiences of all antecedent individuals, who bequeathed to him their slowly developed nervous organizations, etc.—so do I believe that the experiences of utility, organized and consolidated through all past generations of the human race have been producing corresponding nervous modifications, which by continued transmissions and accumulations, have become in us certain faculties of moral intuition, active emotions responding to right and wrong conduct, which have no apparent basis in the individual experiences of utility." Mr. Hutton has taken the pains to refute the Spencerian genesis of morals, and if it be not self-refuting, Mr. Hutton has certainly shown its insufficiency to account for facts.

It may be said that I have been attributing to the Darwinian theory effects which cannot separately and exclusively issue from it, but which belong to Materialism in general, and therefore should be accredited to that. This appears just; but Naturalism* is one phase of Materialism, and the naturalist who assigns every phenomenal result, and every organism, and all moral functions to the agency of natural causes alone, is in effect a materialist. The latter term is mostly confined to metaphysics, but the consequences of both are the same.

In order then to include the consequences of Darwinism and Spencerism with those of Materialism, I proceed to notice them, the latter as briefly and particularly as may be, in connection with Modern Science. For this purpose I must first explain the much-vaunted and certainly momentous modern doctrine of Force.

* By *Naturalism* I mean the explanation of Nature by natural causes entirely, or nearly so. It looks at things only and always on their natural side, and though it may not absolutely exclude the name or idea of God, makes little or no use of it. Thus Nature, which is merely a summary expression for a scheme of things to be explained, itself becomes the general explanation of all its special phenomena. Strict Naturalism is, therefore, equivalent to Atheism, but the latter term is courteously disused. Of course there are degrees and differences in Naturalism, but strict Naturalism dispenses with Personal Deity.

XIV.

INDESTRUCTIBILITY OF MATTER AND FORCE.—THE CONSERVATION AND CORRELATION OF FORCES.

INDESTRUCTIBILITY of Matter.—This doctrine may be illustrated in the burning of a common candle. If a small candle be placed in a glass tube, and the flame of the burning candle be made to pass through a tube containing soda which takes up the disengaged carbonic acid and water, and if we finally collect all the products of the burnt candle, we shall find that they actually weigh more than the original candle, because by the act of combustion oxygen has been united with the component parts of the candle, and by this union carbonic acid and water have been formed.

Weighing these products in a chemical balance, we ascertain the weight of the additional gain of oxygen, and the undestroyed, though changed components of the candle. In like manner if we ignite a piece of the metal called magnesium, it will burn with a brilliant light, and yield a white solid known as magnesia, which is formed by the union of magnesium with the oxygen of the air. Here too, by weighing the magnesia, we shall arrive at a similar result. A great number of accurate experiments with the use of a chemical balance, from the time of Lavoisier, who first established the doctrine, to the present, have proved beyond doubt the indestructibility of matter.

Force and Energy.—It is now believed by most physicists that every change in man, and every change in the chemical constitution of bodies is effected by *Force* or *Energy* in such a manner that light, heat, electricity, magnetism, gravity and chemical affinities may all be considered as convertible the one into the other; that is, that these are not themselves different principles, but different exhibitions of one principle. This one principle or action is termed Force.

It is concluded from observation of the natural laws that there is a fixed and definite amount of Force conducting the entire operations of the universe. Therefore, so far as we can learn, Force in the physical world is not subject to decrease or increase. However or whenever it appears in action, it is one and the same in amount.

As it is subject to no diminution so it is never lost, but it is transferable from one object to another in endless transformation.

Whatever be the true nature of physical power, whether it be merely a mode of action, or an immaterial or spiritual agent, its action is alleged to be always controllable and controlled by what we term physical laws.

Kinds of Force.—Physicists generally recognize five kinds of force, one *Mechanical*, or Molar force, producing movement in mass; and four *Molecular* forces, producing movement in molecules. These four are Heat, Light, Chemical Force, and Electricity. Probably we may add a fifth molecular force—viz., the Nerve Force, which is allied to Electricity. It is now believed that all these Forces, except Light, are interchangeable according to an assignable rate of commutation. An attempt has quite lately been made to distinguish another force termed Psychical, but though the inquiry is curious it has at present led to no decided and accepted result. The term Vital Force has been long in use and widely accepted, whether or not with propriety is a subject of warm discussion amongst living *savants*.

This whole subject is at present incompletely understood and defined, although its principles are regarded as indisputable. Objections, consequently, are frequently raised to particular expressions, which, however, do not materially affect the principles of the doctrine. The Conservation of Force is the generally adopted phrase for its indestructibleness, although some, and particularly Mr. Herbert Spencer, prefer the "Persistence of Force." This expression he adopts to avoid the necessary presumption of a Conservator. With him it is the key to all Science, but he says, " It is considered that the development of all knowledge into an organized aggregate of direct and individual deductions, from the Persistence of Force, can be achieved only in the remote future, and cannot be completely achieved even then." Hence it is impracticable at present to employ terms with satisfaction and accuracy. Sometimes we speak of Force, sometimes of Energy; sometimes of the Persistence, sometimes of the Correlation, sometimes of the Equivalence of

Forces. The same ideas are supposed to underlie all these various expres.ions.

The phrase "Correlation of Physical Forces" has been adopted by Mr. Grove, whose Essay on that subject is so widely known and appreciated. By him, in fact, the doctrine has been shaped into its present form, though it may be carried far beyond it. By him primarily it has been shown that the various affections of matter which constitute the object of experimental physics, namely heat, light, electricity, magnetism, chemical affinity and motion, are all correlative, that is, they have a reciprocal dependence; that not one of them, regarded abstractedly, can be said to be the separate cause of the others, but that every one often becomes convertible into any of the others. Thus heat may immediately or mediately produce electricity, and electricity produce heat. Each merges itself as the other force it produces becomes developed. It is then a fair conclusion from all observed physical phenomena, that no one force can originate otherwise than by devolution from a pre-existing force or forces. Probably the term "Transmutation" would more accurately describe this relation than the term "Correlation."

Subordinate distinctions are drawn between Kinetic and Potential Energy. *Kinetic* Energy is the actual amount of work a moving body is capable of effecting at any instant during its motion, and may be estimated as soon as the mass and the velocity of the body in motion is known. When a moving body reaches the highest point of its course, its Kinetic Energy is spent. But if free to fall to its first position, it will acquire a Kinetic Energy exactly equal to that which has been expended in raising it. Its energy of motion has not been lost, but has been converted into an advantage of position; and this advantage is termed *Potential* Energy. Kinetic Energy of motion may be transformed into heat; for when the falling body strikes the ground, the Kinetic Energy is not annihilated but converted.

When a train in motion is brought to rest by applying a brake, the rails become hot, and sparks are seen to fly from the wheels. Bullets shot to a target, frequently show signs of fusion after impact. In these and similar cases the energy of visible motion is transmuted into heat. The amount of the one form of energy which will produce a given amount of the other has been carefully calculated, and hence is derived the theory of Mechanical Equivalents. If, for example, a weight of one pound be raised to a height of 772 feet, and then be allowed to fall, upon striking the ground, it will generate as much heat as will raise one pound of water to one degree by Fahrenheit's scale on the thermometer.

It is experimentally ascertained that motion of any kind can be converted into heat, and that heat can be converted into motion; and since a certain quantity of motion and a certain quantity of heat are exactly equivalent to each other, it is now a generally admitted doctrine that what we call heat is nothing more than a peculiar kind of motion; but it is a motion not of the mass as a whole, but of its constituent particles, which are supposed to vibrate. The hotter the body, the more rapid the vibration of the particles. When heat is transformed into mechanical force, the motion of the particles is imparted to the mass.

Chemical Force is that which causes two substances like carbon and oxygen to combine. Phosphorus has a strong tendency to combine with iodine, or as chemists say, these have an affinity for each other. The particles of the one seem to rush towards those of the other, and combination ensues. When carbon combines with oxygen, the heat produced by the conversion of the chemical force existing in the elements, is so great as to give rise to combustion. Heat is always evolved during combination, for the chemical force which occasions the combination is always partially converted into heat.

These elementary facts are sufficient to enable the reader to understand the principal inferences derived from them; one of the most important of which, as now received, is that there can be no annihilation of Force or Energy; nor so far as matter or mass can act, can there be any creation of energy; and therefore its total amount is constant through the universe, in which there is an unbroken Conservation of Energy or Force. The attribution of this to the Sun, and the transformation of the solar force into other forces strictly belong to a discourse upon the Sun.

Having established the doctrine of Conservation of Energy, and the possibility of obtaining a numerical equivalence between the various forms of physical energy, exhibited by heat, light, chemical affinity, electricity, or gravitation, we are enabled to examine the complete series of any given amount of actions in external Nature, just as readily as we can trace the successive actions of a train of wheels in a mill. Understanding by Energy something that is intelligible and perfectly measurable—something which, while it produces change in itself, suffers no diminution,—something that in the act of producing or undergoing a change itself, undergoes not a change of amount but merely of distribution, we arrive at an invaluable method of treating physical phenomena. Accordingly physicists employ and apply it to the utmost of their power, and by them it is carried out to a vast extent of comprehensiveness. Biologists in like manner adopt and extend it, and the most objectionable forms of the Evolutional theory are founded upon it, as though upon the firmest foundation. No one English author has carried it out more comprehensively into all regions of nature than Mr. Herbert Spencer. Truly he has made it an all-embracing doctrine. By speculating on the Persistence or Equivalence of Force, Mr. Spencer, and those who speculate with or like him, profess to account for everything and everybody in the most satisfactory manner. In their hands it becomes the clue to a world-wide Evolution.

If we credit these speculators, we pass at

once from inorganic to organic matter, and from that to mind, finding the vital forces to be in direct and exact correspondence or correlation with physical forces. They are the source and media of mind and thought. Mental activity is an exact equivalent of the action of oxydation in the brain. Of that opinion, however, it will be desirable to treat specially under the head of Materialism.

In this page we are endeavouring to represent to all the outline of the scientific ideas of Force and Energy, which is entirely a modern doctrine, and is regarded as controlling, if not remodelling, physical science.

When we accept this doctrine, we accept it and the fundamental truths supposed to arise from it, upon the credit and authority of the great corporation of physicists, with Faraday, Helmholtz, Mayer, and others at their head. But it will be seen that we are by no means bound on this account to accept the conclusions which sceptical materialists draw from it. On the contrary, if we accept the Indestructibleness of Force and Energy, its Persistence, Conservation, Correlation, or Equivalence, we should build upon these dogmas certain conclusions opposite to those of most of the materialists, and should endeavour to show that their conclusions are not necessary consequences flowing from the admission of the truths of the physical doctrine. Let us then accept the Conservation of Energy as it is generally accepted, and also the Transformation of Energy; but not all the inferences derived from them, nor these doctrines themselves as containing the whole truth. As a complementary doctrine I think we must consider Sir William Thomson's theory of the Dissipation of Energy; and here the observation of Professor P. G. Tait, the President of the Section for Mathematical and Physical Science, at the last meeting of the British Association for the Advancement of Science (1871), may be appropriately introduced:

"The Dissipation of Energy is by no means well known, and many of the results of its legitimate application have been received with doubt, sometimes even with attempted ridicule, yet it appears to be at the present moment by far the most promising and fertile portion of Natural Philosophy; having obvious applications, of which as yet only a small per centage appear to have been made. Some indeed were made before the enunciation of the principles, and have since been recognized as instances of it. Of such we have good examples in Fourier's great work on Heat-conduction, in the optical theorem that an image can never be brighter than the object; in Gauss's mode of investigating electrical distribution, and in some of Thomson's theorems as to the energy of an electro-magnetic field. But its discoverer has, so far as I know, as yet confined himself in its explicit application to questions of Heat-conduction and Restoration of Energy, Geological Time, the Earth's Rotation, and such like. But there can be little question that the principle contains implicitly the whole theory of Thermo-Electricity, of Chemical Combination, of Allotropy, of Fluorescence, etc., and perhaps even of matters of a higher order than common Physics and Chemistry. In Astronomy it leads us to the grand question of the *age*, or perhaps more correctly, the *phase of life* of a star or nebula, shows us the material of potential suns, other suns in the process of formation, in vigorous youth, and in every stage of slowly protracted decay. It leads us to look to each planet and satellite as having been at one time a tiny sun, a member of some binary or multiple group, and even now (when almost deprived at least at its surface, of its original energy) presenting an endless variety of subjects for the application of its method. It leads us forward in thought to the far distant time when the materials of the present stellar system shall have lost all but their mutual potential energy, but shall in virtue of it form the material of future larger suns, with their attendant planets. Finally, as it alone is able to lead us, by sure steps of deductive reasoning, to the necessary future of the Universe—necessary, that is, if physical laws for ever remain unchanged—so it enables us to say that the present order of things has *not* been evolved through infinite past time by the agency of laws now at work—but must have had a distinctive beginning, a state beyond which we are totally unable to penetrate, a state, in fact, which must have been produced by other than the now acting causes. Thus, also, in Physiology, it may ere long lead to results of a much higher novelty and interest than those yet obtained, immensely valuable though they certainly are."*

* Sir William Thomson informs me that he treats this subject in the yet unpublished Rede Lecture of 1866. Sir William adds that "Dissipation of energy seems to him strongly against the atheistic theory of evolution, but not against, if anything rather for, evolution." (Letter to the author, 26th January, 1872.)

XV.

THE PRESENT MATERIALISM.

WITHOUT attempting to discuss at length the vexed and probably insoluble metaphysical problems which are associated with Matter, some observations on the principles, character, extent, and assumptions of the prevalent Materialism of our day may be here offered.

Materialism assumes the existence of matter as self dependent, and as endowed with certain inherent and inalienable powers, by which it evolves inorganic changes, and also organic life and growth, and ultimately sensation and thought. This doctrine plainly issues in reducing man to a living machine, affected exclusively by physical impressions, and working out his thoughts by means of the circulations and vibrations felt in the brain and his nervous system.

Every material molecule is affirmed to have

its inherent and eternal properties, which it carries everywhere with it. "A particle of iron," said M. Dubois Reymond, "is, and remains the same, whether it goes through the world in an aerolite, or rolls like thunder in a railway, or circulates in a globule of blood through the temples of a poet." Thus matter and force are inseparable, and have co-existed from eternity. There is an associated immortality of matter and force. Matter never perishes; the same quantity of matter always has existed, does, and will exist. It is in unceasing circulation, during which each accidental combination begins and ends. Nothing comes from nothingness; nothing returns to nothingness. From these principles it follows that the idea of a creative force, of an absolute force, distinct from matter, creating it at first, and governing it afterwards according to certain arbitrary laws, is unphilosophical, a figment of the brain, an impossible abstraction. There can be no such being as the Creating and Governing God of Christianity.

The laws of matter result from its properties. They are the necessary relations which result from the nature of things, and they are eternal and immutable. The laws of matter or nature never have changed and never can change. If the laws of matter changed, such a change would be due to a corresponding one in the properties of matter, or because it assumed properties contrary to its essence, which is evidently impossible, and contrary to the testimony of experience.

The active forces of Nature cannot be separated from itself, and there can be no Design in Nature, no occasion for the operation of Final Causes. Against these the materialists hurl their sharpest weapons of ridicule and reproach. They scorn every conception of their existence, and denounce them as unphilosophical: for it is evident that if we admit Design and Final Causes as the regulating and all-pervading principles of the universe, we at the same time deny and destroy Materialism. Still they cannot always exclude the idea of this principle so manifest in nature, and accordingly even M. Moleschott himself is reported to have said, in an introductory address, delivered at Turin, where he had just been named Professor:—
" Do not believe that I am rash enough, or blind enough to refuse to Nature a design and an end. All those whose ideas I share, by no means, deny the τέλος which they guess, which

they even sometimes perceive in Nature, as Aristotle did before them. But they wish to forewarn the investigator against the maze in which his researches would be lost, if he endeavoured to guess, instead of being satisfied with the *rerum cognoscere causas.*"

In like manner, upon Mr. Darwin's principles, things are not intended for the purposes with which the majority accredit them. They think that colours were designed for human delight, but their opponents point to the number of flowers which the eye of man has never beheld. Beauty is with the majority an intellectual pleasure purposely afforded, with Darwinian naturalists it is a mere motive to and result of Sexual Selection. We see the uses of several organs in our own bodies and the bodies of numerous inferior animals, and their adaptation to the very purposes they were intended to serve; while to Materialists Comparative Anatomy discovers a considerable number of superfluous and rudimentary organs, which though useful to one species are useless to others. Our opponents point out useless complications, and allege that monstrosities are decisive proofs against final causes. Why does the Creator, they ask, create or allow a monstrosity? "The Great

Architect," Whom by traditional influence, we are taught to admire and worship, builds, they say, even worse than a good human architect. He builds a structure defaced by defects and distortions, yet men call this a proof of design and contrivance. All these distortions can be accounted for by Variation and Natural Selection and by transformation of species. Parasites, diseases, sickness, and the manifold continual evils of humanity and organic beings are bad illustrations of, and bad compliments to benevolence; they are the plainest proofs of malevolence. If there be a Supreme Power of Benevolence, whence these evils? If they flow from Malevolence, then, there is an equally potent Malevolent Being.

Such is a condensation of the arguments employed by modern and partly by older materialists, which might be severally assigned to authors of this school. They are here put forth without disguise or softening, in the most sententious form.

Man has a high and spiritual nature, but with materialists this is an evolutionary product developed with the body, and due to the same, or similar material factors as those which effected inferior transmutations.

In respect of the origin of mind and thought there are different shades or degrees of Materialism. All are not as gross materialists as Moleschott and Büchner. The former has announced that "Thought is a movement of matter," and has written the well-known pithy phrase, "Without phosphorus, no thought." Other Germans explain thought as the resultant of all the forces united in the brain, and though it cannot be seen, it may be supposed from the appearances which do present themselves to be only the effect of nervous electricity. "There is," says one of these writers, "the same relation between thought and the electric vibrations of the cerebral fibres as between colours and the vibration of the ether."

Some less decided forms of Materialism regard the percipient principle in man as of one essence with his body, and suggest that as by the senses we can only know the physical laws of Nature, there may be unseen powers inherent in physical objects, and that what we call matter may, besides the physical properties which we know it possesses, contain also, in organized forms, the power of thought and feeling, and thereby become capable of spiritual as well as physical action.

It will be sufficient in these pages to remind the reader that these dogmas of Materialism consist of assumptions incapable of proof, and are sometimes directly opposed to the fundamental principles of mental Science. There are essential differences between the laws of thought and the laws of matter; nor can the physical organism be made the *cause* as well as the *seat* of thought. It is abhorrent to all our conceptions of mind to suppose that matter can so act upon thought as to cause it to think what in its highest exercises it can think. Poetry and art, morals and religions, energies of will, passion and piety, may be attributed by violent effort to the action of matter upon thought, but by the majority of thinking men ever have been, and doubtless will be, attributed to something very different in principle than the action of matter.

The persistence with which thought is declared to be merely a function of the brain, has led many to believe in its truth, and there is a specious simplicity in it, and the arguments brought to support it, which deceive those who do not perceive that the words are but a cloak for our ignorance. It is urged that wherever a brain is observed, there we observe a thinking being, or one with a capacity for intellect;

wherever the brain is absent, thought and intellect are absent. Intellect and the brain increase and decrease in the same ratio, and therefore the cause affecting the one affects the other.

If we should even admit that the brain is the condition of thought, we may yet at the same time deny that it is the cause. There may be a totally distinct cause for the thought, though it be always found to accompany the brain. Spiritualists have also frequently pointed to the unity of thought, and to personal identity as defeating Materialism.

The contradiction derived from Personal Identity is very strong. This is the mysterious principle which cannot be defined, but which is always felt. Every man feels that he remains the same at every instant of the duration which constitutes his existence, and this consciousness is his personal identity. "Thought, memory, and responsibility," says M. Janet, "are the three leading facts which manifest identity with the greatest clearness. The simplest fact of thought proves that the thinking subject remains the same at two different moments." Every thought is successive, certainly as to reasoning. In a demonstration it is the same mind which passes through every stage of it. With materialists, therefore, rests the burden of reconciling the personal identity of the mind with the perpetual mutability of the organized body. "Now we must acknowledge," says Paul Janet,* "that materialists have never taken much trouble to solve that problem, and Dr. Büchner does not even allude to it, and yet it is not clear that the identical can result from the invariable, or the one from the compound."

We may also mention that the Unity of Thought, or what is termed in philosophic phrase —the unity of the *ego* is, unquestionable, and is attested to us by consciousness, which is an important fact. This precludes the supposition that two distinct parts can have a common consciousness. In what parts of the complicative automaton to which Materialism reduces man, can the consciousness of the *ego* dwell?

Imagine a Darwinian to say, "Human consciousness is but the sum total of the minute and imperfect consciousnesses experienced by the lower animals. Natural Selection has com-

* "The Materialism of the Present Day," a critique on Dr. Büchner's system, by Paul Janet, translated by Gustave Masson, 1866. The author effectively carries out his argument against objections which he himself supplies.

bined and perfected these in man." We reply that no conceivable combination of all the scattered animal consciousnesses which they may be said to possess, can compose one individual and sole consciousness. " Unity," says M. Janet, "externally perceived may be the result of a composition; but it cannot be so when it perceives itself from within."

It is certain that we cannot have in the whole what does not exist in any of the parts; therefore all matter is conscious, or consciousness is wholly distinct from matter. " There is no escape from this dilemma," says Mr. Wallace, " either all matter is conscious, or consciousness is something distinct from matter, and in the latter case, its presence in material forms is a proof of the existence of conscious beings, outside of, and independent of what we term matter."

In the books treating of mind and intellect, and emotion that have emanated from authors decidedly of this school, the disposition to resolve psychological into material phenomena is so strong as to appear irresistible. " The influence of these prepossessions," says Dr. Noah Porter, " may be traced in the works of almost every writer on psychology, if not in the conclusions which he reaches, at least in his modes of reasoning, his illustrations, and even in that very language which he naturally employs, and by which he is unconsciously influenced." One reason is that material phenomena are the earliest known to us. The properties and powers with which we become acquainted are those of matter. The laws of mechanism, of fluids, of light, of chemical union, of vegetable and animal life, are the laws which we first study, master, and apply. The phenomena of matter engage the attention of all men, their lives, their trades, their pursuits, being bound up with these laws and obedient to them. Therefore material association so control our minds that they even direct our thoughts, and almost entirely govern our conceptions.

Dr. Porter has clearly pointed out in detail the almost unconquerable influence of materialistic impressions, and our misgivings when we are confronted with new and strange objects in psychological studies. He clearly shows that though the states of the soul have been the nearest to our experience and the most familiar, they have been furthest removed from our observation and our study; so that we ask, are they real, actual, substantial? If actual phenomena, are they distinct and definite? To what substance do they pertain? The readiest answer is—To matter, perhaps in some attenuated form. The soul's functions are explained by the action of animal spirits, or by chemical and electrical changes in the nervous substance. Perception is explained by impressions on the eye and ear, which impressions are referred to motions in a vibrating fluid without, which in turn are responded to by motions aroused in a vibrating agent within. Memory and association are explained by the mutual attractions or repulsions of ideas similar to those to which the particles of matter are subjected by cohesion or electricity. Generalization and judgment, induction and reasoning, are resolved by the frequent and often repeated deposits of impressions, that have affinity for each other, and are then transformed with general conceptions and relations. It is not denied that many of the facts and phenomena which these cerebral psychologists recognize are true and important in respect of the relations which the soul holds to the body, and that most of them exemplify the conditions of the purely psychical activities; but there is no evidence that they *produce* the phenomena observed, nor do they at all explain the original capacity to produce them. This has been insisted upon by opponents of Materialism, and as Dr. Porter forcibly contends, these are only the invariable antecedents, or essential conditions of certain phenomena so long as the agent performing them acts also with those which are purely corporeal or vital. They do not appear among the constituent elements of any psychical state or act; they cannot be found in them by analysis. "These cerebral conditions might be supposed to exist without the occurrence of any of the phenomena in question, without perception, memory, or reasoning. The nervous system might perform any one of its functions without a single psychical result. Its direct and reflex action might occur in every possible form; frequent repetition might increase the flow of nervous energy in certain well-worn paths, and the parts excited might grow in size and strength; new combination of nerve cells might secure growth to the brain, both in mass and complexity, without the occurrence of a single act of perception, memory, reasoning, or mental association, or without any kind of psychical growth or mental development—in short, without the occurrence of a single one of the phenomena which these causes are supposed to explain, and of which they are supposed to be the scientific equivalents."[*]

It is manifest, then, that Materialism is a seductive and specious system, with many attractions and many arguments in its favour, and in one form or another it will probably always find believers and advocates. It presents itself to men with the pretension of being entirely experimental, and as purged from metaphysical hypothesis. It professes to hold as suspected every speculative conception which is not immediately suggested as a direct result, of observation. It vaunts itself as the only system which accords with positive science, and as its most direct and exact application.

In these respects it is contrasted with Pantheism, with Dualism, and all that desires to be imaginary and fanciful. It in effect says, Here is Matter. We do not know what it really is, and offer no analysis of it; we only say that we know nothing else. Man can only reason upon what surrounds him. If there be anything beside, man does not see it, and can not

[*] "The Human Intellect."

know it. All reasoning upon the unknown and imaginary must be unscientific; a thousand theories raised upon the unknown establish no truth. As they can have no logical basis, any one of them is as good as another. We do not contend with speculations, for the contest is absolutely useless. We build upon the known and the visible.

You perhaps found certain objections upon the nature of Matter and its distinctness from Spirit; you say with apparent truth, Matter is an entity or thing occupying space, different in essence from Spirit, and having a self-dependent existence. It is really the substratum of all the qualities observed in physical objects; a substratum which would remain as the only substantial thing if all the qualities were removed. In contrast to and distinct from this substratum, there exists a spiritual substance which underlies all spiritual existence and the spiritual world.

This may possibly be a fair definition of Matter, rejoins the Materialist, but I prefer that of Mr. Mill, that it is a permanent possibility of Sensation. Beyond this no one can securely advance. The following explanation of Mr. Herbert Spencer will at least satisfy

Materialists: "the concept we form to ourselves of Matter is, the symbol of some form of power absolutely, and power unknown to us; and a symbol which we cannot suppose to be like to the reality mentioned, without involving ourselves in contradiction." Mr. Spencer proceeds to affirm that Matter and Motion, as we think them, are but symbolic of unknowable forms of existence. Mind also is unknowable, and the simplest form under which we can think of its substance, is but a symbol of something that never can be rendered into thought. " Mind, as known to the possessor of it, is a circumscribed aggregate of activities ; and the cohesion of these activities one with another throughout the aggregate, compels the postulation of a something of which they are the activities."*

According to this philosophy, the very grounds of safe reasoning are cut from under us, for God is absolutely and for ever unknowable, and Matter and Mind are absolutely and for ever unknowable to us. Hence we can never know that we reason rightly, for all our conclusions are but the effects of the exercise of "a circumscribed aggregate of activities." Be-

---

* " Psychology." Second Edition, p. 159.

hind these there may be a something which causes their cohesion, but that something is absolutely and for ever unknowable. The world, according to another speculator, is one both as to matter and mind, but yet it presents two aspects to us, in one of which it is entirely Mind, in the other entirely Matter.

To argue with the propounders of such propositions, for any ultimate truth, is to beat the air; at every point they can elude your grasp. Do you charge them with Materialism? How can you bring this charge when the nature of Matter cannot be known? Do you desire a distinct definition of Mind? They affirm in reply—It cannot be known. It is another aspect of Matter. The terms of the phenomena of Matter may be translated into terms of the phenomena of Mind; and those who object so strongly to Materialism are fighting against a shadow, against a figment of their own brains, not understanding our philosophy, which at all points is invulnerable.

On the other hand, it is sufficient to accept the opinion which prevails amongst the majority of philosophers, that the world is produced by two independent factors, Mind and Matter; which, however conceived and represented, are always separate and independent. These either actually are present, or are inferred to be present immediately to consciousness, in every instance, of external perception. If we relinquish this opinion we may deduce with the metaphysical ontologists, every thing from Mind, or with the empirical ontologists, deduce everyhing from Matter.

There is one thing which remains to be accounted for, if it be not denied by Materialism, and that is Free-will; for if there be nothing in the world except Matter, free-will cannot exist in man, and there can be no choice. Here the arguments of Materialistic Physicists certainly appear to become mutually destructive; for if all nature be under the rigid rule of physical laws, they exclude human free-will, that being by supposition a mere evolution of matter, a result of certain chemical changes induced in matter. But can free-will be a product of material evolution, and man be the same, when the will governs man and governs matter? It is a power which influences material particles, and causes them to move and take up a new position: how then can it possibly be evolved by the movement of these particles?

The only conceivable method of escaping

this dilemma is to deny the existence of freewill, and inclusively of responsibility, all high motives to moral action, and finally all the higher principles of religion. The highest thing then left to us is "a circumscribed aggregate of activities," and that, too, is absolutely and perpetually unknowable; while we must ever remain ignorant whether in the postulated cohesive something, of which our mental exercises are the activities, there be any free-will. There seems in this philosophy no satisfaction, no soundness, no reality. The universe is, according to it, nothing higher than a coherent aggregate of necessary activities!

XVI.

IMMATERIALISM OR IDEALISM.

FROM such coherent or incoherent aggregate, the perplexed reader may be glad to take refuge in an entirely opposite philosophical system, if such there be. At the opposite pole to Materialism we find Idealism or Immaterialism; an hypothesis which delivers us from difficulties of one kind by landing us amidst difficulties of another. Nevertheless Idealism is a favourite hypothesis with several men of mark now living, and there is reason to expect that during several years to come it will gain acceptance. Probably thinkers of various orders will feel disposed to adopt it as a harbour of refuge from the storms of fierce controversy which now rage around us. Unquestionably it is a ready method of escaping theological difficulties, if it can be relied upon as sound. Unhappily the facility of escaping from difficulties is apt to prejudice us in favour of a system which has too many of its own.

This hypothesis is generally associated with Bishop Berkeley, whose name and character are well known, and of whom Pope sang:—

"To Berkeley every virtue under heaven."

The works of Berkeley have been recently reprinted, and the late criticisms offered upon them seem to intimate that a highly appreciative value of his writings and his theory exists amongst many thoughtful readers. The hypothesis however is by no means exclusively attributable to Berkeley—for in many writers long antecedent to Berkeley, we trace a disposition to discountenance the idea of the actuality of an external world of matter. In the schools of the middle ages, as Sir William Hamilton notes, " the arguments in favour of Idealism were fully understood; and they would certainly have obtained numerous partisans, had it not been seen that such a philosophical opinion involved a logical heresy touching the eucharist. This was even recognized by St. Augustine. Descartes could not with his doctrine of ideas regard the reality of the material world in a friendly manner, and in and after his time it was found difficult to reconcile certain doctrines with the reality of matter. Reid observes "it appears, therefore, that every particular Mr. Locke has hinted with regard to that system which he had in his mind, but thought it prudent to suppress, tallies exactly with the system of Berkeley. If we add to this that Berkeley's system follows from that of Mr. Locke by very obvious consequence, it seems reasonable to conjecture from the passage now quoted that he was not unaware of that consequence, but left it to those who should come after him to carry his principles their full length, when they should by time be better established and able to bear the shock of their opposition to vulgar notions." *

That this theory was entertained by others besides Berkeley is proved by the publication in 1713 of a singular tractate now extremely rare, entitled "*Clavis Universalis*;" or a New Inquiry after Truth : being a Demonstration of the Non-Existence, or Impossibility of an External World. By Arthur Collier, Rector of Langford Magna, near Sarum." Collier

* Hamilton's Edition of Reid ; "Intellectual Powers," p. 287.

pursue the inquiry very closely in arguments substantially the same as those of Berkeley; but with a displeasing style. He meets several objections, and one of the first of them thus:—

"*Objection* 1. Does not the Scripture assure us of the existence of an external world?

Answer 1. Not that I know of. If it does, you will do well to name the text to me wherein this is revealed to us:—otherwise I have no way to answer this objection but that of taking into consideration every sentence in the whole Bible, which I am sure you will believe is more than I need do.

2. To do this objection all the right I can, I will suppose a passage or two in the word of God, and I should think, if such a one is any where to be found, it will be in the first chapter of Genesis, where Moses speaks of the Creation of the Material world. Here it is said that, "In the beginning God created the heaven and the earth," and also that all material things were made some days before the first man, and so cannot be said to exist only relatively in the mind of man. To this I answer—

3. This objection from scripture is taken from Monsieur Malebranche, and is his last resort on which to found the being of an

external world. Here then my answer to this author is that the tendency of this passage of Scripture is not to prove the being of an external (supposed to be an) invisible world, but the external being or existence of the visible world. For it is here supposed that the visible world existed before the first man saw it.

4. It seems to me there is nothing in this passage which affirms the *visible* world to be external; and my reason for this is, because there is nothing in it but what is very consistent with believing the visible world is not external." Collier then carries out this line of argument, and speaks of the importance which some might attach to the "little syllable *The*, which is prefixed in the text to the words *Heaven and Earth*." He adds, "This is a slender thread indeed on which to hang the whole subject of an Universe."

In concluding his tractate, the author refers to the "Use and Consequences of the Foregoing Treatise," and observes "*First*, I know not why my reader should not take my word (I mean till he himself has made inquiry), when I assure him that the consequences of this position are exceeding many in number. If this will pass,

I again assure him that I have found by more than a ten years' experience, or application of it to diverse purposes, that this is one of the most fruitful principles that I have ever met with, even of general and universal influence in the field of knowledge: so that if it be true, as is here supposed, it will open the way to ten thousand other truths, and also discover as many things to be errors, which have hitherto passed for true."

With respect to certain aspects of this theory, whether it be true or false, it does not exclude the government of the Almighty, but as its adherents consider, rather confirms it. "The evidence" says Reid, "of an all-governing mind, so far from being weakened, seems to appear even in a more striking light upon this hypothesis than upon the common one. The powers which inanimate matter is supposed to possess, have always been the stronghold of Atheists, to which they have recourse in defence of their system. This fortress of Atheism must be most effectually overturned, if there is no such thing as matter in the universe. In all this the Bishop (Berkeley) reasons justly and acutely. But there is one uncomfortable consequence of his system which he seems not to have attended to, and from which it will be found difficult, if at all possible, to guard it.

The consequence I mean is this: that although it leaves us sufficient evidence of a supreme intelligent mind, it seems to take away all the evidence we have of other intelligent beings like ourselves. What I call a father, a brother, or a friend, is only a parcel of ideas in my own mind, and being ideas in my mind, they cannot possibly have that relation to another mind which they have to mine, any more than the pain felt by me can be the individual pain felt by another. I can find no principle in Berkeley's system which affords me even probable ground to conclude that there are other intelligent beings like myself in the relations of father, brother, friend or fellow-citizen. I am left alive as the only creature of God in the universe, in that forlorn state of egoism, into which it is said some of the disciples of Descartes were brought by his philosophy."*

Principally to evade the force of all arguments for Materialism, has the Idealism or Immaterialism been more or less confidently

* Hamilton's Reid; " Intellectual Powers," p. 285.

urged. Originating far centuries ago the dreams of sages and the creeds of idolaters, it reappears in the system of Berkeley, and not unfrequently in the modified propositions of more recent philosophers. It has perhaps a wider acceptance at the present day than is commonly suspected, and it is remarkable that even in 1844 Faraday avowed his belief in the immateriality of physical objects, a conclusion at which he arrived while reflecting on the conduction and isolation of electricity.[*]

The Immaterialist asks the Materialist, "What is the nature of this Matter in which you believe?" and the Materialist must answer, "I only know that it is something hard and insensible, having certain properties and particles performing certain work; but what its abstract and essential nature is, I cannot tell." "But," says the Immaterialist, "can this unknown entity possess the power of executing all the operations of Nature, and producing all the organic beings in Nature? Beyond all, can it evolve mind and thought from the action of the brain, as its natural function?" The Materialist replies that matter does all this, and that if it does not, there is nothing known which does.

[*] "Philosophical Magazine," 1844.

Now, says the Immaterialist, I present these propositions* for your consideration.

1. The existence of matter cannot be proved, we never see it perfect, nor can we form any distinct conception of it.

2. Physical properties we imagine to consist of matter; but their active properties indicate the possession of a spiritual, much more rationally than a material essence.

3. Reason does not sanction the existence of an insensible, unconscious, unintelligent entity, possessing active powers; and that such an entity should have the ability to conduct the complex arrangements of the physical world, appears to be a supposition so contradictory and absurd, that few persons will be found willingly to identify themselves with it. For if matter does *any thing*, it does *every thing*; and no Materialist will suppose or suggest a point where its operations cease.

4. *Power*, when we reflect closely on its nature and meaning, presents itself to us as an attribute of an intelligent Spiritual Being, and not of an unconscious inanimate thing. We

---

* See "The World as Dynamical and Immaterial," by R. S. Wyld, 1868, p. 57, from which book the above propositions are principally condensed.

can never conceive of power as an attribute of an unconscious entity, such as we suppose the all-pervading ether to be. And when we see power combined with intelligence, working out useful ends, we can have no hesitation in attributing it to an intelligent, self-conscious, spiritual cause.

5. Physical objects acting in the mass, and physical atoms acting chemically, act externally to themselves, and therefore, through the medium of an immaterial copula. Several phenomena appear to be quite incompatible with the belief in matter as a physical entity.

6. If we assume that the powers of Nature are associated with matter, and sustained in it by Deity, we reduce ourselves to a belief in the existence everywhere throughout Nature of a thing which has no power of its own, and is therefore superfluous, and we involve ourselves in the supposition that the Deity has created a thing which has neither power nor utility, which, in fact, occupies space, while it does nothing in space.

7. It is admitted by all philosophers that we never acquire any direct knowledge of matter, or of anything as a thing in itself. We merely know of things and learn to describe them

by their activities. Therefore we are left at liberty to select an adequate cause to account for the powers exhibited in external nature, and we are under no necessity to select an insensible and evidently inadequate cause, which matter is, even by the showing of the Materialist.

"Seeing, then," says Mr. Wyld, "everywhere around us in the world, marks not only of power but of wisdom, of design, of order, of beauty, the combination of parts, the many antecedents contributing to produce the definite results, we can have but little hesitation in discarding matter as an entirely insufficient cause whereby to account for all this, and for the constant and methodical flux of physical events, and we can have just as little hesitation in coming to the conclusion that the world is not a material entity at all, but an ever active cause, an immaterial and spiritual cause, a manifestation of power ever working in connection with intelligence, therefore an ever present intelligent cause in direct operation. The Infinite subjecting his power to Finity, and manifesting himself in the laws of time and space, and all those other laws which we call mechanical or physical, and which He himself has appointed

as the conditions of this physical world." . . . .
"If the only source of power is Deity, then in perception we are brought into direct contact and connection with the Deity."

The above is plainly Berkeley's theory with some modifications. Berkeley's idealism would give a constant contradiction to reason and natural belief, but this view admits of an external physical world, and our possession of an organic bodily frame. Time and space, too, are in this view attributes with which the Deity clothes himself in arranging the physical world, and wherever the laws of the physical world extend, there the mind, through the senses, is brought into contact with the Deity. Deity is supposed to produce in the mind the necessary sensation which we interpret as caused by the external object. Though there may be no great impropriety in calling external objects *matter* in common language, yet when we wish to give a rational explanation of power, we must conclude that it, together with the world around, is the issue of an immaterial and spiritual nature. Such is modified Immaterialism in its favourable aspects.

As to that world-embracing medium which pervades all space, that subtlest of all things known to us, which we appropriately term Ether, we can only refer to it as something which though known to exist, is definitively unknown to us, and is beyond our experiments. Yet, as Mr. Wyld observes, "Its pressure must almost exceed the bounds of belief," and he illustrates this by the following notable calculation :

"The velocity of the propagation of vibrations in any elastic medium depends on the relation of tension which the medium bears to the *inertia* or weight of the molecules of which the medium consists. The greater the pressure or tension of the medium, and the lighter the molecules composing it, the greater the velocity of the vibrations propagated through it.

"The velocity of sound through air is about 1100 feet a second. The velocity of light is nearly 200,000 miles in the same brief time. We have of course no means of ascertaining the fact, but it is probable that the molecules of this wonderful medium of which we speak may be inconceivably light. Let us assume that they are one-hundredth part the weight of a molecule of air : on this supposition the pressure and tension of the ether must be 960,000 times the pressure of our atmosphere; and if we suppose them to be a thousandth part the weight of a molecule of air, the pressure of the ether will be 96,000 times that of the atmosphere; which, let it be remembered, bears with a force of about 15 pounds on every square inch of the surface of the earth and our bodies. As the ether, however, penetrates all substances, it does not affect them as a weight or pressure. It is only by the movements or vibrations that we have any consciousness of its existence, as it is only by these that it disturbs, or in any way affects physical bodies.

"This subtle medium penetrates all substances, even the densest, and is, in fact, the cushion on which the ultimate atoms of all things rest. It surrounds every atom, and by its movements, which never cease, it keeps them in constant though invisible motion. The mountains, the solid earth, and everything on its surface are thus, as it were, alive with constant motion.

"But though its absolute pressure is so tremendous, yet mark how Nature's agents work for Nature's ends. This vast ethereal ocean which, when in any part it is lashed into violent action, has power to dissolve the most obdurate materials, metals, rocks, cities with their palaces and temples yielding before it, and becoming reduced to ashes, or resolved into their original elements. This same medium whose destructive energy is so great, becomes in its ordinary and tamer moods, like the calm ocean which with soft and musical ripple plays idly with straws and leaves. In these its gentler movements it appears—so perfect is its elasticity—as if it were mastered even by the weakest and most trifling objects. It is entangled by a cobweb; and in furs, and flannels, and feathers, its vibrations become lost in endless reflections, and with difficulty do they extricate themselves.

"It keeps every atom in constant motion, so that one may pass another as they hurry on under the directing energy of the living Organizer, to be built each into its proper place; without it motion were impossible, and the whole earth, organic and inorganic, would become sealed up in the close lock of an eternal stillness, darkness, and death."*

As akin to this subject, some original views of Professor Challis on the Fundamental Ideas of Matter and Force may here be appended:—

"All Matter consists of very minute atoms having no other properties than constancy of

* "The World Dynamical and Immaterial," etc., 1868, p. 67.

form, constancy of magnitude, and an intrinsic inertia which is always the same for matter of the same magnitude.

"All atoms are supposed to be spherical. No other kind of force is recognized than that of *pressure*. The resistance of the atoms, when pressed, to all change of form and magnitude constitutes a physical force which may be called *atomic reaction*.

"All other physical force has its origin in the pressure of a universally diffused elastic fluid medium—the so-called Ether—which pervades all space, and fills those portions of space in the interiors of visible and tangible substances that are not occupied by their proper atoms.

"This ether, when undisturbed, has the same density and elastic force throughout its extent, but is susceptible of variations of density. These variations are accompanied by proportional variations of its pressure.

"The different kinds of physical forces are pressures of the ether acting under different circumstances, and are regulated by the modes of the mutual actions of the parts of the fluid.

"The above hypotheses are in part coincident with those relating to the qualities of bodies contained in Regula III., prefixed to the third book of Newton's *Principia*; and all have been adopted in accordance with rules of philosophy laid down by Newton."*

* "Professor Challis on the Fundamental Ideas of Matter and Force in Theoretical Physics." Philosophical Magazine, 1868

XVII.

LIFE, PROTOPLASM, AND VITAL FORCE.

LIFE has been always considered a special though mysterious endowment, and has hitherto been generally regarded, certainly by the majority of observers, as the consequence of the direct action of the Creator. All our phraseology connected with life has been based upon this view, and if we were compelled to subtract such phraseology from every book, especially our Bible, our religious language, and our common conversation must suffer a very great change, and what amounts to a remodelling must take place in them all. "We are all" says a reviewer of a scientific book, "more or less enslaved by words; but it is the proper business, equally of religion and philosophy, to throw off this thraldom, when truth, as often happens, is fettered or distorted by it." What then would be the revolution in our language and our religious forms, if we were to eliminate all those words or phrases in them which embody the idea of God as the Giver of life, and that in a direct and immediate sense. "It may turn out" says another critic, "that the whole phenomena of life are simply functions of matter;" and this is the opinion prevailing amongst a considerable number of physiologists and biologists. What then becomes of our Biblical and Religious language?

The recent animated controversy respecting the "Physical Basis of Life," particularly in connection with Professor Huxley's notorious Essay thus entitled, has engaged much attention on the part of the reading public at large, who soon perceived what a revolution in their religion and speech must ensue from the general acceptance of an exclusively physical origin of all life. Very few persons were qualified by special knowledge of the subject to form a deliberate judgment upon the hypothesis put forward. In relation, however, to the essay of Mr. Huxley, two replies have been printed which may be referred to as effective, and as I think, any impartial judge would admit, subversive of the theory of the physical basis of life. These replies are entitled, the one "As Regards

Protoplasm in relation to Professor Huxley's Essay, &c." By James Hutchinson Stirling, L.L.D.; and the other "Protoplasm; or Life, Matter, and Mind." By Lionel S. Beale, M.B. The former is a small pamphlet, and the latter a small book. To these any reader desiring detailed information may be referred. Here I need only make such observations as are suitable to the limits and character of this volume.

The main points of this controversy turn on observations made on certain objects under the microscope, and therefore it is desirable to state, that Dr. Lionel Beale, whom I here cite and condense, is an accomplished microscopist; and that of his aptitude for minute and correct observation, or of his long practice with a good instrument of high powers, there can be no question.

In direct contradiction to Mr. Huxley's view, Dr. Beale urges that the several distinct kinds of Protoplasm ought not to be confounded, and he draws a decided and physically impassable line between things living and dead matter. He denies emphatically that the living differs from the non-living only in degree, and the statement positively made by certain authorities that the non-living passes by gradation into the living.

They positively affirm that between the living and non-living there is no considerable difference—no difference except in the rate at which the physical and chemical changes are carried on. He as positively asserts that he has shown and by careful observation established, that *living* matter can be plainly distinguished from *dead* matter, and this even in the case of extremely minute particles in which living matter, and matter that has ceased to live, and matter that is about to live are associated together within a very small area. He, therefore, names living matter Bioplasm, in distinction from non-living matter, or Protoplasm.

In Bioplasm or living matter, wonderful changes take place so long as life lasts, which cannot be explained by physics or chemistry. At any time it can be examined, for it is to be found almost everywhere, and its principal phenomena can be demonstrated under the microscope with a high power ($\frac{1}{17}$ objective). There is not a living being which does not contain Bioplasm, and whose structure, composition, and actions, do not depend upon it. At no period of life, in health, or disease, is there any portion of any tissue of man's body the size of a pin's head (with the single exception of the teeth in adults and in old age), which does not contain some of the living matter or Bioplasm in which purely vital phenomena take place. Nor is there any action characteristic of living beings at any period of their existence in which Bioplasm does not play an important part. At the earliest period the germ is composed almost entirely of it, and from the original bioplasmic germ-mass come the infinite number of bioplasts which subsequently take part in the production of the several tissues and organs.

What is Protoplasm? Dr. Beale states, that this term is now applied to several different kinds of matter, and to substances differing from one another in the most essential particulars. It was thus defined some few years ago. " The name applied by Mohl to the colourless or yellowish smooth, or granular viscid substance of nitrogenous constitution, which constitutes the formative substance in the contents of vegetable cells, in the condition of gelatinous strata, reticulated threads and nuclear aggregations, etc. It is the same substance as that formerly termed by the Germans, ' Schleim ' which was usually translated in English words by ' mucus ' or ' mucilage.' The surface of the mass constituted the 'formative protoplasmic layer,' which was supposed to take part in the formation of the cellulose wall of the vegetable cell. This was regarded by Mohl as a structure of special importance distinct from the cell contents, and it was named by him, in 1844, the "primordial utricle."*

The diverse applications of the same term are of little value to the general reader, for whom it is sufficient to state, that on the physical basis side, the word is assumed to mean that one kind of matter which is affirmed to be common to all living beings, and, therefore, to form "the physiological basis, or matter of life." Mr. Huxley's present conception of Protoplasm then is understood to be that of living matter, living proteine, or perhaps in common language —elementary life-stuff.

Mr. Huxley is charged by Dr. Beale with giving the same name to matter which is alive to matter which is dead, and to matter which is completely changed by roasting or boiling. The matter of sheep or mutton, of a man, a lobster, an egg, is said to be the same, and one may be transubstantiated into the other. How? it is replied " by subtle influences " and "under

* Griffith and Henfrey's Micrographic Dictionary—*Protoplasm.*

sundry circumstances." And all these things alive, or dead, or roasted, are according to Mr. Huxley modes of Protoplasm. He would evolve all organic life, all mind and intellect from one Protoplasm. In order that there shall be no break between the lowest and the highest functions—those of the fungus and of man—Mr. Huxley has "endeavoured to prove that the Protoplasm of the lowest organs is 'essentially identical' with and most readily converted into that of the animal." On this alleged reciprocal convertibility of Protoplasm, he would found an inference of identity, and further derive the conclusion that the functions of the highest not less than the lowest animals are but the molecular manifestations of their common Protoplasm.

In his most recently published little book,* Dr. Beale has given a compendium of his latest opinions on the subject and has illustrated them by several plates of structure which confirm his statements. In this book, though more at large in previous publications, Dr. Beale has shown that the phenomena of living matter differ decidedly from the phenomena of non-living matter. He affirms that "notwithstanding all

* Life Theories: their Influence upon Religious Thought, 1871.

that has been asserted over and over again to the contrary, it has been proved conclusively that the phenomena of the simplest living thing are essentially different from those of non-living matter, and cannot be imitated, and that the living does not emanate from the non-living, or pass into it by gradations. Life is no mere sum of ordinary forces, nor does vital action result from material changes alone. It cannot be shown that the matter of the world and its material forces necessarily give rise to the development of life. We may, therefore, still regard life as transcending mere matter and its forces, and as a distinct gift of an all-wise Omnipotence."

It would be out of character to add any details here upon the controversies now existing about Spontaneous Generation, and the various shades of opinion entertained by a number of experimenters in the obscurer departments of Biology, relating to the origin of life. So replete are the current researches and theories respecting the modes of the origin of the lowest organisms, with shifting speculation, that nothing definite and established can be discovered in them. The main topics for our present purpose are briefly stated in these pages, nor would the reader acquire much advantage from attempted explanations of the Archegenesis of Haeckel, the Abiogenesis of Huxley, or the Archebiosis of Dr. Bastian. It is certain that Spontaneous Generation is not a proved and general accepted truth, though some have adopted it; and it is quite certain that all the flasks and solutions so carefully prepared in the laboratories of chemists, have as yet failed to show to general satisfaction that life has been evolved from non-living matter. It is possible that Nature is so evolving life in some of the lowest organisms; but this is a mere conjecture. Beyond conjecture, human art and science have failed to do as much, except in the opinion of a few.

When the Chemist has really produced life from non-life in his laboratory, it will be proper to consider how this result affects our views. But the circumstance of some eminent men prophesying that one day life may, or even will be so produced, can have no effect upon our present reasoning. Chemico-physiological researches have of late years discovered many of the relations existing between animals and vegetables, and their reciprocal influences. They have shown more to us than we before knew of the accurate and wonderful balance of natural forces in the whole organic kingdom, and it would indeed be agreeable to such a writer as the present, and fully accordant with the object of this volume, to detail the particulars. It is indeed unfortunate that want of space forbids me to add such details to these pages, and especially unfortunate that the unsupported pretensions of this branch of Science in respect of the Genesis of Life, compel me to expose its weakness rather than to show its power. Its weakness, however, lies only in certain directions while in certain hands.

No one of the recent chemico-physical theories of life, however supported by great names, and by the semblance of a scientific basis, need disquiet us greatly. Those who have been or are charged with ignorance or narrowness for not accepting them, pertinently demand where now are similar favourite hypotheses of old? What is there in the present theories to sustain the test of thorough investigation? In this as in other departments of scientific enquiry, the uninstructed are haunted by a vague fear that some wonderfully skilful physicist will discover something which will weaken their belief in the supernatural, or extra-physical view of Life. Extremely few are qualified to form any sound opinion on such enquiries, and therefore a clever essay or a well-delivered lecture may, and for years to come, will throw the multitude into fear and perplexity.

So far as it can be done, it is well to ground men in the conviction that the tiniest particle of living matter exhibits no structure to account for its actions, and that it contains nothing which can by itself explain them. This belongs to a sphere wholly different from the mechanical sphere. The science of centuries has failed to circumscribe it within that sphere. It may be fancifully compared to a clock, but the molecules of living matter are arranged as they never are in dead matter. The living matter exercises a power peculiar to itself, whereby elements which have the strongest affinity for each other are separated from their combinations, and perhaps made to combine with elements with which they have no natural affinity, no tendency to unite. A chemist, by the exercise of his will and knowledge may effect combinations of certain kinds in his laboratory by the aid of complex contrivances, but such a result is at the utmost a mere imitation of what Nature does silently, continually, and without any artificial apparatus. What then is the fair conclusion? simply this, that Nature effects by some influence superior to her what the chemist effects by his art and free will. Therefore there exists an art and freewill as infinitely superior to his, as the whole never-ceasing and all comprehending processes of Nature are superior. As he is in a certain manner higher than the Nature he works upon, so there must be something immeasurably higher than he himself is, which something, or some one, has produced the vital combination in his own person.

Nor do men adequately account for and explain this something or some one by calling it a force, a correlated force, or a force which is so essential to others as to be only one phase of them, and not a distinct vital force. To say that this force is merely a correlate of sun force or heat force; to speak of physical, chemical, and *vital* energy as if they were readily interchangeable and convertible, is merely to assume that they are so without proving it. We may accustom ourselves in physiology as in theology to the employment of phrases which do not explain anything, and we may be as much enslaved by words in the one as in the other. In relation to a vital force, correlated with mere physical force, we ask what does chemical force *construct* by its own unaided efficacy? Does it so construct an organized body? If it does, its presumed correlates do not. Light, heat, electricity, have never been detected in the act of constructing any known organism out of the formless and the non-organized.

Forcibly has Dr. Beale observed, "In all these notions the act of formation, the cause of formation, and action after formation is complete, are confused together. It is held that the organ which changes force has been constructed by force. Force is conditioned by the apparatus it has built up. Force is the architect, the director, the builder, and force is afterwards directed, changed, and modified by the working of the machinery it has designed, constructed, and made. Force is that which conditions, and that which is conditioned. Force forms the instrument which correlates and is correlated by it. It is at one time that which produces the correlating apparatus, and at another is itself correlated by the results of its own constructive power. The constructor is a correlative of the work performed by the mechanism he has produced. The *artificer*, the *machine*, and the *work* done by the machine, are then all correlative."

Conceive that all existing life on our earth were suddenly destroyed; what then would be the power of the physical forces still existing to re-commence and restore life? Assuredly it cannot be supposed that life would re-appear apart from some power able to overcome ordinary tendencies, and to resist and control the operation of physical laws. Moreover, Force is destructive, seen to be so in the largest measure; but, if it be vitally destructive, the same force cannot in the same measure be vitally constructive, or the result would be no vitality. Creative Force postulates the Creator.

Few men will master the scientific terminology of the adepts, but any ordinary reader can judge of the method of reasoning. A fair comprehension of the principles of the modern doctrine of Force is sufficient for this purpose. The aim of the chemico-physical biologists is to show that life is simply an undiscovered correlative of Force—that it is not a distinct and, therefore, cannot be a superior Force. We have just attempted to show how inconceivable this dogma is in consideration of its mutually destructive results. Add also its physical untruth—so far as our knowledge of life has advanced. Life must spring from antecedent life; one antecedent from a like antecedent,—and this appears sound and intelligible. Quite the reverse of intelligible is the doctrine that life may spring spontaneously from antecedent death, just as easily as from life. Yet, if there be only a physical basis for all life, and a common protoplasm for all; if for all existences, the highest and the lowest, the corporeal and the psychical, one common Force correlated with all other forces, suffices to construct all living beings from the lowest animal to man, both the man's body and the man's soul; and if lastly the nature of that common force be utterly unknowable, absolutely and for ever unascertainable, then to call man the wonder and glory of the universe, is the bitterest of all scientific satires, and the cruellest of all modern philosophical mockeries. Surely man was made in vain!

The common tendency of the hypotheses of Mr. Darwin, the philosophy of Mr. Herbert Spencer, and the views of Mr. Huxley, on life and Protoplasm, towards an all-engrossing materialism, must be apparent. However the respective authors may differ in some tenets, they agree in the direction of their issues. This, in the case of two of them, has been well expressed by Dr. J. H. Stirling, in the following passage from his critique on Mr. Huxley:—" It is to be acknowledged that Mr. Huxley would be very much assisted in his identification of differences, were but the theories of the Molecularists, on the one hand, and of Mr. Darwin on the other, once for all established. The three modes of theorizing indicated, indeed, are not without a tendency to approach one another; and it is precisely their union that would secure a definitive triumph for the doctrine of materialism. Mr. Huxley, as we have seen,— though what he desiderates is an autoplastic living *matter*, that, produced by ordinary chemical processes, is yet capable of continuing and developing itself into new and yet higher forms—still begins with the egg. Now the theory of the molecularist, would, for its part, remove all those difficulties that, for materialism, are involved in this beginning; it would place protoplasm undeniably at length on a merely chemical level; and would fairly enable Mr. Darwin, supplemented by such a life-stuff, to account by natural means for anything like an idea or thought that appears in Creation. The misfortune is, however, that we must believe the theory of the molecularists still to await the proof; while the theory of Mr. Darwin has many difficulties peculiar to itself. This theory philosophically, or in ultimate analysis, is an attempt to prove that design, or the objective idea especially in the organic world, is developed in *time* by natural means. The time which Mr. Darwin demands, it is true is an infinite time; and he thus gains the advantage of his processes, being allowed greater *clearness* for the understanding, in consequence of the *obscurity* of the infinite past in which they are placed, and of which it is difficult in the first instance to deny any possibility whatever. Still it remains to be asked, Are such processes credible in any time? Is it true that the objective idea, the design which we see in the organized world, is the result in infinite time of the necessary adaptation of living structures to the peculiarity of the conditions by which they are surrounded? Neither Molecularists nor Darwinians are able to level out the difference between organic and inorganic, or between genera and genera, or species and species. The differences persist in spite of both; the distributed identity remains unaccounted for. Nor consequently is Mr. Darwin's theory competent to explain the objective idea by any reference to time and conditions. Living beings do exist in a mighty chain from the moss to the man; but that chain, far from founding, is founded in the idea, and is not the result of any mere natural *growth* into this or that. That chain is itself the most brilliant stamp and sign-manual of design."

XVIII.

THE ASCENT OF MAN.

ENOUGH of the "Descent of Man." It is to a noble ancestry that the strict naturalists have traced him! An Ascidian is the root of this genealogical tree, abominable creeping things are on the trunk, while in the branches thereof all the unclean birds and flying things do rest. Man is bone of their bones, flesh of their flesh, and mind of their mind. In another aspect, man is a mere coherent aggregate of particles of dust. He is a mass of material molecules, from the biological aggregation of which have been evolved human consciousness and the human soul. "Dust thou art," echoes to him the physico-chemist, "and to dust thou shalt return." Dust thou art in body, soul, and spirit; only let there be changes in the direction of certain forces, and in one moment thou shalt return, all in all, to forceless dust! Thy highest relations are correlations of force. Yes, thy matter, thy spirit, thy thought, thy mind, thy God, are all things of which thou art and must be, absolutely ignorant. Thou mayest indeed be useful to thy fellow-men, and this possible utility is the source and sum of thy virtues, the motive of thy morality, the philosophy of thy societies. Let living dust be useful to living dust. Let human molecular activities benefit other human molecular activities. For this object we are evolved; and yet, even this, without pre-considered purpose!—Such is the sum of our debt to Naturalistic Science. It has wrought hard, by night and by day, to amass this sum, to state it in figures, and to support it by phenomena. But thinking men, not of this school, who yet see the significance of all phenomena when admitted to be real, discover in this Naturalism only a dexterous arrangement, a skilful marshalling, and a specious presentation of visible things. The facts are all made to face one way, and drilled to one system of movements. This philosophy is founded on Natural Phenomena drilled and faced upon Military principles.

Mr. Darwin discharges the office of a veteran

general. He has gathered a vast army of facts or phenomena; he has drilled them during many years upon one system; he has clothed them in one uniform; and then he has given aloud his Napoleonic command—"March! To Creation! Go and overthrow it." The obedient army has marched on, mighty, forceful, irresistible—and lo, Special Creation is no more a stronghold!

But another general might appear in the field; a general on the side of the fallen foe; and he might say, "Give me the same army, the same advantage, the same friends and co-operation, and I will clothe these facts in *our* uniform, lead them to battle on *our* side, and I doubt not that I also could conduct this same army to victory!" After all, then, the whole secret lies in generalship. We have long seen this in war, we now see it in Science—on the one side; it is to be hoped we shall speedily behold it on the other.

"It is dangerous," said Pascal, "to make man see how like he is to the beasts, without showing him his grandeur. It is likewise dangerous to show him his grandeur without exhibiting his baseness. It is still more dangerous to leave him ignorant of the one and the other;

but it is most advantageous to represent to him the one and the other." *

In the copy, though not in the autograph, there follows: "Man ought not to think himself on a level with the brutes, nor equal to the angels; neither ought he to be ignorant of either; but he should know how he resembles both."

Pascal's danger has been incurred on the one side by the strict Naturalists, on the other by the strict Theologians. The strict Naturalists have now done their utmost to show to man, not only his likeness to the beasts, but his direct descent from them, and his intercommunity of nature with them. The Theologians have done their utmost on the other side, though possibly what they have done has not been effected so scientifically and so adroitly. When they have wrought as thoroughly, and asserted as loudly, and have marshalled their forces as commandingly as their foes, it is probable that man will see a little more of the angels, and a little less of the brutes.

There are moods of mind in which, when baffled and repulsed in our higher inquiries, we fall back into a state of hopelessness, and say

* Pensées de Pascal. Ed. Faugère, p. 85.

to ourselves, What is the whole human race but a group of tired children, sitting at the wane of a summer's day in listless society; some half satisfied, some disappointed, some successful, some beaten, some quarrelsome and contentious, some sleepful and heavy; a few hopeful, most, however, neither hopeful nor fearful; all ignorant of the morrow, and meanwhile all waiting for the fast coming, long enduring and dreaming night!

Such is the mood of mind to which we are brought by the study prolonged during some years of the Naturalists and Chemico-Physicists of our world of Science. Assuredly the effect of such study long continued is melancholy. In their atmosphere there is little ozone, it is heavy and spiritless. One desires with an inexpressible longing, the influence of some power above solar force, to lift the miserable human race above the level of precise Phenomenalists. Most men have private sorrows enough of their own to depress them, and they will not be easily consoled by the demonstration of their apish descent, or of their involvement in the universal Evolution which wraps them in its mysterious folds. "After all," they will say, "after all, granted that your Evolutional hypotheses are unassailable and true, what are we as *men*? What are our inalienable characteristics? You determine what we came from. Explain to us whither we are going! What is the significance of the human individual? What is the significance of the human race? If from you we accept our past, of you we ask, What is our future? How does our present bear upon, and influence our future? No Science and no Philosophy can exercise an abiding influence upon us which does not at least attempt to inform us what man is in relation to Time, to Space, to Nature, and to God. This is the quadrature of the philosophical circle."

Such will be the questions asked, and Naturalism must reply, "The answer is not in me."

Let us attempt an approximate and concise solution of these questions; adding two others, which arise out of them.

I. What then is Man in Relation to Time?

A late comer upon earth, whether he came as early or not as some Geological speculators suppose. Not only is he a late comer, but he is a brief sojourner here. In his relation to Time, man is an Ephemera, comparatively the creature of a day. True that most men are old when new men are born, and are still flourishing when he dies. Yet this creature of a day is the measurer and calculator of years—of all the years of human history, and the chronologer of successive empires. He takes all history to himself, and he himself makes all noteworthy history. Moreover, he goes beyond and searches before human history, and scrutinizes the illimitable past. He busies himself with remote geological eras, he calculates or conjectures periods that throw human annals into insignificant brevity. He who seldom or ever lives for one century, grasps in thought a thousand centuries, and even then conceives of an antecedent time. To him the universe is one great dial-face, and *his* eye alone upon earth can trace its hour hand. Of all creatures living here, man alone knows and notes Time. He, first of all creatures, notes the huge pendulum, a few of whose noiseless beats measure his life-span. But though he dies, the pendulum moves on and marks the short duration and hurried departure of generations until the great dial face will be unread.

II. What is Man in Relation to Space?

An atom; an invisible atom if there were but one man, and visible only in the human multitude. Man is an atom in material bulk, but he is above all other things, a *thinking atom*. He is an atom that thinks himself through all space; that measures stars and their orbits and intervals; that circumnavigates the globe, and calculates the courses of futurity; an atom that floats in a sunbeam, yet, while floating, studies the beam, measures its brightness, assigns its several colours to their places, goes far up with the beam to its parent sun, traces light to the remotest planets, resolves rays into spectra, experiments and finds constituent metals in orbs many millions of miles distant from himself.

Yes, he is an atom in space, while he sounds the depths of oceans, makes vapour his charioteer, and electricity his messenger. His first home is a little cradle, his last a narrow coffin; but in the interval between these, man is the King of Space. His first cries reach only his mother's ear, his last, only the ear of his faithful friend; but meanwhile he has laid long wires in the chambers of the deep, and sends his will and his words across the world.

III. What is Man in Relation to Nature?

He is a part of Nature, and yet in mind distinct from it. He is superior to Nature, yet shares its sufferings. He is master of Nature, and yet a fellow-servant with it to a Higher Master. He is a lover of Nature, yet by her unbeloved; an imitator of Nature, yet always her inferior; a copyist, yet never equal to the original. Man is the interrogator of Nature, though she, too, often leaves him unanswered. Speech is his, Silence hers. He paints portraitures of Nature, and, lover-like, sees beauties in her which to loveless eyes are not in her. He is the compeller of Nature, for she does his bidding; her slave, for he does hers. One while he stands up king before her, and she crouches at his feet; another while she rises up in storm, and earth-throe, and fire, against him, and instantly he becomes her victim.

In respect of her, man commonly thinks of Nature as standing between him and God. Rather let us ask, does not Man stand between Nature and God? Man gazes upon her fair and glorious countenance, and sees there a reflection of God. While God Himself is distinct from Nature, she yet reflects God's image to man, and shows to him the presence and power of the Divinity in this world.

IV. *What is Man in relation to the totality of Natural life?* I cannot precisely answer. This is a mystery beyond human solution. That he bears some relation to the living totality, we may be sure. That subtle links bind together the whole organic kingdoms is not a fancy, but a verity. Who can discern those links? No Biologist, no Theologian. The relationship of Man to even a small part of the sum of living things now upon the face of this earth is hardly capable of expression. It is far easier to say where he is out of relation to them all, than to define what his relation is to a fraction of them. Utilitarianism signally fails here, and Positivism is absolutely dumb. Science shows us but little, and Imagination is here feeble and sickly. The vaunted Equivalence of Forces reduces us to a level; Poetry carries us high and far, but soon falls in baffled flight. Atheism pronounces that there is no relation. Religion declares there is. Still it is a great secret, and we can only repeat, "The whole creation groaneth and travaileth until now." The secret lies in the heart of the Creator. In a loftier state of being this hidden thing may be disclosed to us; and if it ever be disclosed, or, be only in slow process of disclosure, we may well look forward to such a revelation as no inconsiderable element of our future felicity. Undoubtedly, all Nature is intimately related to God, and therefore in some manner to man.

V. What is Man in relation to God?

Man is a sinner, and Man is a servant of God. A *sinner*—and if he persist, and perish in his sins, this dark character is perpetuated. As a sinful being, his lower nature is his burden and too often his master. He is dragged down earthwards by tyrannous passions, yet, as a penitent, he is lifted heavenwards by noble aspirations. This twofold nature makes man an enigma, a perplexity, a self-contradiction. There are, then, two homes for him. On earth he may be a centre of evil; or, he may become a source of good; here he is despicable in his deformity, or admirable in his benevolence; here he is seen grovelling in mire, or mounting as on the wings of eagles.

And this twofold nature influences and determines Man's destiny in relation to Time. Yesterday he was sunk in ignorance and despair, to-day he is in pain and bereavement, to-morrow he will be liberated and angelic. Regard man only as a creature of the past or the present, and you see only the enigmatical and the perplexing. Look at him as a being of the future, and you discern his nobler nature triumphant and complete. As a sinner in a sinless world of nature, he alone is against God. As a penitent and a believer, he is as one with Nature and at one with God. The harmony is in human holiness; the perfection, in human purity. " Blessed are the pure in heart, for they shall see God." Apart from its Divine authority, this is a truth of reason and experience. None but the pure in heart can look upon perfect purity and appreciate it. An impure man misreads innocence when he meets it. He thinks it a counterfeit, because he himself is counterfeit. But the pure in heart see God in the ardently desired purity of striving humanity. He who demands perfect objective purity, discerns it in God. All the base passions of our lower nature are consumed in the sacrificial flame which ever burns on the altar of a pure heart. That flame goes up to heaven, and is there accepted. The vestal fire of vestal purity is never extinguished; it kindles evermore in the ardour of Divine worship.

Man is also a *servant* of God. Is he God's servant? then God has given to him inferior servants to obey and benefit him. Nature at large is Man's servant; but in availing himself of Nature's service, let man remember that she ministers to him chiefly that he may minister to God. The King, the Divine Master, is for the present hour away in a far country; and to Man He has committed the keeping and charge of Nature. Man may command and enjoy the benefits of every inferior servant of the absent King; but the King will one day return and rigorously require an account of his servants at the hands of Man. Shame and confusion of face to the viceroy, if in that day he has nothing to render but an account of riotous living and reckless profusion! Who shall deny that the King will justly reward all such according to their doings, and reward them by reversing their former condition; by making the servants masters, and man their former master, henceforth their everlasting servant? Would not this be a just sentence in the eye of all righteous intelligences? "Go, thou riotous and unreckoning profligate; I made thee master over many servants that thou mightest the better serve me. Thou hast abused thy privilege and denied me. Go hence, and instead of being master of many servants, serve thou them as thy many masters!"

And here a momentous question may be

asked, which cannot be fully answered, though by thoughtful men it is frequently pondered.

VI. What is the Destiny of the Human Race?

Naturalists, physicists, philosophers, have not grappled with this momentous enquiry. They have left it in outer darkness, or, perhaps they have made it darker than it was before. Revelation sheds only a partial ray upon it, yet we must use all the light we have. The light of Science, not as it is in our day, but as it may shine in time to come, and with better teachers and reasoners than we now have, may show new ground to Faith. Combining both the light of Nature and of Revelation, we discern, at the present, Hope—Hope, and no more. The enormous extension of Geological Time is a great help in this respect, that it postulates for all Divine action vast periods for the accomplishment of any determinate change. He to whom a thousand years are as one day to us, does not work upon our scale, but on His own. Eternity is His time; and though eternity be but a negative of terminableness, yet that very negative exercises its influence upon our interpretation of His purposes. If He be goodness abstracted from imperfection, and unbounded by limits, goodness in some shape must be the issue of all. For man to speculate how this will be brought about, in what measures and at what periods, would be like the speculation of an Ascidian upon what it will ultimately become. By naturalistic Evolution, the Ascidian becomes Man. Could that Ascidian have forecast this its marvellous destiny? Man may become an angel; but could he have forecast this his ultimate destiny by the teaching of the highest Natural Science?

All ultimate issues not yet accomplished and recognized are mysteries. No man denies this; but mystery in the light of the Higher Ministry of Nature is not Hopelessness—nay, it is the dark ground of Hope. It is the dark ground on which the bright colours of the glorious future are laid. "It doth not yet appear what we shall be;" but Hope prefigures it, and Faith is built upon confidence in the Great Evolver. Faith has a kingdom of her own, and calls Hope to share her crown.

XIX.

DEATH.

LIFE is the field of philosophies; Death is the limit of the field and the test of the philosophies. We may during life indulge in many speculations; death compels us to realize or abandon them. Not many men see others die, not many men reflect profoundly on what they have seen; hence death, under natural circumstances, fails to impress us, and life and speculation go on as before.

There is a picture of Supreme Deity, by Quintin Matsys, painted in so masterly a manner, that the eye seems to look upon you directly in any quarter of the room in which it is suspended. He who writes has tested that remarkably pictured eye, and in no part of the gallery could he escape its piercing glance. Such is the eye of Death; like the eye of a master's portraiture, it follows you wherever you stand. It fixes itself on you at the remotest corner of life; it is impossible to escape it; it pierces you everywhere.

In our youth we are too gleesome to think much of Death, for is it not far away from youth? In middle age we are too busy to think much of Death, for are we not bound to the duties and burdens of life? In old age we think of little else than Death, for are we not at its door? Is not that eye fixed upon us with a perpetual menace? We are fascinated and tremble at its glance!

The counsels of mere men of this world, the conclusions of mere Naturalism, do not avail us much to diminish this fear of death. It is a mockery to console us with the repetition of the fact, that it is a universal law of Nature,—that it is a sure consequence of life; that it is inevitable, must be met, and should be calmly suffered. A hundred Senecas may rhetorize "on the Contempt of Death," but not one man ever despised it the more or dreaded it the less for Seneca. Painters have mockingly depicted the "Dance of Death," but neither pictorial nor rhetorical art can delight or delude us when the reality approaches.

Men die a thousand deaths in fearing one.

Animals do not thus die a thousand deaths; they die but one, and that apparently without anticipation and without dread. What occasions this disturbing fear in man? Is it a consequence of Natural Selection? Is it molecularly evolved? It is not in the Ascidian; not in the Saurian, not in the Anthropoid ape;—whence then does it arise? No materialist can deny that with all its force it is a fear distinctive of humanity; and the more powerful in proportion to the cultivation and sensibility of the individual. No doubt it is unmanly to be continually haunted by the apprehension of death; still, it is truly human, for no being below man is harassed by it.

All who believe in the existence of God are at once able to trace this dread of death to the fear of meeting Him. The enlightened thinker may not expect to meet God face to face literally after death; but he feels assured that he will then enter upon a state in which he must be more conscious of a nearer and comparatively immediate relation to Omnipotence.

In our ignorance, we may continue to call death a meeting with our Maker. However incomprehensible He is, we shall all in some manner after death confront Him. It matters little how, and little where, for the general consideration of the dread change before us.

There are two directions in which our thoughts move when influenced by the anticipation of meeting the Great Deity after death;—one is that of Terror, the other is that of Love.

A study of the universality and rigidity of physical law inspires the former, and intensifies it in proportion to the extent of our knowledge of physical law, and our consciousness of the impossibility of evading it. It is rigid as an iron bar, inflexible as a granite rock, all-embracing as the atmosphere. And if there be nothing but such law in the Ruler of Nature, then we literally live under an iron despotism. Men may as well disport themselves for a few short years, enjoy their scant measure of delights, and then die unreflectingly and resignedly, if there be only physical law for them all. What is death but one penalty or power of this law, the endurance of a sentence long-pronounced?

Represent death physically under whatever metaphor you will, it is in effect the same. Describe it as the running-down of a clock-weight when the winding power is no more renewed; or as the flowing forth of water from a cistern when the plug is removed; or as the dissolution of co-ordinated forces; or as the re-distribution of vital energies; the result is the same, and a variation of metaphor affords no relief. It is no relief to say that in dying we only submit to a universal law; it does not diminish the terror of death to say that it is the condition of living, the pre-destined decay of Nature. A fanciful poet may embellish death with beautiful tropes, but at death every man forgets the tropes and faces the unembellished enemy. From art, then, from poetry, from naturalism, from materialism, and even from idealism, we shall never learn the secret of the Euthanasia.

Has any man discovered the secret of Euthanasia? There appear to have been some men who in long past ages discovered it, and some also now discover and exemplify it. These men have been, and are, of all classes, orders, ages, and measures of ability and cultivation. From slaves to masters, subjects to sovereigns, weak to strong, ignorant to wise, the world has always seen instances of the power to conquer the dread of dying. This has not been the mere victory of Stoicism, because it has passed Stoical bounds. It has introduced hope as the successor of indifference. It has passed the bounds of cold submission. It has ascended above the line of perpetual snow, and has shown itself to astonished spectators in the beautiful Alp-glow, of the serene evening of life.

After that Alp-glow comes death. But gaze *before* death :—What beauty beyond the rhetoric of words, beyond the reach of art, is for a few minutes visible on that countenance turned to the sunlit heavens! Through the whole long day of life we patiently wait to see this final glory. During that doubtful day-time, clouds and mists, damp and heat, hang around the mountain peaks. On them is no joy, no hope; not a single beam. But the expected evening comes; we are standing around, awaiting immediate night. Then suddenly appears the glory indescribable;—at first faint, afterwards full and unearthly. While we gaze spellbound, the flush begins to pale; too soon it fades away, and then succeeds a pure pallor that tells us the sun of life's day has set. Yet that pure pallor, to him who stands long and alone to gaze upon it, has a mournful beauty of its own. It is hueless iciness; but how lately it bore the investing colours of unearthly splendour!

Thus we are led to that other direction of thought, to that which is above the physical law of death—viz. Divine Love.

This is distinctively the Christian direction ; yet, not opposed to physical law, only transcendently higher. We call it another direction because men have made it such; but our aim is to denote a continued operation of the same power in higher regions. We are involved in a scheme of Nature marked by law, and yet, in the highest view, equally under a dominion marked by love. Natural Science leads us to acknowledge the one, Super-natural Science the other. But the Super-natural Science is a continuance, not a contradiction of the Natural. Man has the power of denying and defying both, and must suffer the penalties of his denial and defiance in both worlds. He can acknowledge one and deny the other, and abide by the results of the one alone. He can embrace both, and enjoy the blessings of both.

Love, then, not human but Divine love, is the only antidote to the fear of death. Love is far above all things phenomenal ; the heavenliest thing to be sought for in the world in which we now live, and one of the cardinal doctrines of the Higher Ministry of Nature. Therefore do I thoroughly disbelieve in whatever rejects it, whether by open denial or by unexpressed implication. I so read Nature as to learn that all natural change, which results from decay or death, affords me a freer field of action, and animates me with the hope of a higher life. Natural changes, however slow, lead to marked progress; to enlarged and higher conditions of existence, to grander evolutions. If Nature be Evolution, so is Death. All natural knowledge discovers to me growth within growth, succession to higher shapes; difference and mutation towards higher and more comprehensive order. Many things may appear to retrograde; but in view of the grand whole there is progress, enlargement, and improvement. There is an element everywhere of evil, and of imperfection; but imperfections tend to elimination, and they vanish as do shadows from increasing light, as shadows which are attendants upon light, yet form no part of it. Death is the shadow of life, and yet is no essential part of it, but the negation of it. Life like light will emerge from darkness and death, and shine as brightly as if it had never known an attendant shadow, a concealing cloud, an overpowering night.

As far as respects the present aspect of things around us, both in the natural and moral world, I do not underestimate the amount and the power of evil and sin. Both are here, and both are mighty; but confining myself as closely as may be to my chosen subject, I firmly believe in the truth of what is above advanced, and I further believe that a more ample and more capable survey of even the natural world would display goodness presently mighty, as well as rich with promise for the future.

But, alas! everywhere evil confronts us with its hideous visage, while goodness is forgotten in the horror created by evil, or veiled and unsought.

When, to take an illustration from Nature, I approach a great cataract, I hear from afar, and increasingly as I draw near to it, the thunder of physical power. The turbulent downfall of the river is all mere force—mightiness to subdue impediments, and to descend to the dark and disturbed depths below. It even breaks huge rocks asunder; it abrades, and denudes, and misshapes them when it does not hurl them away. It fills the air with threatening sounds, and the eye with the visible evidence of irresistibleness. It causes the ground underneath to tremble; it flings up to the skies mocking and defiant spray. It makes the silence of the night ever voiceful, and eloquent of unceasing power. One slumbers within hearing of its thunder in troublous dreams. Comes there no glad morning to break over this fearful flood? Will no meridian sun span it with an arch of beauty and of hopefulness? I rise from my broken rest, and I go forth to the disturbing waters. I descend to the falls, and discover a projecting mass of rock, and as I stand thereon, I behold the light of a radiant morning breaking through, and seemingly from the madly bounding cataract. Beams of soft light subtly interfold themselves with the responding and reflecting water-wreaths. I tarry there till the sun advances and gains visible predominance. I bend over and look down towards the boiling rock cauldron, and now I delight my eyes with the vision of an over-spanning iris, small indeed in its bow, but infinite in its beauty. Lo! a smile of heavenly love irradiates the stern face of restless and resistless power!

What are the thoughts and analogies that now arise in the quickened imagination? Here at least and at last is as fair an image as the world can show of celestial goodness illuminating and adorning earthly law! Heaven has smiled, though the swift waters do not a moment pause; though the water-thunder does not for an instant die into silence; though not a rock is unabraded, not a stone is spared.

Do you object that these objects are lifeless and inorganic? Well, then, gaze only on this most delicate and most exquisite of ferns. I gathered it from the top of yonder rock, whence no moisture exudes, and where none abides save the spray dashed upon it most plentifully by the waterfall. There also falls fitfully the light of the sun, the same light that interweaves itself with the foaming waters. Observe that the menacing and mighty cataract, the subduer of rocks, the destroyer of all weak things, combines with the still mightier sun in aiding the growth of a fragile fern.

Is there no force of resistance in fragility to power? Have we no token of radiant love in the very midst of overwhelming forces? The water-bow answers, the fern replies. But you must embrace the fitting moment to perceive the one, and must search diligently to find the other. To a thousand careless and hasty visitors there will ever appear only the emblem of irresistible law—the desolation of a destroying power.

He who wanders alone for long summer days in the High Alps, who dwells by choice in icy solitudes, and who there meditates from sunrise to sunset on the mysteries of life and death, will be likely to muse longer upon the latter than the former. Personally death is increasingly possible to him as he traverses perilous and deeply crevassed glaciers; personally he thinks more of death in regions where his own personality is a presence exceptional to the lifeless solitude. And those immense ice-cataracts streaming down from lofty summits and creeping like messengers of death and destruction into populous hamlets—what are they but the most significant natural images of reigning death Æschylus has sung of the many smiles of the wave-covered ocean. What poet will sing of the many frowns on the face of the rigid glacier? The many smiles wreathing for ever on the face of the ocean represent the Poetry of Life. On the glacier the cold fixed frowns typify the Power of Death.

The long-dreaded approach of Death! What is it under Christian light, but the approach of one who will merely remove us and fit us to be removed? Death is the process of removal from house to home, from the crumbling cottage, the half-lighted, the ever tumbling tenement of an impoverished inhabitant, to a mansion of fitness and fineness, on every side illumined by a sun that never sets, and that never flings its last feeble rays in presage of speedy darkness. True the removal is intensely painful. I must one day stand at the outer door of this my present poor tenement, well knowing its wretchedness, its unfitness, its decay; and I shall doubtless shudder, with unspeakable aversion to the forcible departure. I shall cling to the doorpost, strive, perhaps, with puerile terror to avoid the inevitable dislodgement of my earthly hold. I shall find it unsubstantial in my grasp. What then? Let me now in health, and with some power of reasoning, familiarize myself, despite the delusions of naturalistic dreams and visions, with the truths which the advanced knowledge of physical and psychological science presents to a cultivated mind, in connection with the Christian Faith.

I know that I must die, but "*Non omnis moriar*"—all of me will not perish. My body will be disintegrated, will be destroyed. It is a fleshly body, but in the long ages to come I may have a spiritual body—" This corruptible shall put on incorruption." The elementary molecules of my body are not necessarily subject to decay. Dust I am at the best, and to dust I shall return at the worst; and that last dust is in one view preservable, for it is irreducible, indestructible.

The fact that death must one day dislodge every stone which life, during its appointed term, prevailed to build up in my earthly tenement, is undeniable, and was foreseen at my birth—my birth, which was but a prophecy of my death. Beyond dislodgement, however, death cannot go. It is not totally destructive. Every separated atom may be conserved, as I am led to believe by Jesus Christ, who is the Resurrection and the Life; conserved as dust of gold. Golden dust never ceases to be gold; it may be uncoined, rasped down, rolled away amidst millions of grains of desert sand; but it is still the dust of gold and never loses its nature or its value. That same dust of gold may be regathered, and recoined, and stamped with the image and superscription of the King of Glory.

Every atom of my present body periodically changes, and yet I preserve the same personal identity. The form, the mould are still the same, though molecules are differently arranged. Personally I am ever the same; atomically I am periodically different. Inexplicable corporeal mystery, daily exhibited in millions of living, changing, yet identifiable bodies all over the inhabitable earth! In twenty years not one human being is atomically the same, yet not one personally different. Well then, is it not conceivable that another and similar mystery may be wrought in raising and reconstructing our bodies for their future sphere of spiritual habitation? The transformation may not, perhaps, be so much one of reconstruction as one of recombination. The same indestructible elements may be recombined in a different manner, but with a preservation of the means of self-identification. The manner of combination may be so diverse that it will be evident death has passed over the earthly body, but the whole may be so similar in spiritual personality that the individual shall preserve consciousness, and be sensible of perpetuated identity. Atoms, forces, powers have never been lost, not even in the grave; then what are graves but separate storehouses of precious atoms? If Christ compared his disciples to sheep, not one of whom could ever be lost; not one of whom could ever be plucked from his Father's hand; is it more than this to say that not one esssential constituent of a believer in Him can ever be lost, and that Death cannot pluck it out of His hand? Beyond this, all is mystery, but up to this Science together with Scripture, enable us to advance, and to advance with a confidence which the one and the other mutually and happily corroborate. Life is swallowed up of Death, but again Death is swallowed up of Life, and the second Life will be eternal, uncrossed by the shadow of a second Death!

Change then by death, though apparent destruction, is real elevation. By death we seem to return to elementary dust, dust motionless and hopeless. Yet we know this to be a mere transition, a mysterious, and at present inexplicable metamorphosis. Look, however, for an illustration and a prophecy, at insects, and you find that those which undergo no metamorphosis can never acquire wings. Insects there are which leave the egg fully formed, and only afterwards increase in size. Their development is effected by a series of simple transformations, but they never reach the condition of the perfect insect; as regards external characters they remain larvæ to the end of their lives. So were man never to see death, he would remain a human larva, an undeveloped being for ever. But since all insects of powerful flight, and such as can remain on the wing for a considerable time, pass through marked and complete metamorphoses, so man in order to acquire his full powers, in order to gain his strongest excursive faculty, must pass through the metamorphosis of death. If he would evermore crawl and be close to the clod, let him have his repeated prayer answered, let him live always as he now lives, on the earth. This is what the multitude of mankind seem to wish and pray for; they delude themselves by dreaming that if there were no grave for the body, then there would be no permanent wretchedness; if no death, no dread; and prolonged and laborious life would be prolonged happiness. Could they have their wish, they would discover their delusion and deplore their destiny. If the clod-chained, earth-creeping insect were endowed with consciousness, and could feel envy, how would it look up enviously from its low and its tardy creeping, to the crowd of metamorphosed insects flying and delighting in the summer sunbeams, mounting higher and yet higher towards light, and disporting themselves in the happiest and airiest freedom! *

At the gate of Death our Christian Faith seems to many but a feeble power, and so it is unless previously nourished and strengthened by all suitable aliment; without this, it starves, pines, and perishes. It appears to be like a corporeal element, a material efflux from the brain, a passing current of thought, a failing force which has no correlation with any other force than the failing physical life. Common Faith, the Faith of the general community, what is it? We carry it about with us through life as an instinct evolved by education. We derive it possibly from our parentage, it is hereditary. It may be a mere mental mode of motion, as heat is a physical mode of motion. It may be a religious electricity; another mode of that prevalent Spiritualism which is associated with phenomena not widely accepted, not commonly approved, and certainly at the

* In insects the existence of wings and their functional development are closely associated with metamorphosis. They never exist in the larva, nor are they to be found even in the nymph. They make their appearance only at the very last stage of the animal's existence.—*De Quatrefages.*

best more closely akin to the Descent than the Ascent of man.

The thoughtful believer in God and Christ makes a broad distinction between his faith and the faith of so-called Spiritualists. In this sense, Christians are not to be confounded and classed with Spiritualists.

Christian Faith, feeble as it is amongst many Christians, is the only triumph over bodily death. Every believer bewails its weakness in himself, while he feels it to be his only persistent power. Other possessions make wings to themselves and their flight is speedy and final. The believer can live only in two lights; one beams from the sun of Nature, from things around him of which he is part; the other from things above him and beyond him of which likewise he will become part; but his participation in these latter is seldom sufficiently clear, seldomer strongly realized. The one is the Sun of his day, the other the Moon of his night. There is however to him a Moonrise as well as a Sunrise.

Wandering during a bright autumnal afternoon over one of the loftiest chalk-cliff downs in our island, and often looking out over the great far-stretching ocean that rolled up in monotonous murmurs to the foot of the precipitous white rock walls, on the top of which he then stood, the author of these pages was impressed deeply with a feeling of the limitations of all human knowledge. Down below, some eight hundred feet under him, and for many miles before him was the vast unsounded sea. High up above that was the lofty inaccessible sky. Immediately beneath his feet were solid layers upon layers of accumulated and piled-up chalk. He beheld the sea and the sky under a full sunshine, but he knew nothing absolutely of what was in them, of what was below them, or what was above them. Even of the visible and sea-derived rock underneath him, he knew little more than that it was the white sepulchre of countless centuries, the mighty monument of unhistoric ages, the dead deposit of once boundlessly swarming life, in eras of an antiquity beyond human computation. Full blazing light was *over* all, but light was not *in* all.

Lingering and meditating long upon the same smooth-turfed heights, the sun slowly declined, and his dying beams burnished the ocean with a splendour which never seems less grand and golden, however often it is beheld. Speedily afterwards a grayish gloom fell on sea and shore, escarpment, and turf-down; and a silence unbroken even by the bleat of sheep, came down upon the entire scene. How suggestive of the leaden shadows of Death settling upon the broad expanse of human inquiries and human knowledge, after a life of active and prolonged research into the meaning of things and the mystery of our existence! Does all end in like darkness? Does all light fade, and show its most brilliant colours just in the act and outspreading of departure, as some gorgeously plumed bird, whose feathers are gaudiest when unfolded in act to fly away from the gaze of man? Is there nothing before us but the long and weary night of sleep, or wakeful doubt?

While thus musing, in the distance an unlooked-for brightness flashed up from behind a distant hill. At first it surprised and excited enquiry. Was it a great conflagration? Soon, however, the softer glory of our Lesser Luminary surmounted that distant hill and fell, as if in one gentle fountain flow, upon the face of the waters; and spread over them a beam so tender, so attractive, and yet seemingly so shrinking and reserved, that the tremulousness of the whitened waves appeared fitly to correspond to the moonlight. Was not this a

Faith-like beam? It was not the flashing burnishing beam of sun-like knowledge; it was not cloudless and unquestionable truth; it was the ray of Faith that befits darkness yet dispels doubt. It was the beam that is most timely, parting the shadows of death. It did not dazzle like the sun, nor like the sun did it fail at the approach of sorrow and in the melancholy of desertion.

But lo! the feeble ray becomes strong, the trembling light becomes mighty, and spreads out broadly over the gladdened waves, and the Lesser Luminary now mounts the sky, and goes up joyously upon her fleecy cloud-way, and assumes her nocturnal throne; and welcoming skies above, and resplendent waters below, hail the Queen of Night with an alacrity not inferior to that with which they once hailed the departed King of Day. Now the line of far chalk cliffs grows dimly white again; the scanty sails of slow ships reappear on the softly illumined horizon, and all is again glorious and grand!

So may it be at last with the true and trusting soul of man. The lesser luminary of Faith may become gradually as royal as the lost luminary of slowly fading and forgotten knowledge. The vast dreaded sea of death may spread out before the dying man, not flashing under the all-revealing sunlight, yet not wholly clouded by the all-concealing shadows of night. Subdued tender beams may begin to broaden over it, and its unknown waters may be so softly touched with the ever-widening light that natural fears may be lessened, and the parting spirit may be enabled to contemplate the awful ocean before it without terror, and even with believing peace.

XX.

IMMORTALITY OF THE HUMAN SOUL.

THE prime distinction of the doctrine of our immortality is that it is *personal*. God is a personality, and equally so must be the soul which he made in his own likeness of personality. The immortality of the soul may therefore be termed Incorporeal Personality.

As a doctrine of Holy Scripture this rests upon sufficient grounds. although it is remarkable how little is revealed directly concerning it even there. Although the soul (*Nephesh*) is spoken of four hundred and fifty times in the Old Testament, yet it is rarely referred to in the sense of a disembodied person. In the New Testament the soul (ψυχη) is mentioned about fifty times, not in many instances with direct reference to its separate existence, although the instances in which it is so regarded are of a decisive character.* The strongest proof of

---

* See Luke xii. 20; Matt. xvi. 26; Matt. x. 48; 1 Thess. v. 23; Heb. iv. 12; Rev. vi. 9; xx. 4.

human resurrection rests upon the death and resurrection of Jesus Christ. In these are involved the separation and reunion of his body and his soul. The whole teaching of Scripture and of Theism is distinctly founded on the idea of a conscious, immortal, and responsible soul.

Immortality without personality, is immortality without consciousness, and most materialists will in some sort admit that. Matter is pronounced indestructible, and thus we have an immortality of matter. Force is likewise indestructible, being only convertible, and thus we have an immortality of force. The Pantheists also will admit it, for he who is of one substance with the all-substance is in their view immortal. Hence there may be a play upon the word, widely different from an assent to the Christian doctrine of immortality, which centres in the perpetuity of personal consciousness. Man may conceive of his individual substance being perpetuated under such modifications as would render it indifferent to him. The chief condition of its value is his conscious personality.

Absorption into a universal substance is not much superior to annihilation. Science tells us that all compounded existences dissolve without the annihilation of their component parts. Accept this teaching, but will the non-annihilation, the re-distribution of component parts, include consciousness? If not, we are flung back upon sheer Materialism, or Pantheism, and the colour of the creed will not considerably affect the coldness and the uncongeniality of the conclusion.

So far as Nature can teach or confirm the doctrine of human immortality, it does so in the indestructibility and conservation of force. Science has established that nothing is lost in the material sphere, however frequently it may be changed. Hence though the human body is not immortal in its earthly form, it may be immortal in its constitutive elements. These are indestructible, and may successively enter into new vital combinations without limit. As to the soul originally inhabiting this body, physical teaching is silent; to it we may add a negation or an affirmation of the separate existence of the soul, but the affirmation is founded upon a distinct revelation and belief. In such inquiries we rely on certain intuitions of the mind out of the range of physics.

The persistence of force, therefore, helps,

though it by no means establishes our views of personal immortality. Nor is some such doctrine, as we have said, excluded even from the higher forms of Pantheism, consistently with which it may be affirmed that the soul cannot die, cannot cease to exist, since the idea of an extinction of a substance, of its being nothing, is unphilosophical. The soul's continuance may be involved in endless transformations, during which its imagined personality may be lost, while its actual substance is preserved.

"The more I try to penetrate" says M. Caro *(L'Idée de Dieu)* "into the inner thought of the Pantheists, the more assured I am that the name of immortality has but one sense for them, a sense altogether particular, and so different from the ordinary usage of the word, that one might say it is even its contrary. The immortality of the Pantheist is not relegated to a chimerical future, hidden in the uncertainties of death. It is actual, realizable at every instant by us. It is not a form of future life, but a form of the present. It realizes itself on one sole condition, that of associating ourselves in thought with the eternity of the great Principle, with the absolute of the Substance. One immortality for each of us accomplishes itself here below, by our participation in the Absolute, the Divine. It is puerile to seek for eternal life in any other time, or any other mode. The true time of immortality is the present life,—the true seat of immortality is our soul. Heaven? it is our reason when we think of the Absolute. We become immortal when our thought, escaping from the world of contingency, attaches itself to its principle, and enjoys, by a kind of communication, a consciousness of the necessity of its eternity. To know its dependence, to feel itself sustained as it were and cradled in the bosom of the Eternal Substance, to draw all its strength and all its pride from its relation to the Absolute—which for a moment holds our wretched personality suspended over the abyss of nothingness—this is the only, the true immortality promised to us. All the forms under which humanity conceives of a future life are nothing but the wanderings of imagination and the dreams of infancy. This is enough to content us if we are true men. Each has the immortality he merits. That which constitutes in each of us this immortality, is that which fixes its degree; it is precisely the perfection to which we elevate ourselves. He is fully immortal who the best realizes the Divine in his life and thought, by science or by virtue. Whatever of good his life contains, whatever of truth his thought holds, it is precisely that which establishes his participation with the eternal. The measure of this knowledge and of this virtue is then the measure of immortality."

This view is held as counteractive of the Stoical conception. Those who commit base actions, have low thoughts, vulgar inclinations, and selfish satisfactions only—these men exile themselves from God. It is not God who exiles them from Himself. At every step they take away from truth, their thought is darkened, their taste depraved, and their last degree of misery is to have the desire for the Divine extinguished in them. Such a state is a life in time, but a veritable death.

Obviously this doctrine cannot be reconciled with Spinoza, who formally asserts that after the dissolution of the bodily organs, neither imagination or memory can exist, and by excluding memory from any share in a future life he destroys the conditions of a personal immortality.

Leibnitz reasons thus:—"Our soul is a substance: now no substance can entirely perish except by a miracle of annihilation. And as the soul has no parts, it is not possible that it should be dissolved into separate substances; therefore the soul is naturally immortal." Again in one of his letters, he says, "The I, or principle of unity, is a thing that cannot perish either in us or in brutes. For to perish always implies dissolution : now the principle of unity being without composition, is incapable of dissolution."

Butler also in his Analogy (chap. i.) reasons at length in the same direction—"All presumption of death's being the destruction of living beings, must go upon supposition, that they are compounded, and so discerptible. But since consciousness is a single and indivisible power, it should seem that the subject in which it resides, must be so too. For were the motion of any particle of matter one and indivisible, so that it should imply a contradiction to suppose part of this motion to exist, and part not to exist, *i.e.*, part of this matter to move, and part to be at rest; then its power of motion would be indivisible; and so also would the subject in which the power inheres, namely the particle of matter; for if this could be divided into two, one part might be moved and the other at rest, which is contrary to the supposition. In like manner it has been argued, and for anything appearing to the contrary, justly, that since the perception and consciousness which we have of our own existence, is indivisible, so as that it is a contradiction to suppose one part of it to be here, and the other there; the perceptive power, or the power of consciousness is indivisible too : and consequently the subject in which it resides, *i.e.* the conscious Being. Now upon supposition, that living agent each man calls himself, is thus a single being, which there is at least no more difficulty in conceiving than in conceiving it to be a compound, and of which there is the proof now mentioned, it follows that our organized bodies are no more ourselves, or part of ourselves, than any other matter around us. And it is as easy to conceive how matter, which is no part of ourselves, may be appropriated to us in the manner in which our present bodies are; as how we can receive impressions from and have power over any matter. It is as easy to conceive how we may exist out of bodies as in them : that we might have animated bodies of any other organs, and senses wholly different from those now given us; and that we may hereafter animate these same or new bodies variously modified and organized, as to conceive how we can animate such bodies as our present. And lastly, the dissolution of all these several organized bodies, supposing ourselves to have successively animated them, would have no more conceivable tendency to destroy the living beings, ourselves, or deprive us of living faculties, the faculties of perception and of action, than the dissolution of any foreign matter, which we are capable of receiving impressions from, and making use of for the common occurrences of life."

In his now neglected book, "The Religion of Nature Delineated," Wollaston offered several forcible arguments in proof of the immateriality and immortality of the soul; and these are as sound and as applicable to the contrary suppositions of our day, as of his. Add to these, the detailed and remarkably coherent and convincing treatise of a Cornish writer, of late times, Samuel Drew, and we have in all a body of argumentative support of his doctrine now under consideration, as such a subject can receive.

On the whole there are abundant natural

corroborations of the soul's immortality with personal consciousness, and the proofs of this dogma are not weakened by any scientific discoveries, but rather strengthened by the establishment of the Conservation of Force. Should this favourite doctrine of Modern Science ever be proved unfounded, the old arguments remain in their original strength; should it be indubitably established, they will be so much the more augmented; and the whole taken together will assume a cumulative character.

XXI.

THE CONTINUITY OF OUR KNOWLEDGE OF GOD IN NATURE.

THE modern estimate of the worth of the various kinds or branches of knowledge which men can acquire, is based upon the profitable uses to which they may be turned, and the duration of such uses. More than ever in our time is the value of knowledge determined by these tests. Men, in general, no longer esteem learning because it is recondite, or because it demands long years for its acquisition. They are growingly disposed to measure its value by its immediate fruits and by its readily available issues. Hence a mere knowledge of words, of grammar, of dead languages, of Greek and Latin versification, and of symbols and media of thought, rather than of thought itself, is rapidly and extensively falling in public esteem. Even some professional teachers of such learning are now amongst the foremost and most earnest in their repudiation of a forced and disproportionate instruction in these accomplishments.

We observe, too, at the present time, a general consciousness of the ignorance of otherwise well-educated persons concerning the Philosophy of Nature. Especially has the public feeling been aroused on our need of Technical and Scientific Education, and it has been shown in great detail, and by irrefragable evidence, that the vast mass of our skilled workmen are deficient in proper knowledge of the Science on which manufacturing processes depend. I have elsewhere affirmed, " That no country in the world approaching to England in manufacturing eminence is so radically deficient in special industrial education. Broadly viewed, the whole system of Technical Education has, at this late date, to take root and grow in our soil." *

Reducing the various Knowledges to the test of their actual worth to men, and their effective value in life, we may claim the highest place for that Knowledge of Nature, which we

* Edinburgh Review, April 1868; Article on "Technical and Scientific Education."

are advocating in this volume, and claim it on the grounds herein stated. No kind of knowledge is more elevating, more purifying, and more invigorating to the soul. But the particular topic, on which I now venture more especially to dwell, is a speculative conjecture on the *probable Continuity of this kind of Knowledge in a future state*. Having previously and passingly touched upon this topic, it may be here separately treated.

All varieties of Knowledge excepting that which relates to a recognition of God and the soul of man, will (in the terms of conjecture) die together with the human body. And this seems probable and reasonable, because all knowledge which exclusively pertains to the concerns of the present life, and to our physical condition in it, can have no significance beyond it. We acquire such information slowly, laboriously; and at the various states and ages of life at which we require it. We apply it in action as we need it, and as soon as we need it not, it gradually falls from our grasp, and becomes as uncertain as it is unnecessary. It is one among the many touching failures of aged humanity that those powers which were once so mighty to subdue mental difficulties, and those faculties which were once so ready to retain hard-earned results of thought, finally suffer them to pass away like a dream, and to dissolve into the blankness of forgetful senescence. He who should stand in a large and richly-furnished picture gallery, and delight himself for many hours in contemplating portraits and landscapes of the greatest men and the fairest scenes, and then see the sunlight slowly lessening at evening, and every depicted face and form gradually becoming dimmer and darker, until at last every painting died out in obscurity, might aptly be compared to the studious and deeply learned man, who, in the decrepitude of his last days sees nothing of all the bright and varied pictures which once adorned his mental palace of phantasy, and is painfully conscious that all have faded from his memory, as though they had never found a lodgment there.

If we may speculate on the kind of Knowledge likely to be resumed in the life to come, and to be continued as an important element of it, we may fairly assume that it will be chiefly that which bears direct reference to such future life. If any threads are to be taken up from the web of earthly history, and to be woven into the endless web of eternal history, they can only be such as are suitable to the future texture. Whatever skill has been necessary to our several occupations in this present state, whatever professional lore we may have accumulated during years of study, will probably perish with the body, and will never again be in active use, even if the past should remain in our recollection.

Supposing, however, that a Knowledge of God as he is manifested to us in Nature is an element in our future condition, and an integral part of our joy, we shall at once perceive the probability of a resumption of many trains of thought which have passed through our minds as reverent students of the Natural world. As we can conceive of nothing, naturally speaking, which would so delight the pure and ardent intellects of Christian philosophers here, as an enlargement of the sphere of their clear insight into Nature, so we can conceive of no employment more congenial to their liberated spirits, than an unfettered continuance of the same or similar exercises of thought, in an unlimited sphere of sinless spirituality.

What are the assemblages of men upon earth, which now appear most blamelessly occupied, most united in admirable oneness, and most desirable to perfect and perpetuate?

Are they not those which we join in the earthly temples of the most High God, where He and Jesus Christ His Son are simply but sincerely worshipped and praised? Who that has frequently taken part in such acts of worship does not remember them as amongst the most pleasurable as well as holiest seasons of life? Especially, who that has taken part in some of those grand unartistic strains of psalmody, which swell from the combined voices of many hundreds of singers, does not again and again hear them resounding in memory, and calling back thoughts of Him to whom they were directed?

There are other assemblages on earth to which the same observations would in a more limited sense apply,—namely, those which are gathered to listen to some adept in Natural Science, when he expounds and makes plain a new discovery, or an interesting application of an already known truth. Who that has listened to Faraday, on one of those well-known occasions when he devoted an hour to the instruction of a miscellaneous assembly in some of the great facts of Science, and has witnessed the unfailing and eager attention of the crowded audience to the unfolding of Natural Phenomena, has not felt that this also was a noble assemblage—of another, yet a congenial character,—of willing listeners to a gifted teacher? Who has not felt that here also was the communication of a knowledge which would not perish, for it was knowledge that conducted *ultimately* to God.

Now conceive the two kinds of assemblages just noticed to be united in one, and that they are standing upon a far higher level of knowledge and observation. Conceive them to be disembodied, delivered from many difficulties incident to terrestrial life, possessed of purged hearts and far-reaching vision, endowed with large capacities, and, ranging in free thought over previously unsuspected fields of Knowledge. Conceive that as the issue of all their enlargement of thought, and their clearness of perception of the relations of developed truths, they continually ascribe praise to the Author of Nature, and that ever as they learn, they praise. Conceive this, and surely it is readily conceivable; and what is then wanting to the happy employment of pure spirits, and to the conviction that the continuity of earth's highest and best Knowledge will manifest itself in the final abode of the blessed!

Imagine for a moment the reverse; imagine that all our knowledge of Nature acquired on earth, will be extinguished at death, and that all the conceptions which great and good students, like Newton and Faraday, have obtained of God by a life-long study of some parts of the creation, perish with their bodies and are as fruitless as though they had never been formed. Imagine that our Knowledge of God in Nature has no issues whatever beyond the present life; that the threads of this knowledge are snapped asunder by death like the threads of life; and then the violence done to all the instincts of our higher nature, is at once a proof of the unsoundness of this view. We feel intuitively that, if there be life beyond the grave, there is a Nature of some kind likewise beyond it; and if there be a Higher Ministry of Nature here, the Celestial Nature will exercise a still higher ministry there. Continuity of Life will necessarily bring with it continuity of Knowledge, and this will be a perpetual continuity of Knowledge, for if Nature be immensely extended, so will be our knowledge of it. For all who love God there may be a ceaseless Evolution of knowledge, and corresponding objects of knowledge.

A knowledge of God co-extensive with all that can be known of Him by natural manifestation, would be an unspeakably blessed reward, and perhaps in its full measure will be beyond the attainment of the noblest of intellects. Yet various degrees of such knowledge may correspond to varieties of future rewards. Although we are not in this book treating directly of the manifestations of God in Grace; nevertheless it may be observed that if attainments in grace and knowledge be simultaneous, and if in fact grace and knowledge be correlated, then the continuity of advance in knowing, amongst the highest orders of redeemed spirits, will be interminable.

Is it presumption to suggest that as there is a correlation of forces or natural powers on earth, by which we understand all such forces to be mutually resolvable, and thus arrive at a unity of power; so it is possible that in the future state of felicity, all our spiritual powers may be correlated, and all may be resolvable into the knowledge of God by outward or recognized manifestations of His attributes? We speak of Knowledge, Faith, Hope, Peace, Joy, as distinct, and it is the only manner in which we can speak while on earth of the blessed fruits of the Spirit of God. In the same manner we speak of Light, Sound, Heat, Cold, as distinct physical forces, for this once appeared to be the only mode in which we could know them. But as we are now taught that these physical forces are all correlated and convertible into one solar force, shall we not suppose that the same may be predicated of the soul's spiritual powers? All these may be but modes of knowing and of experiencing or expressing our knowledge of God. As the correlation of natural forces is one of the latest and ripest generalizations of our earthly Science, so may this correlation of spiritual forces and capacities be an after-fruit of the after life.

The doctrine of the Conservation of Force suggests to us another and similar analogy. No physical energy is lost; no matter is destroyed; there is unceasing transformation, but no destruction. Is it likewise so in spiritual energies? Probably no Faith, no Hope, no Joy, are ever lost; probably each one is only transformed, never destroyed. If God has filled our terrestrial dwelling-place with forces and forms of matter which are ever in course of change and conversion, yet never in diminution, if in the waters of our seemingly boundless oceans not one drop is absolutely destroyed; if no particle of our apparently limitless lands is subtracted; shall we err in concluding that no infinitely more precious sentiment of a holy soul is ever destroyed?—Faith? It may be only a requisite for our earthly condition, but it will not be destroyed when it is converted into knowledge. Hope? This may here be only dependent on doubt, but it is not destroyed while it continues to be a correlate with Faith. Love? This assuredly is not extinguished but exalted when converted into knowledge. Joy? What is this but the fruit of the possession, the conscious possession of knowledge. *"Eureka! Eureka!"* was the exultant exclamation of the philosopher who had secured one small portion of knowledge. If such was his joy over a petty acquisition of a fractional part, what will be the joy of the beatified spirit, when it arrives at the conscious possession of the whole? Thus then, it is possible that all the most blessed spiritual gifts may be correlative with and convertible into expanding Knowledge.

Another and principal element in this happy continuity will be the fellowship of the noblest minds of men of all ages and countries on earth, and our introduction into that glorious alliance of truth-seeking and truth-finding spirits. Here we have a faint and temporary type of such an alliance in the societies which men form amongst themselves, of such as are devoted to the cultivation of particular departments of science or art. But subject as these necessarily are to all the imperfections of our humanity, and to all the restrictions of the present time, they can only be alluded to as mere feeble illustrations of what may be suggested concerning the future. Holy Scripture intimates to us in metaphorical language the reunion and the occupation of the redeemed from all nations, and the themes and objects of their praise and worship, and I only seek to add to these intimations, the higher ministry which higher forms or unfoldings of Nature may afford to us, at the reunion of all holy students and reverential admirers of God's works.

If there be conspicuous and acknowledged advantage in the fellowship of men of kindred pursuits and studies on earth, how greatly heightened will be the advantage of a saintly and sinless fellowship of all such spirits in heaven! Each one gladly aiding another:

all jealousies, rivalries, backbitings, and envies, and competitions for fame and human power being abolished; all the impediments of distance, of failure, of infirm health and incapacity, of imperfect communication and representation being removed; it may be inferred that whatever can be gained by the ready, and rapid, and clear inter-communications of high intelligence will certainly be acquired in that celestial company. And with such possibilities it is hard to set a limit to the intellectual achievements of immortal students of God's glorious handiwork. The processes of discovery being far more facile than at present, the progress may be proportionally accelerated. When tens of thousands of ardent souls shall be expatiating in blessed companies over ample domains of boundless space; all intent upon the same pursuit, all finding their true felicity in searching into the admirable plans, the grand designs, and the manifold interdependences of innumerable created things; each momently communicating to each his particular acquisition, all with glad readiness ascribing praise and honour, and glory to Him who has made and who is upholding all these things by the word of His power;—it is indeed impossible to predict a limit to discovery, an exhaustion of knowledge, or a bound to praise. If this be not the Heaven of Mind, it will be difficult to prefigure one that shall better harmonize with our present knowledge.

Such may be the Highest Ministry of Nature, to all who are counted worthy to enter upon its eternal study. Such may be one principal object of the Divine Being in creating and sustaining Nature. That He delights Himself in the contemplation of His ever manifold works is declared in Revelation, and is consonant with all reason. That he should delight himself in the more limited delight which the creatures find in His image, and take in His works, is also consonant to all reason. If in some lofty mode exalted seraphs celebrated the Almighty's praise, when they first beheld His wonderful works, if the Sons of God sang together for joy on the bright morning of Creation, assuredly the human children of God, nurtured in their helpless infancy in a far country, brought up amidst the half-understood marvels of a mysterious land, and departing away from it ere they have obtained more than a glimpse of its exhaustless natural wealth; assuredly these children, when adopted into the heavenly family, and admitted into the societies of angelic hierarchies, and endowed with far-reaching faculties and disencumbered of all impediments, will take up the unfaded notes of the same great pæan of praise to the Infinite Creator!

What gave joy to the elder sons of God, must inevitably give joy to His younger, later, and lower offspring. There is one God alone, and there will be ultimately but one family of God, and one song, though chanted in many parts, raised by that universal family; and at least one grand, inexhaustible subject of praise, of research, reasoning, and rapturous delight. Although this one subject, being so grand and inexhaustible, will present countless aspects to countless investigating intellects, yet it can only be one in origin and one in harmony, as being the product of the One Mind, and having for its object His praise. On earth we learn that Manifoldness in Unity is the law of Creation, and if we learn this while observing but an insignificant part of the Cosmos, shall we not more deeply feel the same truth when it becomes so largely corroborated by our ever-extending observation of ever-extending Nature, through the long ages of futurity?

The two worlds then may be one. A succession of stages may not be a separation of states. If there be a continuity of life there must be a continuity of knowledge. Nature is the outward representation of the Divine to man, and the Knowledge of Nature is so far a Knowledge of God. True that many men have learnt something of God's grace who were wholly ignorant of Nature and of Science. True that babes and sucklings have come to understand the salvation of God by Jesus Christ, and have continued as ignorant as babes and sucklings are. True that the knowledge of Christ is essential to salvation, and the knowledge of Nature is not. All that can be said of this character is freely and at first granted, and it is one of the Divine mercies that things should be so constituted. But we are not in these pages dwelling upon the essentials of salvation. These appertain to other volumes, and to other advocacy, than mine. I speculate concerning the possible attainments and rewards of the noblest students of Nature.

XXII.

ULTIMATE REALITIES—CONCEPTIONS OF GOD.

RELIGION in its simplest or most general form is a potent, and as many men believe, an increasingly potent element in our social life. Whence does it spring? Is it a gift of God, or a product of material evolution? This is the question now addressed to us with an earnestness never before known. Let us first cite the answer of the clearest and best known evolutionist:—

"Two suppositions only are open to us," says Mr. Spencer, "the one that the feeling which responds to religious ideas resulted, along with all other human faculties, from an act of special creation; the other, that it, in common with the rest, arose by a process of evolution. If we adopt the first of these alternatives, universally accepted by our ancestors and by the immense majority of our contemporaries, the matter is at once settled: man is directly endowed with the religious feeling by a Creator, and to the Creator it designedly responds. If we adopt the second alternative, then we are met by the questions—What are the circumstances to which the genesis of the religious feeling is due? and what is its office? We are bound to entertain these questions; and we are bound to find answers to them. Considering all faculties, as we must on this supposition, to result from accumulated modifications, caused by the intercourse of the organ with its environment, we are obliged to admit that there exist in the environment certain phenomena or conditions which have determined the growth of the feeling in question; and so are obliged to admit that it is as normal as any other faculty. Add to which that as, on the development of lower forms into higher, the end towards which the progressive changes directly or indirectly tend, must be adaptation to the requirements of existence; we are also forced to infer that this feeling is in some way conducive to human welfare. Thus both alternatives contain the same ultimate implication. We must conclude that the religious sentiment is either directly created, or is created by the slow action of natural causes; and whichever of the conclusions we adopt, requires us to treat the religious sentiment with respect." *

Adopting from the first the opposite opinion to that of Mr. Spencer, on the source of our religion, I must arrive likewise at an opposite opinion respecting its issue. Believing that it begins with God, I also believe that it ends in Him—with Him as distinctly conceivable, and as made more and more distinctly conceivable by the enlightenment of true Science. "Science," as Mr. Spencer defines it, "is simply a higher development of common knowledge;" and the Religious Ministry of Nature is, as I would suggest, a higher development of common Science. "All Science," continues our evolutionist, "is prevision,"—and prevision is what I claim as the Higher Ministry of Nature.

The study of natural operations, especially when viewed on their largest scale, directly and powerfully tends to expand our ideas of the Divine Being; and in this respect it becomes a useful counteraction to the limited and narrow conceptions which much of our familiar religious phraseology fosters. While the latter has its

* "First Principles," p. 16.

excuse in poverty of language and feebleness of thought, and especially in the customary circumscription of many grand truths by individual selfishness; it is the peculiar ministry of Nature to raise the mind to her own altitude, and to widen thought to her own vast latitude. Common life and daily drudgery debase our highest powers, and confinement to one spot and to one round of duty necessarily dwarfs our religion, renders it sickly and unsupporting, and obscures to us the grandeur of God. In such a state, if we contemplate broad and unlimited Nature, we feel as if chains were struck off from us, and we could walk ever onward with growing conceptions of the Great Creator and Sustainer of all we see and all we are.

When we have once surmounted the trying impediments which intervene between us in our low valley of daily life, and the heights from which we may look over all Nature,—and like God himself in the primitive benediction, pronounce that all is very good—then we may fairly, from far above the mists of lower levels, contemplate in part the exceeding grandeur of the Creator; somewhat of His marvellous and wise government; somewhat of the order of things, and the end of things. We see Him to be the Great and Only Fountain of Omnipotent Will; and in the exercise of Will He becomes eternally the prime mover of all things. He is the Force of all forces,—the one centre of force,—the originator of all motion. We move because He moves in us. "In Him we live and move, and have our being."

To the enlightened and religious student of Nature viewed as the manifestation of God to man, how many inspiriting conceptions of the Great Being arise in the happier moments of meditation and contemplation! As Nature is but a shadow of Deity, so the reason that comprehends its higher ministry is a reflected resemblance of the unapproachable Creator who struck this spark of unfailing light into the human soul. Reason, which is a thought of God, is a delegated thought to man made in the Divine image. God is the intellectual perfection, and man is only becoming perfect as he understands that perfection. In Nature—in the vast and all-embracing Cosmos, we discover God proposing to himself choice designs, and accomplishing beneficent ends. We see Him contriving, ordering, disposing, and accomplishing by the rule of his wisdom, and in the plenitude of his power. Myriads of creatures are constantly instrumental and unalterably subordinate to Him. All second causes, all mediate ministries are ceaselessly and harmoniously active under His supreme activity; and even imperfect human governances, and societies, and mechanisms, only secure their social aims and purposes, as they resemble His undefective plans. Nature is perfect only because He is perfect; men imitate the "perfection of Nature," as they phrase it, while in reality they imitate so much of the perfection of God as they discover in Nature.

Yet the closest, the most apparently successful of human imitations, suggested by our reason and executed by our hands, when strictly regarded, only serve to show us our inferiority to Him. *We* must needs first make rough draughts of our designs—we must studiously re-consider these, and we must amend, revise, and re-shape the primal conception. All our scientific power lies in slow progress from point to point; we cannot pass by clear swift thought; but we cross broad rivers, advance over frail bridges, or ford streamlets on precarious stepping stones. Reversely, at the first glance of His eye from everlasting, He pierced into the depth of all things, into all dimensions of being, and saw what he designed to do, as if it were already done. We behold things in colours and shades. He views them in the pure crystal of his foreknowledge, uncoloured and unshadowed. We take counsel with others, and with wiser ones than ourselves; He doeth all things according to the counsel of His own will. Looking only into His own omnipotence, he discerns all possibilities; into His own wisdom He beholds all degrees and differences of things; into His own purposes He foresees all issues. To Him the beginning and the end are but two beams of the same light!

After studious labour and life-long research we attain to a clear idea of the pervading unity of things created. This unity is an inevitable consequence of the Divine unity. The more numerous the links between things, the more subtle the grades of transition between substances, the greater is our toil in tracing and recording them. Starting, however, from the idea of unity in the Creator, we find that conception expressed and realized in the grand unity of all things natural. "There is One God, and Mohammed is His prophet," say the Mohammedans; let us substitute one word for another, and we have this nobler truth,—

"There is one God, and Nature is His prophet."

The perfection of Science is Unity. Advanced minds foresee this as the end of all Scientific research. "All Sciences approach perfection," said Baden Powell, "as they approach to a unity of first principles,—in all cases recurring to, or tending towards certain high elementary conceptions which are the representatives of the great archetypal ideas, according to which the whole system is arranged. Inductive conceptions, very partially and imperfectly realized and apprehended by human intellect, are the exponents in our minds of these great principles in Nature." And again, "All Science is but the partial reflection in the *reason of man*, of the great all-pervading *reason of the universe*. And thus the *unity* of Science is the reflection of the *unity* of Nature, and of the *unity* of that Supreme reason and intelligence which pervades and rules over Nature, and from whence all reason and all Science is derived."

"All existence is a dominion of reason," said Oersted, "The laws of Nature are laws of reason, and altogether form an endless unity of reason— one and the same throughout the universe."

This one reason in Nature points indirectly to the One God. Even the mere Natural Evolutionist at last arrives at unity. As a final Scientific result this may be stated in the words of Mr. Spencer, at the conclusion of his "First Principles."

"As repeatedly shown in various ways, the deepest are simply statements of the widest uniformities in our experience of the relations of Matter, Motion, and Force; and Matter, Motion, and Force are but symbols of the Unknown Reality. That Power of which the nature remains for ever inconceivable, and to which no limits in Time or Space can be imagined, works in us certain effects. These effects have certain likenesses of kind, the most general of which we class together under the names of Matter, Motion, and Force; and between these effects there are likenesses of connection, the most constant of which we class as laws of the highest certainty. Analysis reduces these several kinds of effect to one kind of effect; and these several kinds of uniformity to one kind of uniformity. And the highest achievement of Science is the interpretation of all orders of Phenomena, as differently conditioned manifestations of this one kind of effect, under differently conditioned modes of this one kind of uniformity. But when Science has done this, it has done nothing more than systematize our experience; and has in no degree extended the limits of our experience."

Such ideas as these lead to what has been called Monism, in opposition to Dualism. Monism, however, is in idea allied to Pantheism, Materialism, Idealism, and Positivism. Monism seeks for nothing behind the Phenomenal, which it unifies. In Pantheism we see the Monism of Consubstantiation; in Materialism we see the Monism of Matter; in Idealism the Monism of Mind or Will, in Positivism that of Science or Knowledge. In Darwinism we have again a phase of Monism; in Evolution we have the same or a similar phase of Monism. Hence it is that Pantheism, Materialism, and Darwinism, and Evolution, are so nearly akin, and hence it is that they possess so strong an attraction for minds so constituted, or habituated, as to think only in the direction of Monism. Moreover, in this respect, they all appear to have a certain kinship with Monotheistic creeds.

It behoves me, therefore, to observe emphatically that Christian Theism is not Monism, but Christianity may partly adopt its style, its method, and language. As a Christian, I rejoice to find that the highest Science points to Unity, though that is not the Ultimate Reality.

In the English language I know of no writer who has so laboriously and so cleverly wrought out (or nearly wrought out) a comprehensive and naturalistic Monism, as Mr. Herbert Spencer. With undaunted perseverance, with rare clearness of statement, though with great inconsistencies, he has built up a system of naked Naturalism, which will hardly be equalled in our time; but it is radically defective. On the Unifying principle he has written forcibly, and conclusively as to the fact of Unity. But at the best in his hands it becomes Natural Monism—subtly shifting its form as you approach to attack and oppose it, yet however you interpret it, you discover that it is Absolute Monism. The "Ultimate Reality," the Μονος—is absolutely and for ever "Unknowable." All that you can ever predicate of it or him is that he or it is the Μονος. That wonderful activity, or force, or entity, of whatever kind, effects every thing, but never can be known by any thing. If you charge upon this the character of Materialism, at once it is translated into Mind. If you claim it as Mind, and gladden yourself with the hope that you have attained to some conception of the Christian's God, at once it is translated back into Matter. It cannot be a nonentity, because it is allowed to be the Ultimate Reality. It cannot be the Christian's Ultimate Reality, because for all purposes of love, reverence, and worship, it becomes a nonentity.

Such is the highest reach of evolutionary reasoning. "Our great philosopher," Mr. Spencer, (in the complimentary language of " our great Naturalist," Mr. Darwin,) has conducted us to this issue; and it appears that no similar thinkers can conduct us higher.

A Christian Naturalist cannot be an advocate of Monism, for in one aspect he maintains Dualism; not the oriental Dualism, in any of its soul-captivating and seductive shapes. He is to this extent only a Dualist; that he believes there are two distinct existences intimately related. One is God, and the other Nature. Both are respectively One, and separately One. So far, and no farther the Christian is a Dualist. He gratefully accepts the conclusions of Modern Science, in all likelihood to be more and more confirmed, that the Cosmos is a Unity. To this he adds that God is unity—totally distinct from the Natural Unity; perfect without it, but infinitely more glorious with it; known to us by it, unknown to us apart from it. This conception of God is perfectly compatible with all Science, while it is entirely incompatible with Scientific Monism.

Accepting this Christian conception of God, you can accept all the established conclusions of Modern Science. Rejecting it, you can also receive them; but in that case you must adopt one or another of the before-named substitutes. There are plausible arguments for each of them, and, as I think, the most plausible for Idealism. If you resolve all the forces acting in Nature into Will-Force, you appear to come very near to Christian Theism. At the least, you obtain a grand conception, but it may be needful to guard and defend it from the charge of Idealistic Monism. In this grand conception you may include God in the form of Omnipotent Will, and you may work this out in a variety of directions. The result would perhaps be the most seductive of all modern views on the side of Nature; but the lines between it and Spiritual Pantheism are very shadowy and shifting. If you will clearly retain the distinctions drawn in these pages, and avoid Idealistic

Monism, the All-Will-Force hypothesis is not only attractive, but allowable.

With the ruling conception of the principle of Unity, it is practicable so to study Nature as to relate every constituent part of it ultimately to God—to the Personal and Omnipotent and Omnipresent God—and so to find in Nature a series of giant altar-steps, leading up to the Great Constructor and beneficent Conservator. It is possible to be a natural philosopher and a natural pietist; and so to combine the two characters that a high and harmonious Christianity may be the happy result. The mere unstudious and unobservant pietist, however personally amiable, will dwarf the idea of God down to his own narrow and inconsiderable individuality. He will view the Great Being solely in his own microcosm, and contract all the scattered thoughts he has ever gained of Him into a relationship to his own petty and atomic self. Nothing can be more contemptible than the manner in which the dread Jehovah is too frequently circumscribed within the circle of some insignificant interests of humanity. Nothing can be more unworthy than the way in which He is so humanized as to suppose him as weak, vacillating, as our ignorant selves. This, however, is not due to religion, but rather to the lack of it, to want of reflection, and especially to unacquaintance with God's action in the grand theatre of natural phenomena. A man who confines his thought and experience to the narrow walls of his own chamber, and the contemptible littleness of his own daily concerns, will never form a worthy conception of Deity. Let such an one go forth into the broad openness of the natural world, and at his first step into the free atmosphere he enlarges his views, amends his misconceptions, begins to grasp the idea of the Infinite God, who has infinite space for his sphere of action, all conceivable and observable worlds for his progeny, and all created beings for his unceasing concern and his parental care. From the first moment that the contemplator of God in Nature realizes this combination of ideas, he begins to be a philosopher, yet need not cease to be a Christian.

As God is in some manner the Creator of each inorganic atom, so likewise he is the Creator of each organic atom, and the minuteness of a molecule does not exclude it from His care. As Creator He is brought within our conceptions by natural phenomena. The Deity reveals Himself to sense by means of the material universe, while He himself is pure Spirit. To our spirits He reveals Himself as the Universal and Unifying Spirit. Nevertheless, though the revelations be twofold in form, they are one in result; for our conception of the material universe is imperfect if it does not include the persistent energy of the eternal creating Spirit.

Thus the twofold nature of Man is brought into relation with the Creator. The Nature that encompasses and contains us, is in every part a work of the living God; the Nature that is within us is the same; but that which is within, is the perceptive and appreciative principle, and comprehends the laws of material nature, and methodizes phenomena, and carries common knowledge up to the higher stage of verified science. This also, rightly regarded, makes the spiritual and material one, and man himself one in his double nature, and in a manner makes man one with God—yea, one with God,—not in substance, not by absorption, but one in image, in likeness, in character. The great Creator looks on Nature, and is satisfied with it; Man looks on Nature, and is gratified with it. Both, with an infinite difference of knowledge, contemplate Nature with delight—in that delight, both are one. At this point of conjunction the Infinite meets the finite—the Creator his noblest earthly creation. Eliminate the idea of God, and Nature remains only as a persistent perplexity—an insoluble problem.

The whole visible creation may be contemplated as God's method of external expression. It is the manner in which He gives out Himself to His noblest earthly image—man. It is the language in which He bespeaks Himself to us—a language which we can interpret; indeed He could not express Himself in any other language which we could apprehend. Even to learn this language is the task of an entire life, and time, if not capacity, would fail us to learn any other. Every listening soul will hear God expressing His voice, His interpretable speech in the utterances of Nature.

Every man, the higher his culture, the wider his knowledge, desires to give an expression of himself to his fellows. Hence reasoning, rhetoric, embellishment, exposition, poetry; and hence art, ornament, decoration, and display. What is true poetry but the outpouring of the poet's soul? What is true art but the externalization of the true artist's conception? Neither of them is, as so erroneously by some represented, the mere self-conceived embodiment of the thinking individual. It is the embodiment of the Creator's creation—the human embodiment of the thoughts of the Divine Creator. Every noble thought, every noble verse, every noble design or pictorial representation is an expression of a thought of the Highest. In proportion as it is the pure expression of a purified spirit, so it is in His.

Mark how the highest works of poetic and representative art transcend the limits of human delight and utility. Were utilitarian advantages their ultimate bound, why the intense striving of true genius to reach something beyond the useful and pleasing? Where does the highest ideal of the highest masters—poets or painters—shape itself and rest? Beyond the present hour, the present generation, the present life. It is aerial, and though intangible and half inexpressible, it is heavenly. If only born for the world that now is, and the race that now lives, it has power beyond its measure, life more vital than it needs; it has potential energies that can never be exercised.

The creations of the highest genius are its outward world, and they are to the inward creative principle a resemblance of what outward Nature is to God.

To those who intelligently believe in Him, God is all or nothing—*all* not pantheistically—but *all* influentially. If He be all, He is in all, and to separate Him potentially from any thing in me or around me, violates a primary relation of His nature. If you remove Him as Creator by an infinite retrospect to a mythical primordial germ, He is not creatively omnipresent; and you remove me likewise afar from Him, and place me in a wilderness of vagrant molecules. I find myself able to think, to design, to invent, to imagine, to paint, to influence my fellow men; and I find myself reciprocally affected by them. I and they have these powers and susceptiblities because God endowed us with them; and I see in their excercise an adumbration of His own image. The creative power always present in Him created me in His image; and sure I am that His ever-operative influence elicits, evolves, developes mentally creative powers, by the conditions in which he places me. Sure I am that He is the Author of every good and perfect gift, which comes down to me from Him as light from the sun.

The sun itself is in position many millions of miles away from me, but it is an accepted conclusion of Science that I could not breathe, or see, or move, without his influential activity. In his far photosphere he is so remote from me that I can scarcely recognize my physical dependence upon him. Nevertheless, Science informs me, and I believe it teaches truly, that whatever I do in ordinary life is in a manner done by the sun; that all my force is due to him, that my physical existence hangs upon him, that my death will result from my inability to appropriate his communicated energy as aforetime. This is never denied. Why then should corresponding truths be denied when I apply them to relations between God and my soul, as well as my body? If it be explained that the sun vitalizes and energizes me by natural laws, then I credit, I acknowledge it, and I affirm that God does the same in energizing my spirit by His spiritual laws. God is light, the Sun of Suns, above and behind them all, and I can no more separate myself from Him than from the sun of our system.

A law of material Nature must satisfy all the

known conditions which it is proposed to explain. It becomes known as a higher law by the all-comprehensiveness of its action. A law of Mind must display the same character. Mind is of God, therefore God influences all that it does, has done, and will do. This satisfies all known conditions of our nature.

Either then there is no recognizable God, or He is all in all, and to all. With avowed atheists we do not here argue; we are solely dealing with those who think the belief in a Creator ennobling and essential, and yet propose such an agency as Natural Selection, or some similar metaphorical factor, as the key to the construction or evolution of the sum of inorganic, organic, and mental and spiritual existences. Rightly regarded, all these, and any other agencies which Science may discover, bring us near to God, and the more sure, ascertainable, and potent they are, the nearer they bring us to Him. They render Him to man the more knowable, and thus I reverse the use which others make of them to prove that He by these becomes unknowable.

A human mechanist employs a particular method of solving a mechanical problem, and accomplishing a desired end. I never saw that mechanist, and I never may see him, but I conceive of him by his accomplishment of a desirable and obtainable result. Am I to be told that, although I believe and admire this result, he has merely availed himself of certain physical properties in matter, which themselves thus become known to me, as directed to a particular end, while the constructor is unknowable? Am I to be informed that he is a mere employer of Force or Forces, and that I can only know these as producing the observed mechanism? Then, am I not right in rejoining "without his mind and action the Force or Forces could have done nothing; they would have been totally inoperative: the mechanism could not have been self-constructed, therefore the constructor is really known to me according to the measure of his mechanism."

If it be objected, "this reasoning may or may not be sound, but in introducing God you are forcibly introducing a personal conception, and adding on to Science what it does not by itself teach," I reply, "your objection is precisely that which I venture to denounce. Science does lead fairly to my conclusions, though it may not lead you to them; and this not because I violently break the logical chain, and insert a new link or chain, but because I follow the chain to its reasonable end. *You* can stop whenever it pleases you to stop: if you have nothing but a natural sequence or law to trace and define, you are right in stopping when you have traced it. If that be your sole object, pause when you have secured it, and no one will blame you; but if you have an object beyond this, and if that be the subversion of a higher, nay, a religious belief, such as Special or Continuous Creation, or Divine interference or action, to employ familiarly known phrases, then I say that your inferences or conclusions no longer possess the character of Science, or partake in any measure of its precision.

"You may be a practised physicist or physiologist, or biologist, and so far as the phenomena submitted to you in these studies are well observed, so far you are well worthy of attention and credit. But when you venture further and impose upon others conclusions having relation to a very different field of thought, these can only be regarded as your personal inferences, which betray the bias of your own mind, which are the consequences of your own habit of thinking, and which possess no authority whatever. Their value is such as may be assigned to your mode of reasoning upon topics which do not belong to your special studies, and upon which you may prove to be weak, while in another department you are wise."

There can be little doubt that all around us able men draw sound scientific conclusions, who in higher departments, reason erroneously upon inapplicable principles. The principles they discover or imagine in Nature, are translated into a loftier region, and are made the basis of sweeping conclusions which have no real relation to the higher kingdom. The rules that govern and direct our observations in the phenomenal world, do not necessarily exercise influence in the super-sensible world. Doubtless there are fixed conditions and laws in both worlds; doubtless, too, in the highest sense both worlds are one, that is, one to the One Ruler, but they are not clearly one to us. The Divine Lawgiver has given laws to both worlds, and works by them in both; and probably works toward some one grand and glorious issue, which it belongs to higher natures than ours to discern dimly and to admire reverently; but to affirm that the laws regulating the phenomenal believer regulates the super-phenomenal world is to say that the unknown must be constituted like the known. This is at the least a presumption with which scientific men claiming to observe with exactitude, should not be chargeable.

Nevertheless this charge cannot justly be brought against our reasoning from Analogy; and it is important to draw this distinction because a specious retort might be otherwise made. We have no other mode of reasoning from the natural into the spiritual world than the analogical. Direct Revelation and Faith being for the moment left out of consideration, our proper business as cultivated human beings is to reason by analogy, from things seen to things unseen. Our care must be to reason fairly from analogy, and, apart from special revelation, this is the true method of arriving at probable opinions concerning things we do not see, and of which we can form no precise or demonstrable conclusion.

Extinguish analogical reasoning, which not a few pure naturalists and some metaphysicians desire to do, and it is not easy to see how one can arive at any truth not absolutely derived from the phenomenal, or physical. Even truths of the latter kind are often arrived at by adopting an analogical course; and in superphenomenal reasoning it is the only method that we can adopt. What Butler did by the careful use of this method is notorious, but even he in his day might have done something more, had he not been influenced by a needless fear of over-stepping his method. In our day the analogical method rightly and skilfully used, would make the Higher Ministry of Nature one of the most powerful and inspiriting of all ministries. Some partial exemplifications of its power have been given in this volume; but in an age of transition like ours, so much time is unhappily expended in combating the specious, and exposing the unsound, that the utmost that an author can hope to effect is to place that ministry on a sure basis, leaving it to others to expand its influence and display its full results. This Higher Ministry will, in its highest results, be the privilege of the future. Only a few of the many natural paths which lead us to Deity can now be traced, and even these are beset with the thorns and briars of controversy. At every step we advance through vexatious entanglements; at every step we have to disengage ourselves from the rank weeds which will one day be eradicated, and cast amongst the refuse. Happy will they be who follow us in happier times, not because the Great Being will be more mightily operant in the universe world than now, not because He will deign to appear in more visible creative grandeur, but because men will look upwards upon a scene from which clouds have been withdrawn. Happier are the men to be born at mid-day, than they who preceded them in the misty morning.

Some pertinent remarks have been made by Mr. Wallace which here deserve quotation. "We are just now living in an abnormal period of the world's history, owing to the marvellous developments and vast practical results of Science, having been given to societies too low morally and intellectually, to know how to make the best use of them, and to whom they have consequently been curses as well as blessings. Among civilized nations at the present day, it does not seem possible for Natural Selections to act in any way, so as to secure the permanent advancement of morality and intelligence; for it is indisputably the mediocre, if not the low, both as regards morality and intelligence, who succeed best and multiply fastest. Yet there is undoubtedly an advance—

on the whole a steady and permanent one—both in the influence on public opinion of a high morality, and in the general desire for intellectual elevation; and as I cannot impute this in any way to "survival of the fittest," I am forced to conclude that it it is due to the inherent progressive power of those glorious qualities which raise us so immeasurably above our fellow animals, and at the same time afford us the surest proof that there are other and higher existences than ourselves from whom these qualities may have been derived, and towards whom we may be ever tending."

Not only do these observations commend themselves to our acceptance, but occurring as they do at the close of a volume which its author has dedicated to an attempt to establish the power of Natural Selection, they are particularly significant. Unquestionably the marvellous development and vast practical results of Science have been given to societies far too low, morally and intellectually, to employ them in the best manner. To such societies they are emphatically curses as well as blessings; and the greatest of all curses is this,—that the higher and nobler inferences and conclusions to which they should have led men have been perverted. Unhappily, instead of strengthening and enforcing that Higher Ministry to which they have a direct tendency, instead of conducting men to the Author, Director, and Controller of all, they have brought many to a mere recognition of second causes, and to the erection of an altar to the Unknowable Deity,—who may be living and energizing all, or may be a lifeless abstraction, a shadow of something inconceivable, a being who is philosophically "unthinkable," an impersonal supreme force, which may or may not be an entity, or nothing beyond a concept.

A word or two may be permitted on the essential difference between Unknowable and Incomprehensible. I may know God now, but I may never perfectly comprehend Him. I know Him in Grace, and in part by Nature, and the more I know of Nature the more I think I know of of Him. So far, indeed, I only repeat what has been a leading thought of this volume, yet the repetition may be pardoned, for the confusion of an Unknowable with an Incomprehensible being seems to be frequent, and to lie at the root of much false philosophy. Should this confusion continue and prevail, the discoveries of Science will be the distancing of God.

The more we discover in Nature, the more we discover of God, and our wider discoveries enlarge our views of Him. Every year He more and more ceases to be the God of vulgar conception, every year he becomes grander and diviner. In truth our knowledge grows up to Him, in proportion as he ascends higher and higher, above our mean and unworthy views. As the light of knowledge grows brighter, He becomes more manifest.

There is an Alpine lake high up and remote from the ordinary tourists' well-trodden ways, which lies at the base of a grand and lofty mountain range, and this it reflects in exquisite perfection. At misty morning time I have visited this hidden lake, and then seen little of its reflecting beauty. At eventide also have I visited it, when lo, in its azure depths every broad outline, and all the snowy purity of the overcrowning mountains have been glassed below, and have been softened down to a tender glory. So perhaps is it with the presently visible glory of the Supreme Being in nature. In the morning time of misty conception, we see little of Him in the mirror, while at the eventide we behold Him in unspeakable loveliness In our cloudy morning the reflection is dim and indistinct, at eventide the mists have dispersed, light is unclouded, and we discern all that Nature can reveal to us of spotless purity and towering grandeur. Rocky pinnacles are higher, and yet seem in reflection nearer. The far-stretching mountain range is loftier, and yet is more distinct. The very fulness of light that elevates and distances it, makes the image truer, and its grandeur more manifest.

In reflecting on the hypotheses and inferences of evolutionists, materialists, and philosophers, one is continually disposed to inquire, How happens it that while to you the whole scheme of visible things is so plainly evolved according to your theory; that while Natural Selection, and Differentiation, and Equilibration, or whatever else be your factors, are so positively working as you declare; that no explanation is offered by you of certain ideas current in the minds of thinking men, which can bear no explicable relation at all to an ultimate reality, if not to the Personal God. Here are two such principal ideas—Unity and Perfection—let us for a moment consider them.

Of Unity as your ultimate scientific reality we have already spoken. It was an idea known in certain old schools of philosophy, but we regard it now as the ruling idea of the day. Whence do we derive the idea of Ultimate Unity, and how do we shape it, if it be not the ultimate idea of an Ultimate *Personal* Unity? Was this idea of Unity evolved naturally out of Multiplicity? Could any number of minute and immeasurably prolonged modifications of species, or any environments, suggest Unity? I, as a student of your books, search everywhere for the origin of this important principle. In undivine Evolution I see everything that would tend to the opposite of such an idea,—such as endless change, enormous lapses of time, continually wider and wider divergences; differentiations amounting to a multitude which no man can number; and the further I go with you, the further I depart from Unity, and the nearer I approach to a broader and boundless multiplicity. While I stand perplexed and confounded in the midst of this amazing multiplicity, I again ask whence comes to you as well as to me the conception of the Ultimate Unity?

Admit for the present that the whole series of varied movements which are commonly called physical forces, can be reduced by analysis to one principle, that is Motion; and that Motion is equivalent to the Ultimate Unity. Then, I have arrived at an approach to the Prime Mover, but *you* only at an impersonal Unity. It seems absolutely impossible that your conception of Unity can be evolved out of perpetually multiplying multiplicity. There must necessarily be One who originated in you the idea of oneness; for if there be no such One personality in the universe, then the supposed ultimate reality of your evolution can be nothing else than an ultimate unreality. Let all be relative except the last. All forces are relative, all motion is relative, all you discover concerning them is verified by Science; but the final discovery which crowns the whole, and to which everything tends is unreal. Every path in a vast labyrinth ends in one point, all wanderers and searchers are coming at length to this point, and when they reach it, they pronounce it to be a point absolutely and for ever undiscoverable!

Now with reference to Perfection; whence does this idea come into our minds if there be no ultimate living reality corresponding to it? It certainly does not spring from things around us, for they are all proverbially marked by imperfections. Nothing is scientifically perfect except a mathematical figure or a mathematical proof. Everywhere there is instability and change; everywhere "the instability of the homogeneous" and to adopt an evolutionary phrase. As of Unity, so of Perfection; whence comes our conception of it? Is it evolved out of imperfections? But can universal imperfection educe the idea of an ultimate Perfection?

Highly educated men possess an idea of moral and physical perfection. No one will deny this, and we are bound to repeat the question, whence does it arise? You as a strict evolutionist announce that religion, like everything else, was evolved by a series of minute modifications. It is one product of your scheme of evolution. But one inalienable element of all rational Religion is the dominant idea of the Ultimate Personal Perfection. This being entirely diverse from the character of all evolutionary processes, and diametrically opposed to them, whence does it originate?

On the other side, and merely as one of the fruits of Nature's highest Ministry, we can distinctly imagine an origin to the notion of an ultimate objective Perfection. We affirm that no imperfect thing, or cause, or being, could have originated it; that it is the precise correlate of a Perfect Personality, to which we logically assign it. In so doing we reason thus—A perfect cause is necessarily intelligent, for absence of intelligence would be, by so much, a serious imperfection. The All-Perfect Unity is not only Himself intelligent, but he acts immediately upon our intelligence, and thereby produces a distinct conception of Himself. This action of His upon any intelligence suffices to prove His presence and His activity. Could I conceive of the cessation of such action, I must conceive that I should lose the idea of objective perfection; just as surely as I know that I should be in total darkness if I were excluded from the light of the sun.

While the action of the All-Perfect Personality is operative upon my intelligence, I derive some radical principles of the philosophy of religion from it. My love of perfection, my admiration for it, my aversion to its opposite, my aspiration towards it, my hope of nearer approach to it, and a full communion with it, all follow logically from my conviction of its existence, and from my experience of its influence upon my spirit. Unless all spiritual religion be a delusion and a dream, I cannot avoid these conclusions, and even were it all a delusion and a dream, Natural Evolution must be a still vainer dream, for it offers no explanation of the origin of an idea which must prove its destruction, in the consideration of Ultimate Realities. If our conception of the Perfect be a direct product of the Imperfect, then the Imperfect evolves the Perfect, itself continuing to be Imperfect while it evolves its contrary!

Within the idea of a living personal Perfection is included the element of Perfect Love. This one essential element is, more than many others, destructive of any theory of naked Naturalism. Pure and unbounded love is far beyond Science, but is folded up in the highest philosophy of Nature. Without Divine Love, Nature, and Man as part of Nature, are meaningless and unintelligible. Without this, Nature is a vast ice-field, and the higher we rise, the more only do we see of its chilling dreariness; extended beneath us like an enormous glacier, walled with massive rocks, and bounded by unalterable rigidity.

Is there such a being as the Loving Creator? An Apostle has told us that "God is Love." Nature confirms this truth, but only when rightly interpreted. Whence do we derive this consoling conviction? Perfect Love cannot be a product of Natural Evolution. It cannot be an acquisition by Natural Selection. It would be a mockery of the commonest sense to endeavour to discover its rudiments in the beasts. It does not exist as an idea in any being below man, and if he does not derive it directly from a Divine source, it is impossible to account for its origin.

This is a fundamental principle of Christianity, and when fully admitted and long contemplated, it is the spiritual sun which enlightens the soul as the physical sun enlightens Nature. And it must be embraced by natural as well as all other theologies. The organic world is by Love held in being, and without it Natural Science is an empty knowledge of loveless laws.

The greatest force in the universe is Divine Love. The Conservation of Love is the loftiest Conservation of Force. Every spiritual force may be ultimately resolved into this; and if as a pure speculation I for a time admit that all force may be Will-Force, as a still higher speculation, rather as an eternal verity,—I believe that the Universal Will is in some way Universal Love.

A conception of the pre-eminence of Love appears to haunt the imagination of the noblest poets, and if I venture to speak of Perfect Love as the omnipotent force in the totality of natural as well as spiritual life, if I venture to connect it with the favourite doctrine of the Conservation of Force, if I regard it as distributed throughout the universe in manifold forms, I do not by such distribution postulate weakness or dissipation of energy. A true poet, commonly called an Atheist, will aptly illustrate my meaning. It was Shelley who thus sang:—

> " True Love in this differs from gold and clay,
> That to divide is not to take away—
> Love is like understanding, that grows bright
> Gazing on many truths :
>
> . . . . .
>
> If you divide suffering and dross, you may
> Diminish till it is consumed away ;
> If you divide pleasure and love and thought,
> Each part exceeds the whole ; and we know not
> How much, while any yet remains unshared,
> Of pleasure may be gained, of sorrow spared :
> This truth is that deep well, whence sages draw
> The unenvied light of hope."

XXIII.

EVIL AND GOODNESS. THE WORLD OF SPIRITS.

IN drawing towards a conclusion, I may be allowed to repeat that I regard the knowledge of the All-Perfect One as the highest object of the life that now is, and its increase as contributing to the happiness of the life to come. Compared with the attainment of this, all other attainments sink into insignificance. This I venture to assert is the Chief End of Man—of Man truly viewed as the wonder and glory of the Universe.

If this be not the highest object of human life, little does it matter what hypotheses are broached and what are buried; for what are scientific reputations, what are ecclesiastical controversies, but the bubbles of an agitated stream that flows in troublous course to final oblivion? We who theorize and philosophize are the children of to-day, and to-morrow other theorizing and philosophizing children will speculate over our graves. "In that very day his thoughts perish," says the Psalmist; and with this conviction there is no more admonitory sight than a museum of preserved or modelled human brains. A marvellous museum of this kind there is in our Metropolis, which contains the finest set of cerebral models and preparations in the world, and often when there has the author repeated to himself the above words of the Psalmist.

Look at those cerebral relics; look at those models fashioned speedily and skilfully after death. All the thoughts that once coursed through those convoluted channels during life have perished. All earthward thoughts, all plans and schemes in respect of self, and time, and this scene, have perished; and so must the like thoughts perish of the living millions who are now passing over the adjacent bridge that spans the river outside of this museum. A million of men cross that bridge in one month—probably more than a million; all busy, care-laden, clever, anxiously scheming, gold-getting, full of fears, rich in hopes. In months to come many of these men may have crossed another bridge which they will never repass. Must all their quick and lightning-like thoughts perish with them? All, probably, that have no reference to God.

If there be an immortality for mind, the thoughts that went up from men to God will with Him remain. If not, like sheep they will be laid in the grave and death shall feed upon them. And if this be their final fate, what matter whether Nature were to them beautiful or not; whether she seemed smiling or frowning; obstinately dumb or full of eloquence? If to the brutes dead men go, what reck we whether or no from the brutes we came? If there be no God; if man know nothing of the God there may or may not be, then his length of earthly life is unworthy of admeasurement. If he be brute-born, why is his laborious life so long? If he be heaven-born, why is it so short? If only brute-born, why lives he so much longer than the creatures from which he has descended? If heaven-born in soul and spirit, why lives he so brief a space?

Why is our life so long? It is hard for Naturalism to conjecture. Why is it so short? It is possible to reply—Because man's future life is eternal. Man's centre of gravity is not here, but in another world, and there he will in the highest sense *live*. A kingdom of mind is beyond us, and to it we are all hastening; a kingdom of pure mind, and of holy beings; a kingdom of perfect holiness and pure thoughtfulness. It is already peopled by the majority, and, as the ancients expressed it, at death we join the majority.

That kingdom of pure mind and thought cannot be evolved out of base impurity and reckless thoughtlessness, for it is the kingdom of God. Both worlds are probably one, but sin is only in the lower of the two worlds, and cannot exist for a moment in the higher. As I cross this crowded bridge,* I look up and see a sunlit and unstained sky,—while a river of foul impurity runs below me in a tortuous course to an ocean I do not see, and do not know.

Perpetually we ask, What is the destiny of this multitudinous human race? It multiplies marvellously, despite fierce struggles for existence. Checks, plagues, pestilences, and wars notwithstanding, it overcrowds cities, it uproots forests, it plants houses in fresh

* London Bridge.

gardens, it swarms beyond all limits; it becomes a terrible and increasing mystery. He who tries to forecast its ultimate destiny is utterly baffled. Science is said to be prevision, but it is hopelessly blind here. Utilitarianism can only reply in mockery, men should be useful to each other. Perfectly true of individuals, but what may be the use of entire generations and of the aggregate race? As one generation dies to-day, and another to-morrow, and another and another, till the last man shall leave this earth, what is the utility of the sum of all generations? When the last man is evolved, and there is an end of evolution, what is its issue? This earth has borne and sustained millions after millions of that creature which is the wonder and glory of the universe! If to no high purpose, then, considering his pains and his fears, and his sufferings and his disorders, and his sins and crimes and death, let us change the phrase and say, Man is the reproach and the confusion of the universe!

"The Survival of the Fittest!" How so, if the ultimate reality be the survival of the unfittest creature for his position and his potentialities, that perversity could have devised? In sowing ruin broad-cast, he has done infinite mischief, and in the blackest estimate he has been a murderer from the beginning. Once he murdered as a savage, now he murders by science. He is vastly more malicious than the beasts, a hundredfold more revengeful, a thousandfold more diabolical, yet he is the fairest fruit of Natural Selection! This ultimate humanity of organic evolution is wise in science and abominable in wickedness. He learns Nature's sciences and then triumphs in multiplied murders! Ah! but this is too severe—this is an unwarrantable charge. Indeed! Well, but if man's soul comes by Evolution, whence comes his sin? If you evolve every organic existence, you must evolve all it does. You bring all out of a fiery cloud; you bring, therefore, Shakespeare, Milton, Newton, and all the sons of Science and Art, from the same fiery cloud; you must also bring every murderer since Cain, every man whose name is a token of infamy, every human being unworthy of the name of Man.

So long as you limit your evolutionary hypothesis to the lower forms of life, its difficulties do not appear so vast; nor do they appear insurmountable in the inferior kingdoms of living things; but when arriving at Man, you evolve him wholly by natural factors: we must look at the evil as well as at the good. How do you evolve the evil along with the good? Natural Selection professedly preserves beneficial variations; how then without a denial of evil do you account for the injurious? Your natural factors are always improving, and from the primeval germ you get the human marvel. But whence do you derive his villany, his terrific passions, and his unutterable crimes?

True that these questions may be retorted upon Theistic or Christian creeds, but with a very different result. We also can decide nothing but the existence and persistence of moral evil; but we do not evolve it along with the good, and by means of the same factors. With us it is a mystery, with you a contradiction. Moreover, Natural Evolution does not afford any hope of its elimination, but Christianity does. By your factors it comes and grows and multiplies indefinitely; and, however many other factors you may imagine, evil will evolutionally accompany them all, and display their inability and defy their sufficiency. We cannot shut our eyes to moral evil. One sentence will comprise our hope—" For this purpose was the Son of God manifested that He might destroy the works of the Devil." In Him, we believe, is the only clue to this perplexing labyrinth. Through innumerable ages to come He will be slowly yet surely eliminating evil. Long ages ago he began this great and Divine task; during ages to which one human generation is as a moment of time, He is proceeding with his task; but this work of elimination is as slow as the passage of geologic changes. One inch of rock, one thin layer of solid coal demands the decadence of a broad primeval forest, and the decay of myriads of plants. Perhaps the elimination of evil and the resultant product of good is as tardy as the processes of earth-building, and perhaps much tardier.

I have previously alluded to the hypothetical resolution of all forces into Will-force, and have admitted this as a grand, if not a perfectly philosophical conclusion. Let us admit it as a provisional hypothesis, in the same manner as Mr. Darwin proposes Pangenesis. Universal Will-force is not only a grand conception, but it clearly realizes the fulfilment of the prayer— Thy will be done on earth, as it is in Heaven!

Let us further carry out the supposition of one Omnific Will in both kingdoms; the material and the spiritual. You find continual correlations in the material kingdom. In heat you find a manifestation of force, which may be changed into light, or into electricity. In life you find a manifestation of force which, as you think, may be transformed from heat, or from light, or from electricity into the organism you examine. Why not the same process, the same interchange in the Kingdom of Spirit? In this man's mind there is force of one kind; in that man's mind force of another; and in a third man's mind, still another. What are these but mental correlations? What are these but manifestations of the primal force in different conditions? Do you find one evangelist or apostle historical, another logical, a third loving, a fourth bold, a fifth speculative? Do you find one believer in God display one cast of thought, and a second another? What are these but effluxes of the One Supreme Force, working out the manifestations of mind according to His own plan?

To what end are all these manifestations tending? To this end—the Education of Spirit; the fitting of Spirit for the highest ultimate excellence. If you find Evolution in things natural, I find it in things spiritual. Moreover,

both evolutions are directed to one final issue.
Perfection is not the accidental or intermediate,
but the latest result. It is the flower; and
cannot show itself before the root, the stalk, the
leaf. An imposing millennium of minds does
not come by sudden and forced marches; but
by slow—almost infinitely graduated growths.
All forces are in action to bring this to pass,
all ages contribute something to it; but the
One Spirit alone is producing it, and no subordinate will can either antedate or delay it.
Come it must; come it shall. It is the beautiful flower; but who shall say when and where
it will blow? Until then, the whole Creation groaneth and travaileth. Unto this end
all Nature ministers in her highest Ministry;
all Grace strives with irresistible predominance.
All correlations of Spiritual force are bringing
it to pass; even the weakest and the slightest,
even the most subtle, and as men think, the
most evanescent. The forces of good do not
die out with the subordinate operants; they
simply change. The manifesting instruments
of to-day may apparently perish; but the
amount of surviving force is imperishable, and
passes into other actors. Not one molecule of
good is ever lost, for it is eternal in right of the

eternity of its Divine Source. Flesh is dissolved, but not Spirit. Evil is transmuted, but not goodness; for that is an ultimate and indispersible quantity. You cannot add to it; you cannot diminish it. You need not add to it, for it is sufficient; you cannot lessen it, for it is indissoluble.

Moreover, it is perpetually in motion. The courses, the complexities, the seeming contradictions of its motions, you cannot understand. How should *you*, an atom, a mere passing actor, comprehend these? How should an insignificant *part* comprehend the whole body? You may possibly perplex, but you cannot explain. Of this vast scheme of evolution you see but one phase; of that you may speak, on that you may reflect; but to unfold the entire plan, to compute its measures, to predict its future phases, to antedate its final issue, is beyond any created intelligence.

Do you ask how any scheme of Grace or Spiritual effluence can comport with the invariableness of the laws of Nature? Do you object that this is a commixture of after-thought with an original purpose? Nature herself will in abundant types show you illustrations. For example, you look down from a lofty precipice upon a still and calm lake environed by mountains, and you see that the beautiful land-locked lake is evermore the same in its outline, and never changes its form or its boundaries. A summer wind alone ruffles its calm surface, or possibly a winter storm raises it by wind and disturbs it by tempest. Afterwards, however, it is still the same; it has neither lost nor gained in dimensions or in depth. It returns to itself, and it finally wears its abiding azure. Is it then a constant and unchangeable thing? —a feature of Nature which thousands of past years have not influenced, and which thousands of future years cannot influence? So it may appear for a moment; but now note that a far-born river is continually rushing towards it and flowing into it, and bringing to it distant materials, drawn from inaccessible heights and unseen depths; poured every minute into its waters together with the unresisted river itself; yet, still the placid lake seems to be unchanged. Still the stern mountains which frame it are unaltered; still they retain and hold their committed charge in unmovable guardianship. Where go all the incoming waters with their included freight? They fall into the lake beheld by the spectator from the lofty eminence, but they do not perceptibly modify one line of the surrounding shores; they do not move one solid custodian from his eternal watch-tower. In like manner, amidst all the apparent invariableness of the broad expanse of Nature beneath us, there may be no traceable change of law, or position, or order; all may be apparently still and undisturbed as in the unknown ages. Nevertheless, all the while the river of Grace may be flowing into it, and mingling with its azure waters, and conveying stores from heights unseen and unscaled by any of mortal race!

Analogy may carry us yet one step farther. In physics it is a fundamental doctrine, as already stated, that the amount of Force is constant. Nothing can be added to it or subtracted from it. May we not, as a moral counterpart to this doctrine, suggest another—that *Divine Goodness is a constant quantity in the universe?* Does this appear too strange for reception? Yet why should not this also be a great and pregnant Spiritual principle? Goodness is the attribute of Deity; it is essential in God, and as eternal and immutable as Himself. Every good and perfect gift is from Him; there is nothing good without Him, and nothing good which does not tend towards Him. The physicist announces that no additional force is ever created; it is but a step in another direction to affirm that no additional Goodness is ever created. All goodness that exists must have existed as long as its source. If there had ever been less of it, there must have been less of a Divine attribute. If there should ever be more of it, there would be an unaccountable excess. God has in all time been perfect goodness, in no future time then can He be more. His goodness, like Himself, is the same yesterday, to-day, and for ever.

It is the motions, the changes, the evolutions of the goodness that we recognize in all great moral phenomena. Successive ages display it in things, and persons created by Him to display it. The transformations of this primal moral force make up all human history. Contemplate human history on a grand scale, grasp it in adequate magnitudes, and in suitable proportions, and you have the long series of Divine manifestations in various transformations of goodness. Here we see more of it, there less, and far back in the darkness of the past, still less. Yet we never lose sight of it on the whole, if we do not restrict it by too minute measurements, and by an inapplicable scale. Like unto light in the sun, it may appear to the vulgar eye to grow from the faint, pale, early streak in the east, until it shines forth with full splendour at noonday. But all men know that this is a deceptive appearance. There is always, so far as we can conjecture, the same amount of light in the solar photosphere; so far as we know, there is always a constant sum of Goodness in the Divine Being.

Such a conception is fertile in satisfaction to the perplexed speculator of the course of man. All moral darkness must in due periods fly before this benevolent light. By whatever names we choose to call this darkness—whether sin, or suffering, or pain, or death; by whatever nomenclature of creeds we baptize it—or by whatever nomenclature of physics or morals, the entire darkness must depart. It is inevitably doomed to defeat and disappearance. Perfect Goodness must in the end be as visible as it is real.

Read the dim roll of Divine Providence by the light of this doctrine, and it at once becomes to our inward eye an illumined record. Goodness is never altogether absent, though oftentimes it has been obscured. Clouds and darkness have long hung round its royal throne, but the King has ever been seated upon it. The inexhaustible fountain of Goodness has ever been pouring out its running waters, and these have at one time and at another flowed in dispersed rills and unobserved channels; yet these pure waters have never been wholly wasted. They will all flow finally together into the undiminished ocean of boundless good.

The various modes of motion of this primal force are seen by us in different dispensations, adapted to different media, and to numerous Spiritual elements. " The earth is full of Thy goodness,"—the earth physically, as *Nature;* the spirits of varied existences, as *Mind.* But Goodness is the prime force; against what is it exerted? Undoubtedly against Evil in all shapes and in all places. Then, is Evil another force, and comes it from another author? No Science, no Philosophy, no Theology, will ever resolve this riddle to man, in his present condition. One belief alone may we rest in, that if Goodness be a constant quantity, Evil is a diminishing quantity. There cannot be two eternal and equipollent opposites. There may be two powerful principles in the universe, at war the one with the other for uncounted ages;

but there cannot be two ultimate Forces. What is impossible in physics, is perhaps equally so in morals. The absolute unity is Goodness.

Assuredly the human mind can scarcely entertain a more inspiriting thought than that in itself it composes a part—an important part of the Universe of Mind which is in perpetual progress towards the knowledge of perfect Goodness. It may thus acquire a conception of its own immense significance, despite the present apparent insignificance of man. The lower, the imbruted, the inherently vicious and obstinately dark minds of our race, may be all sinking in the opposite direction, from darkness to darkness, from various degrees of determined wickedness to ultimate diabolism. This, indeed, is sorrowful and dreadfully depressing. But, on the other hand, while this would lead us to the borders of despair, let us look on the reverse, the hopeful and the bright aspects of God-loving humanity. What bounds shall we set to our hopeful anticipations of its highest advances in time and in eternity? Every good spirit—every pure and purifying intelligence is, or may be, already upon its destined march towards the desired end of knowing the Omnipotent and the All-loving Being. Angelic intelligences are before us, but only before us in the same direction. Disembodied saints are before us, but only in time. All heavenly beings are before us, but only in attainable sanctity and corresponding knowledge. Other, and diversely constituted beings in other, and differently conditioned worlds, are, as we may well presume, before us, but only in respect of their different conditions. The one purpose of all-thinking creation may be in active operation, though, in very varied stages of development, towards the common grand and glorious issue—the Knowledge of the Divine. This may be the invisible chain that joins all holy souls—that keeps them in their several orders, and binds them to their several positions. This may be the electric chain along which traverse the unseen, yet everfelt forces of intellectual vitality.

And in this view we may hope to account for many otherwise insoluble perplexities. The long and intensely distressing sway of evil may be the means of education to many, to us credibly, to others possibly. The slow diminution of evil may be a difficult and painful lesson to humanity. How and whence it came into the course of our teaching let us not attempt to inquire, for, during our days of earthly tuition, all inquiry must be fruitless. Let us only feel assured that it is a medium of knowledge. Why should we dare to assume that we could have been taught without it? And if we are taught by it, why should we dare to pronounce that it might have been avoided? And if it could have been avoided, shall we dare to affirm that we should have been as well instructed in the omnipotence of Goodness, as we shall be by the conquest of Evil? The glory of an earthly conqueror is shown in his visible victory. Is it otherwise with the Divine Victor? When do we crown our heroes with laurels—is it in their repose and inactivity? When does a nation's acclaim applaud its warriors—is it when there has been no combat? When did Cæsar pass through Rome in triumph—was it before or after the signal victory? True, war could have been well spared—but then the public triumph must also have been spared. Is there nothing analogous to this in the highest? Let us listen, and again we hear: "For this purpose the Son of God was manifested, that he might destroy the works of the devil."

Knowledge of the Divine may be communicated to higher intelligences without the intervention of evil. They may be so conditioned as to receive truth more directly; it may shine to them without passing through any refracting medium; but it is the same heavenly light that shines either through or apart from all refraction. God is one, and truth is one.

Different degrees and infinite diversities of attainment must necessarily characterize all minds which are in united motion towards the central truth. As there are varied planetary systems, varied and distinct orbits for individual stars, so are there distinct orbits for individual souls, and perhaps for particular communities of spiritual existence. Still every individual may be separately engaged in taking up, and in pursuing his own line of learning. And in this manner there may exist an Eternal Continuity of Knowledge—eternal in each individual—Universal in the whole kingdom of Sanctified Reason. The mythological fable that represented one of the fatal sisters as ever cutting the threads of human life, may find its realization in the death of the human body, but no Fate shall snap the threads of higher Knowledge. They shall be drawn out continuously and concurrently with the persistence of spiritual life.

Natural Science does not recognize the great World of Spirits, but it cannot deny its existence. It helps the spiritual man upwards to the Spiritual, the Materialist downward to the Material; it concurs with the determining bias of the mind; it elevates the believer to God, it confirms the determined Atheist. Never has it, and never can it adduce any valid argument against the great World of Spirits, because they live beyond its province, and can neither by it be revealed, or by it dispersed. There is a world high above Science, high as the sun above this earth. For this world Faith is prevision, as Science has been called prevision.

There is a wonderful World of Spirits, and there are hierarchies of Ministering Spirits, who, as I believe, influence man through Nature, and by it appeal to his highest capacities. A vast majority of good men in all generations have believed in the existence of these hierarchies; but if they exist, why are they not in communicative sympathy with us? Surely they do not look down upon us merely like pitiless stars on a frosty night; surely since so many of that disembodied multitude have once been men, that in ascending to celestial regions, they have left a long trail of light to mark their upward way. Surely they form a great cloud of witnesses, who, though they sit aloof, and apart from us, intently watch our earthly course, and note with deep interest whether we run our earthly race with patience and zeal. What the stars did in fable, these do in fact. They influence our conduct aright, and encourage us by their unseen but not unfelt presence. They make their helpfulness appreciable to our consciousness. They inspire us with hope, they are ever tarrying for us upon the mountain-top, they become the companions of our solitude, the secret source of unspoken joy to the lonely wayfarer.

They are the ministers by which Nature ministers of her best to us. Some of her whispers they interpret to us in audible speech, others they leave uninterpreted, even while we desire and demand their meaning. They know Nature incomparably better than we do, for our highest Science is their alphabet. By virtue of their purification and exaltation they perceive causations and effects, relations and activities, changes and characters which are hidden to us. Sin does not becloud them, suffering does not distract them, death does not confront them, the grave is behind them. Before them are the infinite potentialities of an endless life!

They remember us always when they remember what they themselves once were. They help us in our earnest efforts to become what they now are. With the speed of light they are able to be present at our side. With the speed of thought they interfuse their holiness into our thoughts. They shine into our earthly homes like morning beams, and they beautify our departure in death with the heavenly splendour of an evening Alp-glow. On our snow-white shrouds they shed the prismatic splendours of their acquired glory.

Blessed and blessing hierarchies! Not one of your innumerable cohorts can be subject to annihilation. You multiply by human death, you increase by Spiritual Selection, you obtain liberty through the grave, you gain light by looking upon the countenance of the Divine! Not one single act of your beneficent ministry to man is altogether lost; every one is a celestial force. You in your beneficent activity are the indestructible forces of the universe of the blest!

You have often been sung, often pictured, often sculptured, and often misapprehended, and not seldom vulgarized. Distorted Science has denied you, scornful Naturalism has derided you, foolish Superstition has degraded you. Nevertheless, you live, and you live for us. Were our eyes duly purged, we should behold you daily; were our ears rightly attuned, we should hourly listen to you in the natural melodies of rill and stream, and river, and ocean; in the sighings of wandering winds, in the labyrinthine mazes of the most perfect music; in that rhythm which attends upon all motion, and which to those who have ears to hear, is the true and entrancing music of the spheres!

One of the most prominent doctrines of Modern Physical Science, is Natural Continuity. "We shall see," proclaimed Mr. Grove in his address on this subject to the British Association in 1866, "that the more we investigate, the more we find that in existing phenomena, graduation from the like to the unlike prevails, and in the changes which take place in time, gradual process is, and apparently must be, the course of Nature." "It would seem as if the phenomenon of gradual change obtained towards the remotest objects with which we are at present acquainted, and that the further we penetrate into space, the more unlike to those we are acquainted with, become the objects of our examination—sun, planets, meteorites, worlds similarly though not identically constituted, stars differing from each other, and from our system, and nebulæ more remote in space, and differing more and more in their character and constitution."—There are, say the philosophers of this school, no breaks in Nature, no new creations, all is gradual succession, ceaseless Evolution. Such is the doctrine which has so often been considered in particular aspects in the preceding pages of this book.

I have ventured to project thoughts of this kind into the supersensible kingdom of existence. My final speculation in this direction is this—If there exist Continuity in the sense of gradual succession, throughout all Nature, why not carry the doctrine one step further and suggest the probability of Angelic and Human Continuity?

When I am assured by luminous teachers of Natural and Physical Science that they cannot draw strongly separating lines between the various provinces of the whole Kingdom of

Nature; that the solid becomes gradually gaseous, that the dead becomes gradually the living, that in the living there are only successive gradations of change, and that between even the vegetable and the animal there is no strong line of demarcation;—then I venture to aver that I am in no want of accordance with the Consensus of modern teachers of Science, if I advance one step higher, to the doctrine of Human and Angelic Continuity.

Why should not the highest development of Manhood be continuous with the lowest condition of Angelic existence? There is here indeed a break—a dark gulph. Death is the strong line of demarcation between the highest man and the lowest angel. Yet death is but transition; it is not a fixed but a passing condition, at least for the good. Death is indeed a severe pang, the severest that organic nature knows. I dread it in direct proportion to my culture; for increasing sensibility to the higher influences of Nature becomes increasing susceptibility to her great changes. So death is the terror as well as the term of my terrestrial life. But it is not a final demarking line; the first wave of the ocean of Eternity will efface it like a sand-mark, and efface it for ever.

I have stood at the death-beds of good, of saintly men, whose painful infirmities have at that hour vanished in the manifested glory of the solemn transition. They were not men of Science, but they were men of Faith, and the highest Christian Faith unites men more lastingly than the highest Natural Science. I have seen hoary and holy age shade off into youthful immortality; I have heard dying whispers merge into angelic song. On the verge of the cold grave I have said to myself,—if there be two worlds, Faith throws a bridge across the intervening gulph, and makes them one. The great unity of all things natural is the prefigurement of somewhat still nobler, the Unity of the Sons of God. Out of all nations and kindreds, and peoples, and tongues, this grand spiritual unity is gradually growing and becoming realized. Nothing in earth or heaven can hinder its accomplishment, for earth foreshadows it, and heaven matures it. A million of years may not bring it to pass; nay, may only evolve one of its phases. But a million of years are a moment to Him who is assuredly bringing it to pass; and since He has endowed me with His own immortality, a million of years shall be to me in my patient yet ardent Faith what they are to Him in his unceasing activity. I have but to wait, admire and adore. Indestructible and irresistible energies are in the Omnipotent One. My name and my fame must soon utterly perish. The name and fame of the princes of this world will perish a little later but as surely. His name alone shall endure throughout all generations!

If I am found capable of awakening in the hearts of good men, some higher and directer and more dominant thoughts of Him and of His works, I have not written, and have not lived in vain. If I am not, I have done my poor best, and may be blameless in unworthily executing so worthy an enterprise. In such a glorious field of effort failure is not a sin, feebleness is not a reproach. The scheme of natural things in which God has placed me, has for many years of personal solitude, apart from all social sympathy, been to me eloquent of Him. I have lived long and alone with Him in Nature. If my superiors in Natural Science smile at me as one grasping at some incognoscible ideal, then I finally say—without Him I cannot, after the most patient efforts, interpret Nature. I have repeatedly tested your Science which dispenses with Him, and I find it to be an empty vanity;

an immense unfolding of aimless life; a sum of causeless effects; an endless series of inexplicable antecedents; an organized delusion, a meaningless mockery!

If my higher belief be a delusion, at least my delusion is better than yours; yours ends in avowed darkness, while mine ends in dawning Light. Of two dreams, one of which terminates in an awaking to Despair, and the other to Hope, which dream is the more dreamworthy? With this simple question of Utilitarianism, I close a volume which has cost its author far more than he cares to confess, and far more than his readers will be concerned to learn.

A Concise Recapitulation of the leading principles, which were in the author's mind, and have been advocated in this volume, may not be inappropriate at its conclusion.

This world of ours, and the universe so far as we know it, form a magnificent manifestation to man, and perhaps to higher beings, of the creative and conserving Deity, without whose creation, and conservation in perpetual exercise, the totality of existing things, organic and inorganic, which we call Nature, would not have come into, and would not continue in existence.

Every relation, or law, or method, we discern and discover in Nature, and in ourselves, is an already accepted, or an additional proof of this fundamental position. The advances and adjustments of scientific research, all, when rightly interpreted, contribute to strengthen and enlarge this view.

Metaphysic, though it raises serious difficulties, and entangles us in some problems which are absolutely insoluble, does not necessarily lead us to hopeless Nihilism, or to any form of irreligion. Monism, Atheism, Pantheism, Spinozism, Buddhism, Godless Naturalism, all have their inherent discrepancies, self-contradictions, and socially pernicious results. However modified in present forms, they still carry with them the same defectiveness which is inseparable from them in any form.

Physical or Natural systems of recent date have many similar, and inherent, and inseparable defects. Endeavouring to displace all theological considerations, they aim to interpret Nature by herself—that is, Nature suffices for her own phenomena without God. With this divorce of principles the author is at utter variance, and has briefly shown how the extreme consequences of such exclusive Naturalism would prove socially degrading and ultimately morally destructive. While holding widely aloof from ecclesiastical and theological narrowness, he holds equally aloof from scientific narrowness. He argues that Natural Science and Advanced Theology are mutually and materially helpful. He has shown in the preceding pages that some of the most pretentious and elaborate Naturalistic systems of the present time fail in many momentous and essential requisites. He has likewise shown that every interpretation of Nature fails which does not include Man as a distinctly and divinely endowed interpreter. All this is concisely shown, because expansion and justification against controversy would demand volumes. No physical genesis of the universe, in whatever form it may be the popular system of the day, will prevail to destroy the great broad principles of Christian Philosophy. Physical agencies are not Spirit or Intelligence, and no confusion of terms can make them such. The ultimate reality is not interpreted by the verbal figment,—Force, unless Man's spiritual faculty be absent, and the materially dynamic becomes tyrannical and autocratic.

The exclusion of a Religious and Theistic

interpretation of total Nature is not logical, but is dexterously perversive. Systems can be presented plausibly and speciously to imperfect perception, while they are utterly wanting in comprehensiveness. They demand the exclusion of fundamental principles of Natural and Metaphysical Science, and become intolerable to those who discern their assumptions, inadequacies, paradoxes, and pernicious consequences.

The author has endeavoured to expose the emptiness of the verbal abstractions which though professedly metaphors, are yet assumptively endowed with personal qualities, with choice, with selective, formative, and constructive powers; and, notwithstanding, definitively represent nothing material or spiritual—nothing that can be a true and sufficient dynamic. They are presumed inherent powers of Nature, which are entirely the figments of theorists. Whatever they represent is, when fairly interpreted, the manner and method of Divine operation.

The substantial value of established Natural Science as an Aid to Christian Faith has been specially dwelt upon. When divested of hypothetical and inconsistent assumptions, it will be found to be invaluable to the cultured Theist. It will supply him with many suggestive analogies, accompany him in religious meditation, disclose new views of God, Man, and Organic Nature. It will in short lead to that conception of Material and Immaterial Unity which is the grandest view of all creation within our conception.

If these positions be well founded and sustained, then God is not the ever Unknowable, but, on the contrary, the ever Knowable Being of beings. Knowledge grows, Science grows, Nature grows; and in their growth the knowledge of God grows. It widens upon the widening intellect of Man,—pervades his whole being, and associates the expansion of his intelligence with all intelligence in the universe in which God displays Himself to Man and Angels. Such is the true, long, and much neglected Higher Ministry of Nature to Man.

www.ingramcontent.com/pod-product-compliance
Lightning Source LLC
Chambersburg PA
CBHW031940290426
44108CB00011B/625